CRITICAL QUESTS
OF JESUS

CRITICAL
QUESTS
OF JESUS

by

CHARLES C. ANDERSON

WILLIAM B. EERDMANS PUBLISHING COMPANY
GRAND RAPIDS, MICHIGAN

Acknowledgment is hereby made to the following publishers to quote from the books cited: A. & C. Black Ltd., and The Macmillan Company, *The Quest of the Historical Jesus* by Albert Schweitzer; Harper & Row, Publishers, *Form Criticism* by Rudolf Bultmann and Karl Kundsin, translated by Frederick C. Grant, Copyright 1934 by Willett, Clark & Company, renewed 1962 by Frederick C. Grant; *Christ without Myth* by Schubert M. Ogden, Copyright © 1961 by Schubert M. Ogden; Fortress Press, *The So-Called Historical Jesus and the Historic Biblical Christ* by Martin Kähler, Copyright © 1964 by Fortress Press.

To my mother and father
through whose encouragement and gentle discipline
I first came to know the meaning of the love of Jesus.

PREFACE

The outward course of Jesus' life has increasingly drawn the attention of critical scholarship since the beginning of the nineteenth century. The theological debates that have centered around the investigation of this subject have been intense. In order to understand these debates we must first understand the various historical approaches scholars have taken.

The following treatment, which seeks to trace the main movements in the critical study of the life of Jesus, is an attempt to overcome some of the inadequacies of previous accounts. The writer has made conscious effort to avoid any step-by-step criticism of the movements presented. This is possible in part because succeeding critical schools point out the inadequacies of earlier movements. The author also hopes that a more thorough analysis from his own point of view of the critical studies treated in this volume will be presented in a succeeding volume.

There are rare occasions where criticism of a particular position will be made independent of that found in succeeding critical analyses. When this is the case, it is done to inform the reader of the reason for the decline of a particular critical approach when succeeding critical treatments do not make it evident why there was such a decline.

In an attempt to narrow the study to particularly crucial areas, the investigation has been centered around the six questions asked at the end of Chapter One. It is felt that the answers given to these questions will to a great extent determine the historical portrait offered to us by any specific group of critics.

CONTENTS

CHAPTER ONE

STUDIES TO THE CLOSE OF THE NINETEENTH CENTURY

BEGINNINGS

It may be a surprise to some to learn that the story of the life of Jesus from a historical perspective was neither a primary interest nor a problem until the second half of the eighteenth century. It was well after the time of the Reformation that this issue first attracted the attention of biblical scholarship. As J. Klausner has put it, "Neither the question 'What is the historical value of the Gospels?' nor its corollary, 'What was the historical character of Jesus?' (as we understand the problems) were [sic] raised in the Middle Ages or in the Reformation."[1]

Prior to this time, the typical Christian depended more upon the portrait of Jesus painted by the church to which he was joined — whether Catholic or Protestant. The inability of the rank-and-file Christian to read the Gospels and interpret them for himself meant that the church with its interpretation was left as his supreme authority. The chief efforts expended in the church were in connection with attempts to form "harmonies" of the four Gospels and to paraphrase them in order to make them more understandable.[2]

Perhaps the most noteworthy of these harmonies was the *Diatessaron* of Tatian, prepared for the Syrian churches in the second century. It is fortunate indeed that such a harmony did

---

[1] Joseph Klausner, *Jesus of Nazareth*, trans. Herbert Danby (New York: Macmillan, 1925), p. 75.
[2] Maurice Goguel, *The Life of Jesus*, trans. Olive Wyon (New York: Macmillan, 1933), p. 38.

not find a place in the Greek- and Latin-speaking churches, as the result doubtless would have been the disappearance of our four Gospels and the substitution in their place of a patchwork harmony having none of the value of the four separate records.

Other types of works prepared in these centuries have even less value. They are mainly literary compositions, the chief aims of which are edification and instruction.[3] Typical of these is the *Historiae evangelicae libri quatuor*. This epic poem of more than three thousand verses was written by the Spanish priest Juvencus about A.D. 300. His work was followed about a century later by a paraphrase of the Gospel of John by Nonnus of Panopolis.[4]

The period of the Middle Ages was little more productive, although three works deserve mention. Bonaventure wrote his *Vita Christi* in the thirteenth century; Ludolph of Saxony wrote *Vita Jesu Christi a quatuor evangeliiset scriptoribus orthodoxis concinnata* in the fourteenth century; and this was followed by *De Gestis Domini* of Simon of Cascia.[5]

At the time of the Reformation there were voices raised against the divinity of Christ, and some who regarded him as nothing more than a prophet or the founder of a new religion; but these conclusions were not based on a critical study of the Gospels or on the application of the methods of historical criticism to the Gospel accounts. In this category we should mention particularly the Italian Laelius Socinus (1525-1562) and the Spaniard Michael Servetus (1511-1553).[6]

In 1602 Hieronymus Xavier, nephew of Francis Xavier, composed a *Life of Jesus* in Portuguese, which was later translated into Persian for the use of the Mongol King Akbar.[7] In the seventeenth century, the Persian text was translated into Latin by the Reformed theologian Louis de Dieu in an attempt to discredit Catholicism. "It is a skillful falsification of the life of Jesus in which the omissions, and the additions taken from the Apocrypha, are inspired by the sole purpose of presenting to the open-minded ruler a glorious Jesus, in which there should be nothing to offend him."[8]

The English deists John Toland (1671-1723), Peter Annet (d. 1768), and Thomas Woolston (1669-1731) applied a more

---

[3] *Ibid.*, p. 40.

[4] *Ibid.*

[5] *Ibid.*, pp. 40-41.

[6] Klausner, p. 75.

[7] Goguel, p. 41.

[8] Albert Schweitzer, *Quest of the Historical Jesus,* trans. W. Montgomery (New York: Macmillan, 1910), p. 14.

consistent critical method to the Gospels, and their work was featured by a denial of the miracles and a subsequent attempt to rationalize them. Their estimate of Jesus was as a great prophet. He had founded a religion that was not really new. He merely gave this "natural religion" a more profound and adequate expression.[9] Rather than get involved in historical problems, the deists devoted themselves to such questions as Jesus' messianic claims, his environment, the beliefs of contemporary Judaism; however, they did not look upon these questions as being in any need of scholarly research. Where reconciliation of the Gospel accounts seemed impossible, it merely meant to them that the Evangelists were untrustworthy. Preference was given to the Gospel of John over the Synoptics, because of its fewer miracles, greater emphasis on Jesus' religious and ethical teaching, and its more philosophical approach.[10]

The influence of these English deists on French writers of the period was pervasive. Voltaire (1694-1778) agreed with them that Jesus was only a prophet. The miracles of Jesus and his advanced ethical code were merely the inventions of priests to take advantage of the ignorance of the people.[11]

Rousseau (1712-1778) ranked Jesus with Socrates and declared that his desire was to set the Jews free from the Romans. Jesus thus sought to revive enthusiasm for freedom via his ethical teaching. However, the Jews did not understand him, and he lacked the forcefulness of character to bring about a political revolution. Rousseau was unalterably opposed to those who felt that Jesus was an invention of the Evangelists. He demonstrated this very vividly when he stated that the existence of Socrates was far less certain than that of Jesus, and that no one doubted the existence of Socrates.[12]

SAMUEL REIMARUS (1694-1768)

How little fruit all these labors had borne is indicated by Schweitzer as he states, "Before Reimarus, no one had attempted to form a historical conception of the life of Jesus."[13] It is from this Hermann Samuel Reimarus, professor of Oriental languages at Hamburg, that the critical study of the life of Jesus takes its beginning. His thought is contained in his work "Von dem Zwecke

---

9 Klausner, pp. 75-76.
10 *Ibid.,* p. 76.
11 *Ibid.*
12 *Ibid.*
13 Schweitzer, p. 13.

Jesu und seiner Jünger," published ten years posthumously by
Gotthold Lessing in 1778.[14]

Reimarus himself was an advocate of Natural Religion, and so
it should be no surprise to us that his approach was from the
beginning a militant one. His basic attempt is to discredit ecclesiastical Christianity.[15]

One of Reimarus' main contentions was that Jesus was a complete Jew in his religious thinking. The idea of founding a new
religion was far from his mind. Reimarus agreed with Rousseau
that Jesus wanted to re-establish Jewish national independence. He
looked upon himself as the Messiah, but this term had no
metaphysical significance in his thought.[16] He merely looked upon
himself as the one who would bring this desired occurrence to
reality.

As a consequence, the preaching of Jesus is contained in two
commands, both of which meant the same. "Repent and believe
the gospel," and "Repent, for the kingdom of heaven is at hand."
Because Jesus never explained what he meant by the kingdom
of heaven, we must suppose that Jesus used it in the way intelligible to the Jews, i.e., in the usual Jewish sense.[17] As a consequence, it is not difficult to understand why Jesus attracted such
a large and enthusiastic following, as there were many Jews who
were waiting for the kingdom to appear.[18] Jesus himself was waiting for a popular uprising to sweep him into office. On two
occasions he felt that such an uprising was at hand. The first was
on the occasion referred to in Mt. 10:23, when in sending out his
disciples he stated, "Ye shall not have gone over the cities of
Israel before the Son of man comes." The second was on the
occasion of the triumphal entry.[19]

His life, however, ended in tragedy when the populace refused
to support him, and he went to the cross crying as he exited this
life, "My God! My God! Why hast Thou forsaken me?" This
was fundamentally the cry of despair of one whom God had failed
in his attempt to lift political oppression from his people.[20]

This unexpected turn of events left the disciples completely
without resources; however, after an initial period of gloom, when
they regained their composure, they realized that they could

[14] Klausner, p. 77.
[15] Goguel, p. 43.
[16] *Ibid.*
[17] Schweitzer, p. 17.
[18] *Ibid.*, p. 18.
[19] *Ibid.*, p. 19.
[20] *Ibid.*, pp. 19-20.

maintain themselves by activity similar to that which they had engaged in during Jesus' life, i.e., preaching. As a consequence, they arrived at the following plan of action. They stole the body of Jesus and after a wait of fifty days, to be certain that if any-one found his body it would be beyond recognition, they pro-claimed that Jesus would soon return.[21]

While a polemical work of this nature may not seem to be of any great importance in getting at the facts of history, his work was of great importance to the critical school in that he was the first to raise several issues of importance. For the first time in his work we see a preference for the Synoptics over against the Gospel of John. He was also the first to deal with Jesus within the context of Jesus' historical and national environment. Similar-ly, he was the first to portray Jesus as basically at harmony with contemporary Judaism, and this harmony carried over to Jewish eschatology with its teaching of the future life and the kingdom of heaven. Finally, we see for the first time in his work the twofold conception of the Jewish Messiah, i.e., the apocalyptic and the prophetic, or to put it in other terms, the material and political on the one hand, and the spiritual and ethical on the other.[22]

The significance of Reimarus can perhaps be summarized more finely another way by saying that there were two areas of great importance in his work for future critical study: (1) Jesus gave to his disciples, and emphasized to them, hopes for the future; (2) even more importantly, Reimarus emphasized the develop-ment that took place between the death of Jesus and the forma-tion of the church.[23]

THE RATIONALISTS

The rationalistic lives of Jesus revolve principally around the question of miracle. They may be divided, for convenience, into three periods. In the early period, while there was no attempt to eliminate the idea of miracles from the Gospels, there was an evident attempt to explain at least some of the miraculous incidents in the Gospels as resulting from natural causes.[24] In the middle period, there is the complete rejection of the miraculous and with it an attempt to account for the miraculous in the Gospels in natural terms. In the final period, there is somewhat of a lessening

21 *Ibid.,* p. 21.
22 Klausner, p. 79.
23 Goguel, p. 44.
24 *Ibid.,* p. 45.

in the ability of the rationalistic explanation to account for the miraculous.[25]

The basic approach of the rationalists is well stated by Schweitzer: ". . . It is a firmly established principle that the teaching of Jesus, and religion in general, hold their place solely in virtue of their inner reasonableness, not by the support of outward evidence."[26]

The first person of importance in the early period is Johann Hess (1741-1828) of Zurich. His life of Jesus is in the form of a paraphrased harmony of the four Gospels. His attitude to miracle marks him as an early representative of this school. He sees the miracles as at once being a stumbling block and as essential to revelation. Miracles must not be valued for their own sake, but rather for their ethical teaching. His semirationalistic position is emphasized when he points out the danger in either the overuse or the elimination of the miraculous. It was the error of the Jews that they became too involved in the miraculous itself and forgot its moral teaching. It is a modern danger to eliminate completely the miraculous and with it essential events in gospel history bound up with revelation.[27]

In accordance with this mediating position, Hess retains some of the miraculous elements in the Gospels. The virgin birth is retained, because it assures the sinlessness of Jesus. The bodily resurrection of Jesus is retained, because upon it depends the general resurrection of the dead. Similarly, Hess holds to the miraculous character of such events as the temptation of Jesus and the resurrection of Lazarus.[28]

On the other hand, many events in the Gospels are rationalized. For example, in the case of the Gadarene demoniacs, it was not the demons but the demoniacs themselves who rushed among the swine and caused them to plunge over the precipice. By this accommodation to the ideas of the demoniacs, Jesus was able to effect their cure, and also perhaps taught the people a lesson that the value of the men far exceeded that of the swine.[29]

The second of these early rationalists that we shall briefly consider is Franz Reinhard (1753-1812) of Wittenberg and Dresden. His position with respect to the miraculous in the Gospels is stated as follows:

---

25 Schweitzer, pp. 51, 58.
26 *Ibid.,* p. 28.
27 *Ibid.,* pp. 29-30.
28 *Ibid.,* p. 30.
29 *Ibid.*

All that which we call miraculous and supernatural is to be understood as only relatively so, and implies nothing further than an obvious exception to what can be brought about by natural causes, so far as we know them and have experience of their capacity. A cautious thinker will not venture in any single instance to pronounce an event to be so extraordinary that God could not have brought it about by the use of secondary causes, but must have intervened directly.[30]

Jesus' primary significance for Reinhard was that of being an extraordinary "divine" teacher. In this class he stands by himself. Jesus attached his teaching to Jewish eschatology; but this has reference only to the form of his teaching, for it was at its heart universal. Jesus went voluntarily to his death in order to destroy the mistaken belief that he was trying to establish an earthly kingdom.[31]

For Reinhard, however, the point of singular importance in the life of Jesus was its union of religion and reason. "Reason was to maintain its freedom by the aid of religion, and religion was not to be withdrawn from the critical judgment of reason."[32] He thus concludes that the universal religion Jesus founded bore the three necessary elements of any religion that could pretend to be universal. It was ethical; it was intelligible; and it was spiritual.[33]

A third representative of these early rationalists is Johann Jakobi, of Waltershausen. He acknowledges in a work of 1816 that much of the miraculous is a later supplementation of the facts, but distrusts some of the explanations of these miraculous elements given by the rationalists, finding them more strange than the miracles themselves. The purpose of the miraculous is not to "authenticate the teaching of Jesus, but to surround His life with a guard of honour."[34]

The final representative of these early rationalists that we shall consider is Johannes Herder (1744-1803) of Weimar. In his two books of 1796 and 1797 he advanced the idea that while the Synoptics were Palestinian and historical, the Fourth Gospel was not so much historical as it was doctrinal. He also felt that the Fourth Gospel was the last of these Gospels composed. His advance in documentary analysis was very marked, as can be seen also in that he was the first to recognize that Mark's was the

---

[30] Quoted *ibid.,* p. 32.
[31] *Ibid.,* pp. 32-33.
[32] *Ibid.,* p. 33.
[33] *Ibid.*
[34] *Ibid.,* p. 34.

earliest Gospel. Before his time, the value of Mark's Gospel was usually looked upon as being less than that of the other Synoptics. He was a mere epitomizer or abbreviator of Matthew and Luke. He felt that at the roots of all three Synoptics lay a primitive oral gospel which had been narrated by the apostles in Aramaic.[35]

In his attitude toward miracles, he was clearly a member of this early rationalistic group. The miracles are not subject to proof and belong in the area of church belief. On the other hand, in a limited sense they are to be accepted on the basis of historical evidence. Jesus' performance of miracles was in part a concession to a miracle-loving age, but the real value of the miracles lies not in their performance but in their symbolic value.[36]

As an example of the middle period of the rationalists, or the thoroughgoing rationalists, we shall mention only one representative, Heinrich Eberhard Paulus (1761-1851) of Heidelberg. His chief importance to us is in the realm of explanation of the miraculous. We have called him a thoroughgoing rationalist because of his belief that every miracle in the Gospels, with one exception, is subject to naturalistic explanation.[37] Underlying his treatment are two points of primary importance: "(1) that unexplained alterations of the course of nature can neither overthrow nor attest a spiritual truth, (2) that everything which happens in nature emanates from the omnipotence of God."[38] He agrees that the Evangelists intended to give accounts of miracles, and since many events of Jesus' day were the result of inexplicable causes, they appeared to be miraculous; however, "since that which is produced by the laws of nature is really produced by God, the Biblical miracles consist merely in the fact that eyewitnesses report events of which they did not know the secondary causes."[39]

Our only problem, therefore, is to discover the secondary causes of the miracles of Jesus. With respect to the miracles of healing several possibilities are evident. Jesus worked on the nervous system of the sufferer; he used medicines known only to him; or he prescribed diets and treatments after the initial "healing." The nature miracles are explained as optical illusions, etc. The raisings from the dead were cases of coma. At any rate, the love of miracle on the part of the Jewish people caused them to attribute everything to God and to overlook secondary causes.[40]

---

35 Klausner, pp. 80-81.
36 Schweitzer, p. 36.
37 Klausner, p. 82.
38 Schweitzer, p. 51.
39 *Ibid.*
40 *Ibid.*, p. 53.

The one miracle that escapes rationalization for him is that of the virgin birth. He does not attribute Jesus' conception to natural generation, but rather, at least indirectly, regards it as a self-conscious act of Mary.[41]

From the final period of the rationalistic lives we select two men, Karl Hase (1800-1890) of Jena and Friedrich Schleier-macher (1768-1834). Schweitzer points out the approach of these final representatives. "They still cling to the rationalistic explanation of miracle; although they have no longer the same ingenuous confidence in it as their predecessors, and although at the decisive cases they are content to leave a question-mark instead of offering a solution."[42]

The chief contributions of Hase can perhaps be grouped into five areas. (1) He is fully in accord with the rationalists in that he very frequently explains the miracles by rationalizing them. Thus, for example, in the instance of the baptism of Jesus, the transfiguration, the coin in the mouth of the fish, the stilling of the storm, and the feeding of the five thousand, completely rationalistic explanations of the occurrences are given.[43] (2) In certain instances, he holds that either a naturalistic or supernaturalistic interpretation is possible. Such, for example, is the instance of the resurrection of Jesus. "Either . . . the creator gave new life to a body which was really dead, or . . . the latent life reawakened in a body which was only seemingly dead."[44] (3) A third significant feature of his work is his comparative evaluation of the Synoptics and John.

> For the rationalists all miracles stand on the same footing, and all must equally be abolished by a naturalistic explanation. If we study Hase carefully, we find that he accepts only the Johannine miracles as authentic, whereas those of the Synoptists may be regarded as resting upon a misunderstanding on the part of the authors, because they are not reported at first hand, but from tradition.[45]

Thus, for him, a comparison of the value of the Synoptics and John comes out in favor of John. (4) Certain elements in the Gospels he relegates to the category of myth. Included in this category are the birth-story of Jesus and certain events in his infancy, the miraculous happenings at the time of Jesus' death,

41 *Ibid.*, p. 51.
42 *Ibid.*, p. 58.
43 *Ibid.*, pp. 59-60.
44 *Ibid.*
45 *Ibid.*, p. 60.

and the ascension.[46] (5) Finally, he was the first to create the historico-psychological picture of Jesus which was so much used after his time. He noted two periods in the life of Jesus. In the first period he held more or less to the traditional Jewish idea of the messianic age, and in the second period he developed his own conception of the Messiah.[47]

Schleiermacher's life of Jesus did not appear until sometime after his death in 1864. His position with respect to the resurrection of Jesus is very similiar to that of Hase. That is, it may have been either a return to consciousness from a trance or a supernatural resurrection; however, it makes very little difference which was the case. He does say that Jesus spent a period of time with his disciples after the event of the cross. Jesus' life during this time was consequently less public in order that he might keep down an inappropriate messianic movement.[48]

He too classifies the miracles on a scale according to their probability. At one end of the scale are the miracles of healing, which he feels may be explained largely on the basis of the removal of some mental difficulty on the part of the recipient. At the other end of the scale are the miracles of the birth and childhood of Jesus, which must simply be given up.[49]

Schleiermacher, like Hase, preferred John to the Synoptics. It is, in the first place, the only Gospel in which the consciousness of Jesus is properly reflected. There is a steady development toward the idea of divine Sonship. Furthermore, it is only in John that we have an authoritative outline of the life of Jesus. The Synoptics are merely compilations of various traditions which their authors have put together. It is true that Luke used greater care in his compilation than did the others, but even his work is inferior to that of John.[50]

DAVID STRAUSS (1808-1874)

It is certain that there has neither before nor since appeared a book on the life of Jesus that has caused more excitement in the scholarly world than did the *Life of Jesus* by Strauss in 1835. Its significance is to be found both in its refutation of the past, and in its presentation of a radically new concept of the life of Jesus as we have it presented in the Gospels. He made use of the Hegelian dialectic to develop his theory. The thesis is represented

---

[46] *Ibid.*
[47] *Ibid.,* p. 61.
[48] *Ibid.,* p. 64.
[49] *Ibid.,* pp. 64-65.
[50] *Ibid.,* p. 66.

by the supernaturalistic explanation of the events of the life of Jesus, which had made everything supernatural. The antithesis is represented by the rationalistic explanation of the events of the life of Jesus, which had made everything intelligible as natural causes. From the opposition of these two rises the synthesis and a new solution — mythological interpretation.[51]

Somewhat surprisingly, Strauss is more critical of the rationalistic explanation than he is of the supernaturalistic one. He feels that the latter at least represents the plain sense of the narratives, while the former results in forced interpretation and artificiality to a very marked degree.[52]

Perhaps the most important element to try to understand in the work of Strauss is his concept of myth. For him, myth did not so much have the connotation of nonreality but was rather a vehicle for the symbolical expression of a lofty truth.[53]

> He regards the Gospel discrepancies as proofs that the Gospels are not historical works, but rather historico-religious documents written by men with a deep sense of faith unable to describe actual events without letting their own and their contemporaries' religious feelings and ideas colour their statements.[54]

From this point, he goes on to show how he feels the miracles of the Gospels developed. The same general pattern prevailed here as in the religious literature of the Greeks and the Romans. That is, the Gospel miracles are the product of *mythenbildender Glaube* (legend-creating faith) on the part of the early Christians. This faith was particularly anxious to find Jesus as the fulfillment of the prophecies of Hebrew Scripture, and to demonstrate how he surpassed the work of the prophets of Israel.

We may note some examples here from Strauss' point of view. The genealogical tables of Matthew and Luke make Jesus a descendant of David. The temptation of Jesus as well as his suffering and death parallel the temptation of Job by Satan. Many of the healing miracles of Jesus and the raisings from the dead are paralleled by similar events in the lives of prophets like Elijah and Elisha. The transfiguration is a more spectacular instance of the kind of thing that happened to Moses when he came down from the mount and his face shone after he had received the law. Even Jesus' ascension is made after the analogy of the calling of Elijah into heaven in a chariot of fire.[55]

---

[51] *Ibid.*, p. 80.
[52] *Ibid.*, p. 84.
[53] Goguel, p. 48.
[54] Klausner, p. 83.
[55] *Ibid.*, p. 84.

However, Strauss did not dissolve the life of Jesus into an absolute myth. In particular, he regarded the messianic consciousness of Jesus as an historical fact. He felt that Jesus went through a progression here. First Jesus regarded himself as the forerunner of the Messiah, and this gradually developed to the point where he felt himself to be the Messiah. He expected the help of God and his angels in the bringing in of the messianic kingdom. Finally, at the end of his life, he had developed the conceptions of his atoning death, resurrection, and second coming.[56]

A second important element in the work of Strauss was his historical evaluation of the Synoptics in comparison with John. He felt that the attempted combination of the data of the Synoptics with the Gospel of John was impossible, and decided in favor of the Synoptic Gospels,[57] inasmuch as he regarded John's Gospel as being dominated by theological and apologetic interests.[58] Although there had been some earlier vacillation on the part of the critics with respect to the comparative historical value of John and the Synoptics, it appears that from the time of Strauss onward, the preponderance of critical opinion was on the side of the Synoptics.

While Strauss was successful in elevating the Synoptics above John as historical sources, he did not go on to assert the priority of Mark as the vast majority of modern scholarship has done. He regarded Mark as the epitomizer of Matthew and, on that account, an inferior Gospel.[59]

It should be noted as an appendix to the work of Strauss that his conclusions were apparently too severe even for him to hold, because in 1864 he wrote a second life of Jesus in which he drew a picture of Jesus in conformity with liberal theology and retracted the opinions he had given in his life of 1835.[60]

CHRISTIAN WEISSE (1801-1866)

To this Leipzig professor belongs the credit for the theory of the priority of Mark, or as it is sometimes called, the Markan hypothesis. It will be recalled that most often even when the Synoptics were preferred by biblical scholars to the Gospel of John, Mark was looked down upon as an abbreviated account of an originally much more full account occurring in Matthew and

---

56 *Ibid.*
57 Goguel, p. 49.
58 Schweitzer, p. 87.
59 *Ibid.*
60 *Ibid.*, p. 95.

Luke. Schweitzer summarizes very well the arguments Weisse used to arrive at the Markan hypothesis.

> (1) In the first and third Gospels, traces of a common plan are found only in those parts which they have in common with Mark, not in those which are common to them, but not to Mark also.
>
> (2) In those parts which the three Gospels have in common, the "agreement" of the other two is mediated through Mark.
>
> (3) In those sections which the First and Third Gospels have, but Mark has not, the agreement consists in the language and incidents, not in the order. Their common source, therefore, the "Logia" of Matthew, did not contain any type of tradition which gave an order of narration different from that of Mark.
>
> (4) The divergences of wording between the two other Synoptists are in general greater in the parts where both have drawn on the Logia document than where Mark is their source.
>
> (5) The first Evangelist reproduces this Logia-document more faithfully than Luke does; but his Gospel seems to have been of later origin.[61]

In comparison with the Synoptics, Weisse holds a very low view of the historical reliability of John. He feels that the accounts of the continual conflicts of Jesus with the Jewish rulers in John are in error. According to Weisse, Jesus enjoyed unbridled success in his ministry until the final week. He further feels that the historical Jesus could not have preached the doctrine of the Johannine Christ. "It is not so much a picture of Christ that John sets forth, as a conception of Christ; his Christ does not speak *in* His own Person, but *of* His own Person."[62] However, Weisse is not willing to go to the extreme of asserting that John had no connection with the Gospel that bears his name. He feels that John had reflected long on the teaching of his master in combination with John's own inventive insight. He finally decided to draw up an account of the didactic portions for his own use. However, after John's death these brief accounts, which he had not intended to publish, fell into the hands of some of his disciples. These disciples decided to develop them into narrative form and give to the world a life of Jesus. In accordance with this plan, they put between the speeches narrative sections. In this way the Fourth Gospel originated, and for this reason little weight can be placed on its claim to accuracy.[63]

It appears that one of the determining factors in Weisse's con-

---

[61] *Ibid.*, pp. 123-24.
[62] Quoted *ibid.*, p. 125.
[63] *Ibid.*, p. 126.

struction was a feeling that while Strauss had dealt severe blows to the rationalistic and supernaturalistic positions, he was running the danger in his conception of myth of dissolving the connection of the gospel with history. He thus in his Markan hypothesis opened the road for an historical basis as a solution to this problem. To be sure, Weisse did not feel that even the Gospel of Mark contained a detailed, accurate life of Jesus; on the contrary, he regarded it as only the main outline of the life of Jesus. "He [Weisse] does not, therefore, venture to write a Life of Jesus, but begins with a 'General Sketch of the Gospel History' in which he gives the main outline of the Life of Jesus according to Mark, and then proceeds to explain the incidents and discourses in each several Gospel in the order in which they occur."[64]

BRUNO BAUER (1809-1882)

In his chapter on Bruno Bauer, Schweitzer gives as a subtitle, "The First Sceptical Life of Jesus."[65] This is an accurate designation of his work, for its importance as well as the conclusions it reaches are almost completely negative. This critic from Berlin and Bonn takes his point of departure from the Fourth Gospel. For some of the preceding scholars, as we have just noticed, the difference of John from the Synoptics indicated to them that the Synoptics stood on a much firmer basis than did John. But this conclusion was reached basically by paying primary attention to the Synoptics and casting only a casual glance at John. It appears that Bauer looked more carefully at John, and afterward the idea dawned upon him that perhaps the other Gospels were similarly constructed. That is, as he felt that John had purely a *literary* origin, he came to believe that the other Gospels might have been similarly constructed.[66]

The further Bauer studied, the more extreme his position became. He went so far as to assert that everything that is known about Jesus is a product of the imagination of the early Christian community, and as a consequence the conception that developed had no connection with any concrete personality called Jesus in the history of the world. Or to put it more succinctly, the historical Jesus never existed.[67]

The biggest obstacle left to Bauer was, consequently, to account for the origin of Christianity. He felt that it was a product of Greco-Roman civilization. From the Roman side there was

Stoicism, which had been aided by the introduction of Neo-platonic ideas. But this in itself was insufficient to account for the arrival of Christianity. Added to it was a particular kind of Judaism which was being freed from its nationalistic shackles, as is seen, for example, in the work of Philo and of Josephus. "Thus was the new religion formed. The spirit of it came from the west, the outward frame was furnished by Judaism. The new movement had two foci, Rome and Alexandria."[68]

ERNEST RENAN (1823-1892)

The *Vie de Jésus* by Renan is not of interest primarily because of its scholarly worth, but rather on the basis of the great popularity it enjoyed. Although Renan had been a Catholic, as a result of the kind of thinking that went into his book, he withdrew from the church. But he found no other religious association more acceptable. Moreover, his withdrawal from the traditional forms of religion in his day was not prompted primarily by critical objections, but rather was on the basis of aesthetic feeling.[69] This aesthetic approach best explains the popularity that his book enjoyed. As Klausner states, "It is rather a historical novel than a work of scholarship."[70] Renan's countryman Maurice Goguel summarizes its popularity very well.

> Owing to its literary qualities, Renan's *Vie de Jésus* (the first *Vie de Jésus* to appear in a Catholic country) reached an enormous public. Renan's book is as easy to read as that of Strauss is difficult; consequently it was read by hosts of people who were neither initiated into nor even prepared for exegetical research.[71]

Renan feels that John is the best biographer of Jesus. But while he would class all of the Gospels as biographies, Renan does not mean biographies in the historical sense of the term, but rather legendary biographies. All of their texts need interpretation, and the clue to proper interpretation is to be found in aesthetic feeling. "They must be subjected to a gentle pressure to bring them together, and make them coalesce into a unity in which all the data are happily combined."[72]

In accordance with his aesthetic approach, he refuses to let the reader be upset by critical questions. He refrains from taking either a negative or positive attitude toward miracles. He merely

[68] *Ibid.,* pp. 157-58.
[69] *Ibid.,* p. 180.
[70] Klausner, p. 87.
[71] Goguel, p. 50.
[72] Schweitzer, p. 183.

reports them and then adds, "We do not say miracle is impossible, we say only that there has never been a satisfactorily authenticated miracle."[73]

The difficulty of a presentation like this is pointed out by Schweitzer.

> Renan professes to depict the Christ of the Fourth Gospel, though he does not believe in the authenticity or the miracles of that Gospel. He professes to write a scientific work, and is always thinking of the great public and how to interest it. He has thus fused together two works of disparate character.[74]

* * *

One may question the value of a sketch like this, which covers only a few of many treatments and covers even these briefly. To be certain, there are several books that give them a more adequate treatment, but enough has been said here to give us some indication of the work done to the beginning of our century. Furthermore, and most important to our discussion in this book, we see in the representatives here sketched the emergence of several questions with which all subsequent writers have had to deal:

(1) *Is it possible to write a biography (history) of Jesus?*

(2) *What is the place of miracle in the life of Jesus?*

(3) *How should the resurrection of Jesus be interpreted? Literally or in some other way?*

(4) *What is the nature and place of mythology in the New Testament?*

(5) *What is the historical value of John as compared with the Synoptics?*

(6) *What is the central significance of Jesus?*

---

[73] Quoted *ibid.*
[74] *Ibid.*, p. 191.

CHAPTER TWO

LIBERAL[1] LIVES OF JESUS

The whole movement of which we have been writing to this point was a product of the Enlightenment. It originated in the desire of men to be free from church dogma and to find out the essentials of Jesus of Nazareth as he actually lived in the first century. This movement developed more uniformly in the last half of the nineteenth century. At the roots of this movement were the great advances that had been made in the natural sciences, the application of psychology to the study of Jesus, and a particular concept of history. We shall evaluate these features more in later chapters.

Schweitzer in his chapter "The 'Liberal' Lives of Jesus"[2] deals only with writers from the second half of the nineteenth century. We shall deal in this chapter with five writers from the first third of the twentieth century. One criterion of selection has been to choose men of diverse national backgrounds. Thus we will discuss a German theologian, Harnack; a French writer, Goguel; a British author, Mackinnon; an American presentation, that of Case; and finally a Jewish analysis, by Klausner.

A second reason for selecting these particular authors has to do with their importance to the movement. Thus, Harnack is in at least some respects the most significant of all these liberal theologians. His summary of the essential message of Jesus is the classic expression of the liberal faith. Goguel has written what

---

[1] The term "liberal" as it shall be used in this book refers to theological liberalism, the movement that had its beginning under Schleiermacher and was carried on by such men as Ritschl, Harnack, and Schweitzer. We do not use it, in the sense in which it is sometimes improperly used in lay terminology, to refer to everything to the theological left of orthodoxy.

[2] Albert Schweitzer, *Quest of the Historical Jesus*, pp. 193-222.

25

many scholars consider to be the best historical study of Jesus.[3]
The work by Mackinnon is perhaps the best and most comprehensive work from a British point of view. Case represents the
most important American biography from this group.[4] Finally,
the work of Klausner is the best written from the perspective of
Judaism.

A further word should be said about the religious background
of these authors. The critical movement itself has arisen primarily
from within the less conservative element in Protestantism. All
of the above writers with the exception of Klausner are from
this group. Klausner is included because, while he is a Jewish
scholar, he shares many of the opinions of this school.

It would of course be impossible to analyze all the writers who
belong to this theological approach. This is part of our reason for
selecting five authors. But, furthermore, it is impossible even to
analyze these five thoroughly within the confines of this book.
For this reason, we shall examine their works in an attempt to see
what their probable answers would be to the six questions we
raised at the end of the last chapter.

HARNACK — "WHAT IS CHRISTIANITY?" (1901)

Harnack asserts that our sources do not afford us the possibility
of writing a biography of Jesus. He notes, for example, that the
Gospels tell us nothing about Jesus' early development, but rather
confine themselves to his public ministry. He notes that Matthew
and Luke do contain the infancy narratives, but he disregards them
as historical sources, since they never recur in any other context
of the New Testament. After these introductory passages, the
Evangelists never refer to Jesus' early life again. Jesus himself
never talks of his early life, and Paul similarly is silent. From
this Harnack concludes that the earliest tradition about Jesus did
not contain anything of his early life.[5] This being the case, it is
of course impossible to write the biography of a man about whose
first thirty years we know nothing.

Even though the Evangelists give us no adequate materials for a
biography, Harnack does feel that they provide the essentials —
that which we need to know.

They are weighty because they give us information upon three

---

[3] Cf. Dwight Marion Beck, *Through the Gospels to Jesus* (New York:
Harper, 1954), p. 80.

[4] Cf. James M. Robinson, *A New Quest of the Historical Jesus* (London:
S.C.M., 1959), p. 10.

[5] Adolph Harnack, *What is Christianity?* trans. Thomas Bailey Saunders
(New York: Putnam, 1901), p. 33.

important points: In the first place they offer us a plain picture of Jesus' teaching, in regard to both its main features and its individual application; in the second place, they tell us how his life issued in the service of his vocation; and in the third place, they describe the impression which he made upon his disciples, and which they transmitted.[6]

He believes further that even concerning the thirty years of silence we can formulate some negative conclusions. In the first place, it is unlikely that he attended a rabbinical school. In this respect he compares Jesus with Paul, who everywhere exhibits his theological training. Second, he does not think Jesus had any vital contact with the Essenes. His manner of life, particularly his non-separatist tendencies, demonstrates this. Third, Harnack does not believe there is any evidence that Jesus made a radical break with his past. There is no evidence of any revolution in his inward life. Finally, clearly, and somewhat surprisingly, there is no evidence that Jesus had any meaningful contact with any of the important Greek thinkers. The surprise here is in view of the Greek influence in Galilee,[7] which was considerable.

Harnack next proceeds to analyze what can be learned from the Evangelists about Jesus' life.

With respect to the question of miracles, Harnack begins by making four generalizations. "In the first place, we know that the Gospels come from a time in which the marvelous may be said to have been something of almost daily occurrence."[8] The world of Jesus' day was a world filled with wonders. Back of these marvelous acts stood some god to whom the people were related. As a matter of fact, miracles only become meaningful in a context of knowledge of the laws of nature. This being the case, miracle is only meaningful in the context of a society that knows these laws. Furthermore, not only beneficent beings performed miracles, but also malevolent ones. For that reason, the performance of a miracle and its significance was a cause of endless controversy in Jesus' age.[9]

In the second place, he notices that miracles are attributed to famous persons almost immediately after their death. He therefore regards as prejudicial the attempt to explain miracles that are ascribed to the founder of any religion as the result of the inventive tendency of a later age.[10]

---

[6] *Ibid.,* p. 34.
[7] *Ibid.,* pp. 34-37.
[8] *Ibid.,* p. 27.
[9] *Ibid.,* pp. 27-28.
[10] *Ibid.,* p. 28.

"In the third place, we are firmly convinced that what happens in space and time is subject to the general laws of motion, and that in this sense, as an interruption of the order of Nature, there can be no such things as 'miracles'."[11] He proceeds to examine the dual nature of man's existence in the realm of ideas and perceptions and observes that that which makes man free is perceived as a mighty power working upon Nature and directing its course. He then concludes, "This notion, though it belongs only to the realm of fantasy and metaphor, will, it seems, last as long as religion itself."[12]

In the fourth place, Harnack acknowledges that while the laws of nature are inviolable, we do not understand all the operations of the forces of nature, either working separately or in combination with other forces. He says that while this is true even with respect to material forces, it is much more so the case with psychic forces. Here he is interested in such things as the effect of faith and the will on the body. He thus concludes, "Miracles, it is true, do not happen; but of the marvellous and the inexplicable there is plenty."[13]

Having made these generalizations, Harnack proceeds to classify the miracles into five categories. (1) There are first of all the stories that are exaggerated narrations of natural events. (2) There are those stories which are a mere projection on the external world of sayings, parables, or inner experiences. (3) There are stories that arose out of a desire to fulfil some Old Testament statement. (4) Some stories of cures can be attributed to the spiritual force of Jesus. (5) Finally, there are certain stories the secret of which is not available to us.[14] He concludes, "The question of miracles is of relative indifference in comparison with everything else which is to be found in the Gospels."[15]

In dealing with the subject of Jesus' resurrection, Harnack points out that we must make a distinction between two categories of evidence: the empty tomb and the appearances of Christ on the one hand, and the Easter faith on the other. If we base our faith on the empty tomb and the appearances, it will always be subject to doubt, for no orderly account can be constructed on the basis of the New Testament evidence. On the other hand, we may give up this miraculous appeal to our senses and rest our confidence in the Easter faith. As to the meaning of the resur-

---

11 *Ibid.*, pp. 28-29.
12 *Ibid.*, pp. 29-30.
13 *Ibid.*, p. 30.
14 *Ibid.*, p. 31.
15 *Ibid.*, p. 32.

rection in the New Testament, he writes, "Whatever may have happened at the grave and in the matter of the appearances, one thing is certain: this grave was the birthplace of the indestructible belief that death is vanquished, and there is a life eternal."[16]

When it comes to a discussion of the nature and place of mythology in the New Testament, Harnack is keenly aware of the work of David Strauss. He treats this in conjunction with his dealing with miracles. He notes that in an attempt to make Jesus' history a fulfilment of Old Testament prophecy and to make his person and ministry more significant, the miraculous element has been intensified. To Strauss, he says, the above evidence means that the Gospels contain a great deal of material that is mythical. He responds that this "has not been borne out, even if the very indefinite defective conception of what 'mythical' means in Strauss' application of the word be allowed to pass."[17]

Harnack then proceeds to observe that from his point of view it is only in the accounts of Jesus' childhood that the mythical can be traced, and even in this part of the narrative its use is very sparing. Furthermore, he does not feel that any of these mythical elements disturb the "heart of the narrative." For him the answer to problems is to be found in careful historical study and the comparison of the Gospels with one another, not in taking the easy way of attributing a great deal in the Gospels to myth.[18]

In dealing with the subject of the comparative value of the Synoptics as against John, Harnack is, once again, very mindful of the work of Strauss. He notes that sixty years previous to the time of Harnack's own writing, Strauss felt that he had completely destroyed the historical credibility of not only John, but the Synoptics as well. Harnack believes, however, that in the two generations between himself and Strauss, the credibility of the main outlines of the Gospels had been restored. He admits that neither the Synoptics nor John are historical works. That is, he does not think they were written with the objective of giving simply the facts. To the contrary, they are works written for the purpose of evangelization. As such their primary purpose is not history, but rather a desire to awaken faith in Jesus' person and mission. "Nevertheless they are not altogether useless as sources of history, more especially as the object with which they were written is not applied from without, but coincides in part with what Jesus intended."[19]

16 *Ibid.*, pp. 173-75.
17 *Ibid.*, p. 26.
18 *Ibid.*
19 *Ibid.*, p. 22.

In support of his assertion of the historical value of the Synoptics, Harnack notes the care with which Matthew and Luke go about writing their Gospels, in the main, in conformity with Mark's Gospel. This indicates to him that the Markan tradition was firmly established in the church.[20]

Harnack does not deal at length with his estimate of John as compared with the Synoptics, but what he says is significant. He notes that the Synoptics confine the activity of Jesus almost exclusively to Galilee with the exception of the events of passion week. This is very significant for him, because he feels that if there had not been a strong tradition demanding this presentation of the facts, the early church would likely have represented Jesus as working mainly in the city of Jerusalem. "That our first three evangelists almost entirely refrain from saying anything about Jerusalem arouses a good prejudice in their favor."[21]

Harnack summarizes his estimate of the significance of Jesus in what is generally known as the classic statement of the liberal theological position. For him, Jesus' primary significance is seen in his message as it is included in his teaching. Harnack writes,

> If, however, we take a general view of Jesus' teaching, we shall see that it may be grouped under three heads. They are each of such a nature as to contain the whole, and hence it can be exhibited in its entirety under any one of them.
>
> Firstly, the kingdom of God and its coming.
>
> Secondly, God the Father and the infinite value of the human soul.
>
> Thirdly, the higher righteousness and the commandment of love.[22]

These he regards as the main elements in the message of Jesus. It is our task as Christians to orient our thinking to them. "His words speak to us across the centuries with the freshness of the present."[23]

KLAUSNER — "JESUS OF NAZARETH" (1925)

Klausner is in agreement with Harnack that it is impossible to write a biography of Jesus, but the problem for him lies not in the scarcity of the available material, but rather in its lack of order. He begins with the remark of Papias, included in the history of Eusebius, that Mark wrote "accurately all that he remembered

---

20 *Ibid.,* p. 24.
21 *Ibid.,* p. 25.
22 *Ibid.,* p. 55.
23 *Ibid.,* pp. 55-56.

of the words and deeds of Christ, but not in order." Klausner finds this lack of order perpetuated in all the subsequent Gospels, which used Mark. This being the case, it is very difficult for us to present a complete life of Jesus, because we do not know the chronological order and settings of his deeds and sayings. This lack of order was perpetuated from the first, for the material came from the apostles spontaneously as they happened to recall it. This material was later taken by the disciples of the apostles, the Evangelists, and put in a narrative form according to the purpose each of them had in writing. This subsequent rearranging was not done with any malicious intent, but rather was in keeping with that particular purpose. That is, their chief aim in writing was not to present a biography or history as ours might be, but rather to present Jesus from a religious perspective.[24]

After pointing out the difficulties with our sources, however, Klausner hastens to add that this is no justification for casting "wholesale doubt on the historicity of the Synoptic Gospels." He does find a certain artificiality in the way the Gospel writers represent Jesus as being in mortal conflict with the Pharisaic Judaism of his day; but beyond this, the actions of Jesus, as well as his words, fit very nicely into what we know of the Jewish life and Pharisaic teaching of first-century Palestine."[25]

According to Klausner there are primarily three devices at our disposal in our attempt to decide what is historical and what is dogmatic. First, we have the literary criticism of the Gospels. Second, we may study the life of Jesus as it is presented in the Gospels. Third, we may study contemporary Judaism from sources independent of the Gospels. As a result of this,

> the mystical and dogmatic atmosphere which enveloped Jesus is removed, and we know what in the Gospels to accept and what to reject, what is early and what is late, what the Evangelists unconsciously attributed to Jesus owing to their living under the influence of the post-Pauline Church, and what, still unconsciously, they have preserved of Jesus' national Jewish features.[26]

Klausner feels that only after we have gone through such a process of selection will we find the historical Jesus, which for him is the Jewish Jesus. Although he believes that Jesus must have risen out of a Jewish environment, he apparently does not feel that the entire non-Jewish presentation of him in the New Testa-

---

[24] Klausner, *Jesus of Nazareth*, p. 126.
[25] *Ibid.*, pp. 126-27.
[26] *Ibid.*, p. 127.

ment is in error, for he hastens to add that the Jews could neither accept him as the Messiah nor his teachings as a means to their redemption.[27]

Klausner admits that the problem of miracle is a difficulty with which every life of Jesus since the time of Reimarus has had to wrestle. He refuses to take the easy way out and say that miracles are the creations of early religious leaders in an attempt to strengthen their religious position. He then proceeds to classify the miracles into five types: (1) "Miracles due to a wish to fulfil some statement in the Old Testament or to imitate some Prophet."[28] It will be noticed that this is precisely the same as the third type given by Harnack. Klausner says that the works of Elijah and Elisha are particularly in view here. If Elijah and Elisha are represented as having raised the dead, then Jesus must have done so also. As a consequence, we have the incidents of the raising of Jairus' daughter, the raising of the widow's son at Nain, and the raising of Lazarus. Similarly, if Elisha was able to supply the widow with an unfailing supply of oil, and to make twenty loaves of barley be more than sufficient for the needs of a hundred men (I Kings 4:1-37, 42-44), Jesus must be able to feed *five thousand* with *five* barley loaves, with *twelve* baskets left over. Furthermore, whenever the prophets predicted marvelous events to transpire in the messianic age, these events of necessity had to be fulfilled in the ministry of Jesus. He notices, for example, the words of Isaiah concerning the messianic age, "then shall the eyes of the blind see, and the ears of the deaf be opened; then shall the lame man leap as a hart and the tongue of the dumb sing" (Isa. 35:5-6). It can be seen very easily how these predictions are fulfilled in the life of Jesus presented in the Gospels.[29]

(2) "Poetical descriptions which, in the minds of the disciples, were transformed into miracles." This, we can see, is very much like the second type given by Harnack. Inasmuch as Jesus' disciples were simple folk, they "transformed an imaginative description into an actual deed which stirred the imagination."[30] A primary example of this is seen by Klausner in the cursing of the fig tree in Mark (11:13-14, 20, 21) and Matthew (21:19-21). Luke merely tells an incident of a man who planted a fig tree in his vineyard, and after three years of patient waiting cut it down

27 *Ibid.*
28 *Ibid.*, p. 267.
29 *Ibid.*, pp. 267-68.
30 *Ibid.*, p. 268.

because it failed to produce fruit (Lk. 13:6-9). From this Klausner concludes, "This apt parable was, therefore, transformed in
the circle of the disciples or by the evangelists into a strange
miracle inflicting a gross injustice on a tree which was guilty
of no wrong and had but performed its natural function."[31]

(3) "Illusions." Here, once again, Klausner emphasizes that the
disciples of Jesus were really very simple people. Among such
people the marvelous was an everyday occurrence. Such, for example, is the incident of Jesus walking on the Sea of Galilee. A
storm arose late at night when the disciples were weary; they
had an apparition, which later was transformed into a miraculous
occurrence.[32]

(4) "Acts only apparently miraculous." In this category Klausner puts the story of the stilling of the storm. He relates how
the Sea of Galilee is subject to such sudden changes, as occurred
on one occasion when Klausner himself was on it.[33]

(5) "The curing of numerous 'nerve-cases.'" This is very similar to the fourth type listed by Harnack. His emphasis here is
on Jesus' powers of suggestion. He notes that this is nothing
unique with Jesus, but has been practiced by many men throughout the ages. "Certain men, gifted with a peculiar will-power and
an inner life of special strength, can, by their exceptionally penetrating or tender glance or by their inner faith in their own spiritual power, influence many kinds of nervous cases and even cases
of complete insanity."[34]

After listing these five types, Klausner proceeds to discuss
another element in the miracles of Jesus. He notes that Mark in
particular emphasizes Jesus' dislike for publicity in connection
with his miracles. He points out that the majority of Christian
scholars have attributed this to Jesus' not wishing to be regarded
as a mere "wonder-worker." He feels that his own estimate of
Jesus' dislike for publicity is simpler. "His miracles were not
always successful and he was afraid to attempt them too often;
he even disliked publicity for the successful miracles lest the
people insist on more."[35]

In considering the subject of the resurrection, Klausner at once
discards the possibility of deception or mere invention on the
part of the disciples. "The nineteen hundred years' faith of mil-
lions is not founded on deception." He says that the resurrec-

---

[31] *Ibid.*, p. 269.
[32] *Ibid.*
[33] *Ibid.*
[34] *Ibid.*, p. 271.
[35] *Ibid.*, p. 272.

tion must be accounted for on the basis of a vision by some of
the Galilean disciples. He emphasizes that the vision was spiritual and not material. He finds justification for this in a comparison of the experience of the disciples with that of Paul. He
notes that Paul deliberately compares his own experience with
that of the disciples; and because Paul definitely states that he
had a "heavenly vision" (Gal. 1:16), this is obviously the experience the disciples had.

> This vision became the basis of Christianity: it was treated as
> faithful proof of the Resurrection of Jesus, of his Messiahship,
> and of the near approach of the kingdom of heaven. But for
> this vision the memory of Jesus might have been wholly for-
> gotten or preserved only in a collection of lofty ethical precepts
> and miracle stories.[36]

On the subject of the nature and place of mythology in the
New Testament, Klausner is completely silent. This is understandable considering his treatment of the miraculous. Evidently
he feels that mythology has no large place in the New Testament,
and that any elements of mythology that are included may be
accounted for in a way consistent with his discussion of the
miraculous.

Klausner's estimate of John as compared with the Synoptics is
perhaps best summarized in the following statement. "The Fourth
Gospel is not a religio-historical but a religio-philosophical book."
He goes on to say that John was not written until about the
middle of the second century and as a consequence was not written by John the apostle. By the time of its composition, Christians had become a group distinct from Judaism, and they no
longer had any dealings with official Judaism. Also, by the time
of its writing, many pagans had been converted to Christianity.[37]

The chief purpose in the writing of the Gospel was to give to
Jesus the meaning of the *Logos*. This was done in accordance
with the interpretation of Philo. For this reason the author passes
over such features in the life and death of Jesus as would make
him appear too human. He does not deny that the Gospel may
contain some historical fragments which came to the writer by
tradition, but he concludes, "Its value is theological rather than
historical or biographical."[38] Thus, while Klausner would tend to
discount the historical value of much in the Synoptics, in the
case of John the historical is minor even in comparison with them.

---

[36] *Ibid.*, p. 359.
[37] *Ibid.*, p. 125.
[38] *Ibid.*

Since Klausner is a devotee of Judaism, our final question as
to the central significance of Jesus should perhaps be rephrased,
"What is the secret of Jesus' influence?" In the first place, his
influence is not to be found in that he presented something radically new. In discussing the teaching of Jesus he writes, "There
is in it nothing that is new (i.e. not already contained in Judaism)
except its arrangement and construction." The secret of his influence lies rather in a combination of Jesus' remarkable insight
to grasp a truth in all of its profundity and his ability to express
it "in a short, shrewd proverb, grasping the idea in its fulness and
drawing from it some conclusion which can never again be
forgotten." In this way the personality of the teacher and his
teaching came to be mingled and inseparably united. His influence
was indelibly etched as a result of his death. "The tragedy of the
dreadful death which came upon Jesus wrongly (though in accordance with the justice of the time), added a crown of divine
glory both to the personality and to the teaching."[39]

CASE — "JESUS: A NEW BIOGRAPHY" (1927)

It should be self-evident from the title of his book that Case
feels it is possible at least in some sense to write a biography
of Jesus. Moreover, in his chapter "The Return to the Historical
Jesus,"[40] Case develops what he believes to be a sound basis for
historical investigation into the life of Jesus.

In the first place, he notes some of the limitations of the work
of the Evangelists. They did not, of course, use the modern scientific method in procuring their information. For this reason,
they tended to portray a Christ who fitted the needs of their
own contemporary situation. Thus in many cases the Evangelists'
interpretation of Christ had an effect on the way in which they
portrayed him. Case concludes, "A successful return to the real
Jesus is possible only if one is able to distinguish clearly between
unhistorical features in the documents and such objective data
as may have constituted the raw materials, so to speak, used
by his ancient biographers."[41]

The great problem then for Case is how to get at the element
in the Gospels that is historical; or, to put it in another way,
how to separate the original, historical element in the Gospels

---

[39] *Ibid.*, p. 412.

[40] Shirley Jackson Case, *Jesus: A New Biography* (Chicago: University
of Chicago Press, 1927), pp. 57-115.

[41] *Ibid.*, pp. 57-58.

from the interpretive additions that were added to them down to the time of their writing.[42]

He then goes on to note some traditional approaches to this problem. One approach has been to say that the canonical Gospels are good history and the apocryphal gospels are not. He does not consider this to be demonstrable, since the formation of the canon was more due to a demand for standardization than because the Gospels contained pure history.[43]

For many, an important element in support of the historicity of the canonical Gospels is the claim to their traditional authorship. He similarly discounts this as a reliable criterion inasmuch as the books themselves contain no necessary internal evidence to back up the claim, and also because the ascription of individual books to individual authors is very late. According to Case the development of interest in apostolic authorship of the various books is a development of the canonical period, when individual books were either accepted into or rejected from the canon. Consequently, a book that could be traced back to an apostle or near apostle had attached to it a strong argument for inclusion.[44]

Case disputes the traditional authorship of all the canonical Gospels with the partial exception of the Gospel of Mark. He says, for example, "Today Lucan authorship of Luke-Acts is in serious doubt. . . . A traveling companion, it is thought, could hardly have been so ignorant of the real Paul and so completely unaware of his correspondence."[45]

Case summarizes his position by saying:

> Neither the canonicity of a gospel nor tradition about its authorship is of any real value for determining the historical quality of the narrative. Not what the church has said about a book, but what the document lying before us today contains, remains the sole ground for judging its historical worth.[46]

Case goes on to explore other areas that might yield information with respect to the historical Jesus. He investigates the contribution of Acts and the letters of Paul, but decides that it is slight. The two-source theory (i.e., that the two basic sources behind the Synoptics are Mark and Q) is not of much help either, because it tells us nothing of the time up to the composition of the two

---

[42] *Ibid.*, p. 58.
[43] *Ibid.*, pp. 59-60.
[44] *Ibid.*, pp. 61-63.
[45] *Ibid.*, pp. 65-66.
[46] *Ibid.*, pp. 73-74.

sources. The investigation of the literature itself may be helpful, but it will not be very fruitful unless one goes back of it to investigate the living conditions of Jesus' time and the time of the emergence of the Gospels.[47] Thus he concludes,

> Every statement in the records is to be judged by the degree of its suitableness to the distinctive environment of Jesus, on the one hand, and to that of the framers of gospel tradition at one or another stage in the history of Christianity, on the other. When consistently applied, this fact will prove our safest guide in recovering from the present gospel records the life and teaching of the earthly Jesus.[48]

Case notes that all four Gospels show a great fondness for the miraculous. Even though books like Mark and John show restraint in regard to the infancy narratives, they share with the others a depiction of Jesus as one being very easily able to overcome any difficulty by the use of his miraculous power.[49] As far as Case is concerned, the reason for this is to be found in the need of missionary Christianity in its Gentile mission fields. In these areas, the new faith had to compete with others which claimed the power to heal through divine agency. He hastens to add, however, that appropriate as this may have been on foreign soil, it was completely inappropriate for a preacher of reform in Palestine.[50]

Acknowledging that this was an age of belief in the supernatural, he points out the difference in the significance of miracle in the Gentile and Jewish environment. To the Gentile, the ability to work miracles added to the prestige of the performer. To the Jew, however, the ability to work miracles was merely the righteous man's prerogative. "It meant that God was with him in especial measure, but not that he himself was constitutionally different from others or was in any sense entitled to worshipful reverence of his fellows."[51] Thus, Case deals even more briefly with the subject of miracles than do Harnack and Klausner, and apparently takes the miraculous element in the Gospels even less seriously than they do.

With respect to the resurrection of Jesus, he notes that it is definitely a tenet of the faith of the early church. But for Case, the problem is in going from this belief to the corresponding

[47] *Ibid.,* pp. 79-114.
[48] *Ibid.,* p. 115.
[49] *Ibid.,* p. 354.
[50] *Ibid.,* pp. 356-57.
[51] *Ibid.,* pp. 358-59.

objective fact. As a matter of fact, he holds that the movement from the belief to the fact is no longer possible. Furthermore, he sees a weakness in the foundation of this belief. "The point of departure for the early belief in Jesus' resurrection is said to be a conviction on the part of certain persons that Jesus had been seen by them after his burial, and these visions may have been due to a combination of purely natural circumstances."[52]

He goes on to point out that the disciples had been under a long and severe strain, and that after their tragic experience in Jerusalem they returned to the places of their former association with him. In these circumstances they experienced a rebirth of their former hopes. "These circumstances brought about unusual psychic experiences interpreted by those who shared them as visions of the risen Jesus."[53] For Case, therefore, the greatest importance is to be attached not to the resurrection, but rather to the Easter faith on the part of the disciples.

The nature and place of mythology in the New Testament are discussed in a chapter, "The Mythical Christ of Radical Criticism."[54] In this title "mythical" refers to the denial of the existence of the historical Jesus. For Case the alternatives are clear: "Thus modern radical criticism sets up its mythical Christ over against the historical Jesus of liberal theology." He describes the work of those in this radical school. First of all, they assert that there is no reliable evidence for the existence of the historical Jesus. This involves the positing of a second-century date for the writings of the New Testament; then advocates of this position go to great length to show the scarcity of early non-Christian references to Jesus.[55]

With these negative conclusions as their starting point, says Case, they begin to construct their positive conclusions. While he states that there is great diversity here, he finds a common element in their work in that ideas rather than persons are considered of primary importance in the origin of Christianity. Correspondingly, the origin of Christianity is to be found in a Christ-idea, not in an historical Jesus. After a very lengthy critique of the proponents of this school, he concludes, "If the possibility of his non-historicity is to be entertained at all it must be brought about by reconstructing, without reference to him, so strong a theory

---

[52] Case, *The Historicity of Jesus* (Chicago: University of Chicago Press, 1912), pp. 15-16.

[53] *Ibid.*, p. 16.

[54] *Ibid.*, pp. 32-61.

[55] *Ibid.*, p. 56.

of Christian origins that the traditional view will pale before it as a lesser light in the presence of a greater luminary."[56]

As to the comparative value of John and the Synoptics, Case has little to say, but what he does say is definitive. He characterizes the representation given of Jesus in Matthew and Luke as a "literary mosaic." In comparison to this the Gospel of John cannot claim to be a more historical work. On the other hand, "It is manifestly the work of an artist who, however true to life he may strive to paint, at the same time has an irrepressible genius for interpretative decoration."[57]

The central significance of Jesus lies for Case in the ideals he proclaimed. "Jesus proclaimed that the good life was the perfect life." He was tolerant neither of mediocrity nor of moderation in the sphere of the spiritual life. His uncompromising attitude toward both the ideal of religious life and the effort required to attain it was always emphasized. One must not let any obstacles stand in the way of achieving that goal. Thus one must be willing to cut off a hand or pluck out an eye in his effort to reach the kingdom. One must be willing to suffer persecution, hunger, affliction, and poverty on the road to that goal, and not merely by way of endurance, but as blessings. Membership in that kingdom was compared to the possession of a costly pearl. The value of this achievement must make a man ready to give up everything else, even his life if necessary, as he strives toward the goal. Case points out — and this is perhaps the most significant element for him — that Jesus did not merely preach a message for others, but gave in his own life the supreme manifestation of the seriousness with which he preached his ideals. "His own loyalty to the ideals that he preached carried the prophet from his carpenter's home in Nazareth to Christendom's cross on the Golgotha hill."[58]

MACKINNON — "THE HISTORIC JESUS" (1931)

Mackinnon agrees with the previous scholars that it is impossible to write a biography of Jesus in the modern sense. He notices, for example, that we do not have sufficient information from the early period of Jesus' life. With the exception of the nativity stories in the Gospels of Matthew and Luke and a single story of his boyhood contained in Luke, we have no reliable information on him until the time of his public ministry.[59]

---

[56] *Ibid.,* pp. 56-61.
[57] *Jesus: A New Biography,* p. 45.
[58] *Ibid.,* p. 441.
[59] James Mackinnon, *The Historic Jesus* (New York: Longmans, Green, 1931), p. viii.

Knowing this, the critic must realize that an attempt to write on the life of Jesus must be concentrated on his public ministry, which covers only two or three years of his life; consequently, it is only possible to write a history of Jesus' mission — not his life. But even here there are great problems. The nature of the record gives us difficulty. In the first place, it is not a carefully worked-out body of historical documents with which we deal, but rather a record that is largely incidental and as a consequence fragmentary in nature. For Mackinnon part of the problem lies in the silence of the record at crucial points, and part of the problem lies in what he considers to be the defect in the record. "There are ever so many critical problems, arising out of the imperfection of the record, to be weighed before we can arrive at a knowledge of the facts, and even then we cannot by any means always be sure that this knowledge is certain and final."[60] He says we are often left to conjecture and to greater or less degrees of probability, but the defect of the record has to do principally with its lack of comprehensiveness. He therefore concludes, "Nevertheless, such record as we have, if critically treated, cautiously weighed, is of the highest value."[61]

Mackinnon also has some things to say about the nature of the Synoptic Gospels, which have an effect on our attempt to write a history of Jesus. He notes that their primary purpose is not to give a history of Jesus' ministry, but rather they are intended as didactic or apologetic treatises. The question then arises for him: How far has this purpose modified the records?[62] He concludes that this imported or foreign element has not substantially affected the Gospels and their value to us as sources for the life of Jesus. "A cautious and judicial criticism, which strives to eschew subjective presuppositions, too facile reasonings, and fanciful conclusions, will win from them a fairly adequate and substantially real *apercu* of the historic Jesus, as far at least as he is made known to us in these sources."[63]

While Mackinnon admits that there are difficulties in arriving at an accurate history of Jesus' mission, he is even more certain that a skeptical position with respect to this subject is unnecessary. He notes critics who emphasize the accidental nature of the record and then go on to assert that the record is filled with later inauthentic additions.[64] "These critics seem to me to be all too

---

[60] *Ibid.,* p. viii.
[61] *Ibid.*
[62] *Ibid.,* p. xi.
[63] *Ibid.,* p. xiii.
[64] *Ibid.,* p. ix.

pessimistic. The case is by no means so hopeless as they make out. It is, in my opinion, possible to construct, in accordance with scientific historic method, a fairly adequate account of the mission of Jesus, as far at least as it has been recorded in the first three Gospels."[65]

Mackinnon's treatment of the questions regarding the miraculous and the resurrection is more comprehensive than that of the other authors we are studying. He begins his treatment of the miraculous by dealing with the subject of the healings. He sees in them actions in conformity with the Hebrew conception of God. God does intervene in the lives of men and even in the course of nature to bring things into accordance with his will. These miracles, so conceived, are evidence of a visitation of God through a new prophet. In this connection Mackinnon notes, as have the other writers, that belief in the miraculous is characteristic of the time.[66]

However, Mackinnon is not content to explain the healings merely in terms of a particular religious or social climate which said they may or must happen. The will of a God-inspired person like Jesus, he says, in cooperation with the faith of a subject of a healing, could bring about the cure of a number of diseases recorded in the Gospels. "The modern study of psycho-therapeutics, or healing by mental and spiritual means, has incontestably gone far to vindicate the reality of these cures, which an older generation of critical writers, like Strauss and Renan, too readily assumed to be the creations of myth or legend."[67]

With respect to the supernatural works of Jesus other than the healings, Mackinnon shows much more hesitation. He does not approach the subject with the presupposition that any interruption of the forces of nature is impossible. The faith of Jesus was infinite, and we dare not say that to such a one a given occurrence must be ruled out without further investigation. However, the real question for Mackinnon lies in the kind of faith these nature wonders would require on the part of Jesus. He questions if Jesus would "deliberately risk experiments of this kind." He questions whether one who in the temptation story refused to turn stones into bread, and refused to cast himself down from the pinnacle of the temple at the promise of divine protection, would attempt to walk on water, or attempt to multiply the loaves and fishes in the manner represented in the Gospels.[68]

---

[65] *Ibid.*, p. x.
[66] *Ibid.*, p. 339.
[67] *Ibid.*, p. 351.
[68] *Ibid.*, pp. 361-62.

He develops this further. In the story of the temptation Jesus refused to use God's providence magically for his own benefit. Furthermore, on another occasion Jesus refused to give the Pharisees a confirmatory "sign" to demonstrate his Messiahship (Mk. 7: 11-12). He notes that this kind of sign is typical of the Fourth Gospel, which on this account as well as others he sees to be of less value than the Synoptics.

After discussing the incident of Jesus' walking on the water, he concludes,

> Even if he stood in a unique relation to Him [God] in virtue of his supreme moral and spiritual elevation, he was, nevertheless, a real human being, and we are in danger of reducing him to a mere docetic figure and surrendering his real humanity if we exempt his body from the law of gravitation, as such stories naively do.[69]

He makes three other observations in conjunction with these wonders on the part of Jesus. (1) Like some of the other authors considered in this chapter, he thinks certain of these miracles may be the result of the combination of a natural event with faith or imagination on the part of early believers.[70] (2) In the case of incidents of a wonderful or magical kind, more proof is needed than that supplied by our Gospel writers. That is, our standard of adequate evidence is higher than they can meet.[71] (3) The reason for the inclusion of the miraculous is not to be questioned. The wonder would have been if these events had not been included in an age in which the miraculous played so large a part.[72]

Finally, Mackinnon deals with the significance of the miraculous in the Gospel records as it applies to the present. "The time is now past when, in eliminating from the Gospel the miraculous in the traditional sense, we may seriously expose ourselves to the charge of eliminating what is essential to Christianity."[73] He finds the real value of Christianity in the area of the moral and spiritual, and not in the area of what he terms the "magical."[74] He concludes,

> God's working in Nature is at once natural and supernatural. It is natural because God works through means to ends. It is supernatural because He, who is above nature, is present in this working. To explain the miraculous in terms of the natural is not, therefore, to explain the supernatural in and behind all Nature.[75]

---

[69] *Ibid.,* pp. 371-72.
[70] *Ibid.,* p. 367.
[71] *Ibid.,* p. 369.
[72] *Ibid.*
[73] *Ibid.,* p. 372.
[74] *Ibid.*
[75] *Ibid.*

In his examination of the resurrection, Mackinnon begins with the accounts of Paul, which are the earliest New Testament records. From these accounts he learns primarily two things. First, it is evident that the disciples, very soon after the death of Jesus, by means of appearances that he made to them, gained an unshakable belief that Jesus had triumphed over death. In the second place, the appearances that he made were in a spiritual body, not a physical body. It is in accordance with this that Paul's emphasis is on the burial and resurrection of Jesus (I Cor. 15: 3-4), not on the empty tomb.[76]

When we come to the later accounts preserved for us in the Gospels, there is no doubt but that they assume belief in the bodily resurrection. But while they agree with regard to the bodily resurrection, they do not agree with respect to the sequence of events following the resurrection. Furthermore, the more distant the narrative is from the event, the more the account is embroidered.[77] Mackinnon finds the reason for this emphasis in the Gospels primarily in two areas: (1) "the craving for more tangible proof that he had overcome death and had vindicated his Messianic mission and destiny, and this proof is found in the bodily raising and appearances"; and (2) "indirectly the tradition is influenced by the desire to maintain the real humanity of Jesus against the Docetic view that he only appeared on earth in a seeming body."[78]

Mackinnon then turns to an evaluation of the physical versus the spiritual resurrection. "Those who cling to a bodily resurrection, as related in these stories, assume that, if they are questioned, the resurrection faith falls to the ground."[79] He denies the validity of this position, pointing out that Jesus himself shared Pharisaic belief on this issue and that this belief was broad enough to encompass a spiritual resurrection.[80]

Having established the possibility of a spiritual resurrection from the point of view of first-century Palestine, he goes on to defend it from a modern point of view. He considers indefensible the conclusion that all spiritual phenomena are illusory. "Such an attitude is very superficial, and scientists are happily today emphasizing the spiritual reality underlying the material manifestation of it."[81] He claims for example that such a phenomenon

76 *Ibid.*, p. 286.
77 *Ibid.*, pp. 291-92.
78 *Ibid.*, pp. 293-94.
79 *Ibid.*, p. 294.
80 *Ibid.*, pp. 294-95.
81 *Ibid.*, p. 296.

as telepathy is a proven reality, and that intercourse of mind with mind is possible apart from a physical confrontation.[82]

Mackinnon then deals with the objection that Jesus did not appear to any other than the disciples, i.e., his friends. If he had really risen, why did he not appear to his enemies as well? This question dates back to Celsus in the second century. Here Mackinnon uses his conception of a spiritual resurrection to advantage. In the case of Jesus' enemies, the conditions for receiving such an experience were not present. Two essentials for such an experience are sympathy with and aspiration after the object. "We cannot come by these experiences without the receptive mind, the spiritual atmosphere to which they belong. For there is really nothing supernatural in them. They are the facts of the spiritual life, and without the conditions of them they cannot be, as it were, extemporised."[83]

He calls attention to the tendency to posit material proofs for what is spiritual, but notes that the essential meaning of the resurrection is to be found in that Jesus was great enough to transform the faith of the disciples, in spite of the cross, into a spiritual communion. It is in this belief in a higher spiritual, divine life, which we see exemplified in Jesus, that we have our own belief in a blessed immortality. "Only let those who cherish this belief not risk it by resting it on other than rational, spiritual grounds."[84]

Myth, to Mackinnon as to most others discussed in this chapter, means the nonexistence of the historical Jesus. His position in this regard is not left in doubt. "The myth theory is an absurdity in the face of the evidence of Paul, let alone the Gospels."[85] He goes on to show how those who hold this theory must deal very arbitrarily with the literature of the Synoptic Gospels. They are forced to transform the narratives of the Gospels into mere symbolic representations of a body of beliefs and hopes centering about a cult deity called Jesus.[86]

For Mackinnon, the mythical school represents the opposite extreme of the orthodox school. "Whilst the orthodox theologians have tended to transform him into an abstraction in the course of their dogmatic controversies, the mythicists have sought to deny his historical existence and transform him into the unreal creation of a Christ cult."[87] He notes that this "craze" has been

---

82 *Ibid.*, p. 297.
83 *Ibid.*, pp. 297-98.
84 *Ibid.*, pp. 298-300.
85 *Ibid.*, p. xv.
86 *Ibid.*
87 *Ibid.*, p. 396.

refuted repeatedly, and that it is something on which we "need no longer waste our time. Without the historic Jesus there would have been no Christianity and no Church to found."[88]

Mackinnon feels that the Synoptics are as history on a much higher level than John, although even they cannot be used without discretion. On the other hand, one cannot ignore the historical importance of John absolutely. The reasons for the correspondingly less value placed on John are several. In the first place, it is the latest of the Gospels, coming from around the turn of the second century. In the second place, it is much more deeply colored than are the Synoptics by the conditions of the time of the writer and by his own theological position. "The writer depicts him and his mission in the light of his Christian thought and experience and the conditions of the age in which he himself lived and taught."[89] Thus the writer is predisposed to idealize Jesus and to transform him into a personality acceptable to Paulinism and Hellenistic philosophy. "It is a very mixed record of fact and the individual conception of fact."[90]

On the other hand, Mackinnon feels that people who completely ignore the historical element in John make as much of a mistake as those who accept it as an historical document. The separation of the historical from the interpretation of the author is a difficult task, but a necessary one.[91]

In trying to pinpoint the significance of Jesus, Mackinnon begins by stating that Jesus is different from and subordinate to the Father. However, "He is immeasurably great in the spiritual and ethical sphere."[92] As such, his chief greatness lies in the inspiration he gave to his disciples. We see in him "The combination of the highest moral and spiritual ideal with the firm belief in an ultimate renewal of the world."[93] Or as he also puts it, "Jesus laid hold of the ideal as a means of transforming the real."[94] He describes Jesus as "the greatest of Utopians." Out of his leadership and the inspiration of his character has arisen the church, which through his influence "has made and moulded history to the highest ends wherever his spirit and his teachings have taken a grip on men's souls."[95]

---

[88] Ibid.
[89] Ibid., pp. xiii-xiv.
[90] Ibid., p. xiv.
[91] Ibid.
[92] Ibid., p. 394.
[93] Ibid., p. 395.
[94] Ibid.
[95] Ibid.

GOGUEL — "THE LIFE OF JESUS" (1933)

Goguel begins his study of the question of history by noting that those who passed on the early traditions were not fundamentally interested in either biography or history. This lack of concern for historical accuracy is to be found in several areas. The transmitters had no primary interest in history for the sake of history. They did not have the particular mentality to write history even if they had desired; and finally, such things as apologetic motives prevented them from writing history in the modern sense.[96]

In connection with this he says, "The facts did not interest them so much as facts but as the revelation of a transcendent reality." Goguel therefore concludes that it should not surprise us that the presentation of the facts has been worked over and altered to some extent. The real surprise is that early Christian tradition did not completely submerge the historical and replace the accounts we have in the Gospels "with a myth which would have been an interpretation and explanation of the Christian faith at once more homogeneous, more direct, and more integral."[97]

Consequently, the answer for Goguel is found neither in the historical accuracy of the Gospels, nor in a skepticism with respect to their historical accuracy. "It will never be possible to reconstruct the story otherwise than in a fragmentary and conjectural manner, and thus to resolve the problem of the life of Jesus."[98]

Goguel approaches the subject of miracle with some hesitation. He feels that this question belongs more to the sphere of the philosophical than the historical.[99] He notes, as have others in this chapter, Jesus' refusal to give the Pharisees the "sign" they desire (Mk. 7:11-12). He also notes Jesus' refusal to use miracle in the narrative of the temptation (Mk. 4:3-7). From these two incidents he concludes that the working of miracles was not very important in the ministry of Jesus. "They were not at the center of his work, but on the circumference, and even on the fringe."[100]

Certain categories of miracles he summarily dismisses. For example, incidents like the healing of the ear of the servant of the high priest in Lk. 22:51 must be rejected since the other Gospels do not mention it. It is to Goguel unthinkable that the other Evangelists would have omitted such an incident had it occurred. Another category he would omit is that of what he regards as

---

96 Goguel, *The Life of Jesus*, p. 180.
97 *Ibid.*
98 *Ibid.*, p. 183.
99 *Ibid.*, p. 216.
100 *Ibid.*, p. 219.

theological explanations. In this class are the accounts of the virgin birth and the transfiguration, along with others.[101]

Ultimately, however, for Goguel, the miracles as a whole may be explained by one of two possibilities. They may be the result of pious imagination, or they may be regarded as interpretations given by spectators to natural events or coincidences.[102]

Goguel deals with the resurrection in the second volume of his trilogy on Jesus and the origin of Christianity.[103] He feels that by a careful analysis of the tradition contained in the Gospels, we can get an idea of the sequence of events that led to such a belief. It appears that the disciples were discouraged and dismayed as a result of the crucifixion of Jesus; however, after a period of time the length of which we are unable to determine, they regained their courage. They began to meditate on what Jesus had told them about the meaning of his suffering and death. As a result of this they began to think of Jesus as living, not dead. Subsequently, they began to think of Jesus as one who would return to fulfil his office as the Messiah. "Jesus first rose in the heart of his disciples who had loved and believed in him."[104] He notes that according to Renan belief in the resurrection resulted from a miracle of love on the part of the disciples. Goguel says that "Rather than speak of a miracle of love it would have been better to speak of a miracle of faith which prevented those who had for a few months lived with tremendous expectations believing that they had been snatched away from them."[105]

The sequence of events for Goguel would thus be somewhat as follows. The belief in the resurrection of Jesus originated in the hearts of his disciples, especially Peter. "The appearance of Christ to him created both the idea and the belief simultaneously." Subsequently, he appeared to others who were acquainted with the initial appearance to Peter but needed yet to give their full loyalty to Jesus. These appearances led to the idea of the empty tomb, which at first was a consequence of belief in the resurrection, but gradually assumed an independent status and was relied upon more and more as evidence.[106]

Goguel approaches the subject of mythology in much the same way as have the other writers discussed in this chapter. The pri-

---

[101] *Ibid.*, pp. 218-19.

[102] *Ibid.*, pp. 219-20.

[103] Maurice Goguel, *The Birth of Christianity*, trans. H. C. Snape (New York: Macmillan, 1953), pp. 218-19.

[104] *Ibid.*, p. 74.

[105] *Ibid.*, pp. 74-75.

[106] *Ibid.*, p. 75.

mary question for him is: Are we to see in Jesus an historical person or a creation of religious myth? His answer to this question is very direct: Jesus is an historical person. His objection to the myth theory is twofold. In the first place, myths break down under careful examination; second, they raise difficulties that are much more difficult to solve than the problems they pretend to solve. For these reasons he states, "Without any hesitation I affirm the historical character of the person of Jesus."[107]

Goguel joins the other writers in attributing less historical significance to John than to the Synoptics. The author of the Fourth Gospel has altered his material, has adapted it to his specific purposes, and has introduced additions into it; consequently, the value of his Gospel is not to be found in its framework or general construction, but rather in the traditional material he has incorporated into his work.[108]

What guided the author in his selection of his materials? His chief purpose was the edification of his readers, and their up-building in the Christian faith. For this reason we have in this Gospel a collection of incidents which are really independent of each other. The guiding purpose in their selection was the enlightening of the Christians or their confirmation in different aspects of the Christian faith. "It is a series of meditations on the Gospel story, set in a framework composed of narratives relating to John the Baptist and the story of the Passion."[109]

The Gospel was consequently not written to present a history of the life of Jesus, but rather to edify the Christians at the time of its writing and to strengthen them in their faith. "The attempt, therefore, to discover a history of the life of Jesus in the Johannine Gospel is due to a misunderstanding of the nature of this Gospel."[110]

What is the central significance of Jesus from Goguel's point of view? He states at the outset that Jesus did not intend to begin a new religion. In his attempt to reform and correct the Judaism of his day, he was largely unsuccessful, and this caused him to lose some of the hopes that he had cherished in his early ministry; but regardless of his dismay with the Jews themselves, he never condemned their religion. They had become enslaved to the letter of the law and had failed to grasp the great principles laid down in the Law and the Prophets and to put them into application in their daily lives. "It was through fidelity to the ideal Judaism that

---

[107] *The Life of Jesus,* p. 200.
[108] *Ibid.,* p. 157.
[109] *Ibid.,* pp. 156-57.
[110] *Ibid.,* p. 157.

Jesus became detached from empirical Judaism and condemned it, and did not feel that he was the founder of a new religion."[111]

But while Jesus himself did not intend to found a new religion, his work resulted in just that. Goguel's point of departure is Jesus' cry from the cross, "It is finished."

> The work of Jesus was finished. The faith which he had been able to plant in the hearts of a few men, feeble and hesitating as it was, had roots which were too deep to be ever eradicated. Nothing was finished; in reality, everything had just begun. The faith in the Resurrection was about to be born, and with it that Christianity which was destined to conquer the Ancient World and to march through the centuries.[112]

SUMMARY

While the material in the five authors just surveyed may appear on first glance to be very diverse in nature, upon closer examination it will be seen that their works give evidence of a remarkable similarity. For this reason, as a summary to this chapter and as an attempt to get at an overall view of these liberal lives we shall put our six questions to the group as a whole. In so doing we must be aware that the summation in each case might not be acceptable in every detail to any single author; however, it will be in most cases representative of the school.

1. *Is it possible to write a biography (history) of Jesus?*

Although one of the books by Case contains the word "biography" in its title, it is certain that he is agreed with the other authors that the writing of a biography of Jesus in the modern sense is not possible. Although there is a difference in emphasis on the part of the five authors, three reasons for this impossibility occur rather frequently, and are somewhat constant. (1) The lack of comprehensiveness of the material makes it impossible. Our Gospel records tell very little about the early life of Jesus. Aside from the nativity stories of Matthew and Luke and one brief incident in Luke about Jesus' early childhood, there is nothing on his life until we reach the years of his public ministry. Or, to put it in even more pointed form, the only very significant material we have in the Gospels at all concerning the life of Jesus is limited to a period of two or three years.

(2) Although this point is not nearly as much emphasized as is the first, Klausner in particular, and other authors to a lesser extent, emphasize the lack of order of the material. While the

---

[111] *Ibid.,* p. 585.
[112] *Ibid.,* p. 586.

explanation for this is variously traced, the reason most constantly given is that the writers of the Gospels lacked historical judgment. Sometimes it is said that this lack of historical judgment is because the scientific method had not yet arrived, and consequently it is unwise for us to posit of these authors what is true of our society in the twentieth century.

(3) It is emphasized in the third place that the Gospels are not historical in intent. That is, the writers of the Gospels had no primary interest in history. Their chief motivation for writing was "religious," to use the most general term. This religious motivation had a twofold aspect. Positively, it was to evangelize, instruct, exhort, and inspire. Negatively, their writings served as an apology to the pagan world.

But while the five authors are agreed that a biography in the modern sense of the word is not possible, they are equally agreed that our records do not lead us to an absolute skepticism so that we must give up any attempt to write a more limited historical account of Jesus' ministry, or, as some have thought, give up completely the idea of the existence of a person called Jesus.

These factors being the case, the liberal scholars feel that the way to proceed is to enter on a process of selection from the Gospels in order to arrive at historical truth regarding Jesus. The technique foremost in the minds of these authors is what has come to be called literary criticism, in all of its multitudinous facets. A consideration of the source of the material in our Gospels, the attendant questions of authorship and date of a given book, the analysis of the life of first-century Palestine — its geographical, political, social and religious structure — are only some of the areas that come up for investigation.

Out of this long and laborious process, these scholars are confident that we can at minimum obtain a sketch of Jesus as he really was in first-century Palestine.

2. What is the place of miracle in the life of Jesus?

All of the authors start with the assumption that the miraculous — i.e., revelatory acts of direct divine volition operating outside of any known or unknown secondary laws of nature — is impossible. They go on to state that the world of the New Testament era was one saturated with belief in the reality of miracles. This being the case, it is not at all surprising that we find them in our Gospels.

The authors note that Jesus is represented at least on occasion as having an extreme dislike for performing miracles. On other occasions he seems to have experienced some difficulty in trying to bring them about. They even go so far as to question whether he would attempt to work any miracles, for they see in such acts at least an implied temptation of God.

This being the case, what are presented as miracles in the Gospels must be accounted for on thoroughly rationalistic bases. The miracles that are treated the least drastically are some of the instances of Jesus' healings. As a result of Jesus' profound religious insight and spiritual depth, he was able to see the difficulty involved in many of these cases and to bring about a cure, much the same way modern physicians have done, by realizing the effect of the mind on the body.

A second class of miracles is to be explained as faulty sense perception on the part of the disciples. In this category Jesus' walking on the water is a favorite of these writers.

A third and much larger class of miracles arose from the pious imagination of the early Christians. Some of these arose from meditation on a parable or poetic saying of Jesus, which was subsequently enlarged into a miraculous event. As a story was subject to embroidery in passing it on, so was an event. Consequently, an event that was perfectly natural in its origin sometimes came to have a miraculous interpretation as it was passed along. Another group of these miracles arose out of a desire by the early church to have Jesus fulfil some prophecy given in the Old Testament. Finally, some authors suggest that certain of these stories may have been invented by incipient Christianity in order to compete more favorably with rival faiths.

In a fourth class are miracles that, while certainly not being miraculous in the sense stated, must simply be left without explanation. We cannot tell what was involved in their origin or transmission.

Finally, the five authors are agreed that the occurrence of miracles cannot be regarded as an essential element in the literature of the New Testament. For these writers, that they did not happen as related is of little consequence.

3. *How should the resurrection of Jesus be interpreted?*

This question is of course very closely linked to the previous one, and thus it is no surprise to us that they agree that a physical resurrection did not occur. They all admit that the Gospel record says a physical resurrection did in fact occur. This being the case, the writers are forced to choose between one of two alternatives. Either our Gospel records are inventions pure and simple on the part of the early church, or they are developments from an historical nucleus. The invention theory is at once thrown out.

There remains in these authors some uneasiness in the rejection of the physical resurrection, but where this is the case it is merely stated that historical verification of such an event, even if it had occurred, is impossible.

These writers most often find the origin of the resurrection in a vision to the bereaved disciples. After a period of depression, the disciples regained their composure and had a vision of Christ in which they perceived that he had not been taken from them at all, but now continued with them in a new, spiritual manner. While most of these authors refer to this resurrection as a vision, Mackinnon uses the words "spiritual resurrection." The difference here, however, seems to be not so much in content as in choice of terminology.

This idea of vision is also helpful in explaining why Jesus did not appear to any other than his friends. In order to receive such a vision, one must be receptive to it. Jesus' enemies were not receptive, and as a consequence, he did not appear unto them.

4. *What is the nature and place of mythology in the New Testament?*

The idea of myth in connection with Jesus is frowned upon if not disdained by these authors. The most usual connotation it has for them is that of the denial of the existence of the historical Jesus. Harnack appears to use it in the more limited sense of an arbitrary invention with no historical truth and to apply it to individual incidents in the life of Jesus rather than to his life as a whole, but even so it gains little more favor with him than it does with the others. If myth is accepted in the terms in which these writers think of it, it means that Jesus had no historical existence, but that he is rather the creation of a bizarre Christ-cult of the first century. This they deny categorically.

5. *What is the historical value of John as compared with the Synoptics?*

The liberal scholars are in agreement that none of the Gospels was written primarily for the sake of presenting historical facts. This being the case, they must all be used with care and discretion in attempting to construct an historical account of the life of Jesus. Evangelization and other concerns related to it were foremost in the minds of the Gospel writers. But while this may be the case, the Synoptics stand on a definitely higher level than does John. They may not be primarily historical works, but they are religio-historical. At least there is not in them a point of view that is opposed to history.

On the other hand, John is recognized as a work that is religio-philosophical rather than religio-historical. Its chief concern is with theology. It is a work that is written chiefly to edify and not to give account of events. Furthermore, it gives evidence of being a very carefully designed artistic work, and as such its value is found much more in its style than in its history. On the other hand, these authors are not willing to throw it out as an historical source. It does contain some historical material, but this must be carefully separated from the bulk of the material and used very cautiously.

In addition to its general nonhistorical character, there are one or two other things that militate against the Gospel of John as compared with the Synoptics. In the first place, according to these writers, it was written very late. Those who express themselves date it anywhere from the end of the first to the middle of the second century. Also, the Synoptics present Jesus' ministry as taking place primarily in Galilee, while John places it primarily in Judea and Jerusalem; and these writers hold that the Synoptics are right on this point and John is wrong.

6. *What is the central significance of Jesus?*

Here the writers are agreed both by direct statement and by implication that Jesus was not the metaphysical Son of God or deity. The difference of Jesus from us was not one of kind, but only one of degree. On the other hand, these writers agree that he was looked upon as deity by the early Christians.

If then we are to attempt to estimate the significance of Jesus, it must be from the point of view of his excellence as a man. Here various terms are used by the various writers, but they may be all summed up in the following. He is revered primarily for his ethical thought, his spiritual force, and his moral excellence. He was a man of high ideals, and he made these ideals effective in the lives of his followers because he had exceptional ability as a teacher, and he practiced perfectly what he taught — even to the extent of going to his death for his beliefs. Therefore, he was not only effective as a reformer, but through his leadership he was able to inspire in his disciples the same zeal, which was instrumental in forming the church, the continuing evidence of his significance.

* * *

In the critical school in French and Anglo-Saxon scholarship, the work of the liberal school has continued with only slight

modification.[113] However, in German theological thought, a kind
of approach to the New Testament has developed that has
emphatically rejected the methodology and approach of these
liberal writers. We shall trace this German development in subsequent chapters.

---

[113] Cf. James M. Robinson, p. 9.

CHAPTER THREE

HISTORY OF RELIGIONS SCHOOL

GENERAL APPROACH

During the final decade of the nineteenth century a movement originated in Germany that began to question the legitimacy of the liberal approach to the life of Jesus. It had basically two questions to ask of the liberal scholars. (1) What right had the liberal scholars to assume "that the full and final revelation of God has been mediated through the facts of history"?[1] History is a very relative and transient factor in the story of mankind. Jesus comes from an era that is far removed from our own. Why should contemporary man build his faith upon so remote and uncertain a foundation as the historically demonstrable facts of the life of Jesus?[2]

(2) Another question asked was, What right had liberal scholarship to treat Christianity as an isolated phenomenon in the history of man's religious experience? To be sure these scholars had discussed Christianity in its relation to the Old Testament, but why had not the Hellenistic background of the early church been explored? Out of these unanswered questions arose the movement generally referred to as the History of Religions school. It sought to understand Christianity in terms of the contemporary Hellenistic world.[3]

Wilhelm Heitmüller, an early advocate of the History of Re-

---

[1] Hugh Ross Mackintosh, *Types of Modern Theology* (New York: Scribner, 1964), p. 182.

[2] *Ibid.*

[3] *Ibid.*, pp. 182-83.

ligions school, put it this way: "Early Christianity lived in an atmosphere which was saturated by Mystery-bacilli and grew up in a soil which had been fertilized and broken up by the decay and syncretism of the most varied religions, a soil which was thus especially fitted to provide new life for old seeds and shoots."[4] Once the questions had been asked, the development within the school was very rapid. Every facet of Christianity was compared with similar concepts that appeared in other religions. More and more it was discovered that what was previously thought to have been unique in Christianity was not so at all, and the devotees of this school came to the conclusion that Christianity was the product of syncretism.[5] As another of the school put it,

> Christianity is a syncretistic religion. It contains, and has to advantage transformed, strong religious themes deriving from abroad, both Oriental and Hellenistic. For it is the character-istic, we might almost say providential, feature of Christianity that it had its classical period at that moment in history when it moved from the Orient into the Greek world. . . . These foreign religious themes must have infiltrated into the com-munity of Jesus immediately after his death.[6]

The advocates of this school consequently proceeded to identify the great variety of movements that went into the formation of early Christianity. With respect to areas of the ancient world, Jewish, Greek, and Oriental thought all made their contribution. From within the circle of Judaism itself, some elements were taken from the more orthodox rabbinic sector, and others were taken from the more liberalized Hellenistic sector. Philosophical insights gained from Stoic ethics were combined with emotional elements taken from the Greek mystery religions. Rigorous asceticism was combined with the esoteric features of developing gnosticism, and an undeveloped form of rationalism was combined with the ecstat-ic experiences of mysticism.[7]

It was therefore felt that Christianity was more a product of ancient thought than a challenge to ancient thought. It was more a result of religious development of the first century than an initiator of that development. It was more a consequence of a powerful religious movement from the East into the West than a transformer of ancient religious thought. Its significance was more

---

[4] Quoted in Heinz Zahrnt, *The Historical Jesus*, trans. J. S. Bowden (New York: Harper, 1963), p. 57.

[5] *Ibid.*

[6] Hermann Gunkel, quoted *ibid.*, p. 57.

[7] *Ibid.*, p. 56.

in the different names that were used to express old concepts than in a presentation of radically new concepts to the ancient world.[8]

WILHELM BOUSSET

Because this movement was relatively short-lived and also because it was mainly a German movement, it is possible to gain an understanding of this school of thought by studying only one representative scholar. Perhaps the chief representative of the school was Wilhelm Bousset of Göttingen.

Bousset is even less optimistic than were the members of the liberal camp as to the possibility of writing a biography or history of Jesus. He begins his work by noting that the only segment of the life of Jesus that we have any knowledge of at all is the comparatively short period of his public ministry. Anything previous to that contained in our Gospels belongs to the realm of legend. He goes to considerable length to point this out. In the first place, it is significant to him that our earliest Gospel, Mark, has nothing to say on the events of Jesus' infancy and that "even the fourth passes them over in silence."[9] He proceeds to show that even Matthew and Luke disagree on almost every particular except that Jesus was born in Bethlehem. Luke assumes that Nazareth was Jesus' native town, while Matthew apparently designated Bethlehem as the former home of Jesus' parents. If one chooses the apparently more historical account of Luke, which gives an attempted explanation for the presence of Jesus' parents in Jerusalem at the time of his birth, one is little better off, for this account, which brings them to Jerusalem for the purpose of a census in the reign of Augustus, "is full of historical impossibilities."[10]

Furthermore, the story of Jesus' miraculous birth is merely "a piece of dogmatic legend." He feels that this idea is refuted elsewhere in the Gospels when they refer to Jesus as the carpenter's son or talk about Jesus' brothers and sisters. Even more significantly, the genealogies in Matthew and Luke are traced to David through Joseph. From this he concludes that these genealogies must have been developed before the birth stories, because in connection with the birth stories they lose all their meaning. Finally, the apostle Paul knows nothing of the virgin birth and apparently even refutes it in at least two passages. In Rom. 1:3 he calls Jesus "the seed of David according to the flesh," and in

---

[8] *Ibid.,* pp. 56-57.

[9] W. Bousset, *Jesus,* trans. Janet Penrose Trevelyan (New York: Putnam, 1906), p. 1.

[10] *Ibid.,* pp. 2-3.

Gal. 4:4 he refers to him as "born of a woman." Bousset therefore concludes that if the "dogma of the miraculous birth" is of
no importance to Paul, it can be of no importance to us.[11]

As a consequence, we know nothing of importance concerning
the life of Jesus until he was a grown man at about the age of
thirty. But of how much more historical value is the material in
the Gospels regarding the period of Jesus' public ministry? Here
Bousset is little more optimistic, at least with respect to chronology.

> We are no longer in a position to reconstruct an historical pic-
> ture of the ministry of Jesus in Galilee according to its chron-
> ological development, for the narrative of our Gospels, with
> its prevailing timelessness and its frequent arrangement of the
> words and deeds of Jesus in a designedly material order, does
> not provide the means necessary for such a picture. Only a few
> scanty data can be established with certainty.[12]

As a consequence, we cannot be certain of the outward course
of Jesus' life; and when it comes to an analysis of Jesus' internal
development, "we find ourselves plunged in uncertainties and
obliged to be content with conjectures of a greater or less degree
of probability."[13]

Even a superficial comparison of the views of Bousset with
those of the liberal school will reveal how different is his approach
from theirs. To be sure, the liberal theologians saw problems in the
sources for writing an account of the Jesus of history, but their
doubts were not nearly as deep as those of Bousset. The liberals
were skeptical of the value of the larger part of the narratives of
Jesus' birth and childhood, but they did not totally reject the
tradition as does Bousset. The liberals felt that the Gospels must
be used with great caution in attempting to get at the Jesus of
history, but there was not nearly the lack of confidence in the
ability to reconstruct a chronology of Jesus' life that we see in
Bousset. Thus, as one modern writer has put it, "the confidence
of the liberals, who had believed themselves capable of reconstructing a picture of the historical Jesus, gave way to the scepticism of the historians of religion, in whose hands the picture of
the historical Jesus began to disintegrate more and more."[14]

If we ask further why it was that the History of Religions school
adopted this position of historical skepticism, we may perhaps
find the answer in a later work of Bousset. "The purely historical

---

[11] *Ibid.*, pp. 3-4.
[12] *Ibid.*, pp. 11-12.
[13] *Ibid.*, p. 14.
[14] Zahrnt, p. 55.

is really never able to make an impression, but rather only the living present symbol, in which one's own convictions are transfigured and presented."[15] While we shall say more of this presently, we here note only that from Bousset's point of view the relationship of Christ the Lord in the New Testament to Jesus of Nazareth "was both historically questionable and theologically irrelevant."[16]

Thus, it is basically the idealism of this school that led it to question the importance of history. Salvation is not to be found in history but rather in metaphysics. The need for a reference to a person at all is to be found in the need for a cult symbol around which to gather. "Community and cult are formed only around an historical person. Men want more than myth, they want real, vivid life. A symbol is only a symbol for men of faith if it is a real man, who has lived, fought and conquered."[17] As a consequence of this, we see in the History of Religions school a replacing of historical interests with those of metaphysics and sociology.[18]

Like the liberal writers, Bousset makes a distinction between the healings of Jesus and his other miracles. With respect to the healings, "Jesus made use of religious and spiritual means alone."[19] Moreover, Bousset states, "His method of healing may be called a psychical one."[20] The clue here lies in the resources of Jesus' inner life. He had such an immense faith in God that he was able to awaken similar faith in the subjects of his healing. "Thus his healing activity lies entirely within the bounds of what is psychologically conceivable, and this feature of the life of Jesus has nothing absolutely unique about it. The history of religion offers countless analogies to it down to the most recent times."[21] He goes on to mention cases in our own day, like those at Lourdes, which have pointed out to us the great effectiveness of such things as suggestion, autosuggestion, and hypnotism. If we carry our knowledge back to the day of Jesus himself, we can see how much more likely it is that something of this character would happen then. We have there not only the very forceful personality of Jesus, but we have along with it the confidence of the people. These people of a prescientific day entertained no suspicions as to the

---

[15] W. Bousset, *Kurios Christos* (Göttingen, 1913), p. 75, quoted in James M. Robinson, *A New Quest*, p. 75.
[16] Robinson, p. 75.
[17] Zahrnt, p. 59.
[18] *Ibid.*
[19] Bousset, *Jesus*, p. 47.
[20] *Ibid.*
[21] *Ibid.*, p. 48.

possibility of the miraculous. Thus Jesus was able to accomplish
in them much more than would a similar wonder-worker in our
day, because their confidence in his ability pushed them to the
limits of what was psychologically possible.[22] This is confirmed
for Bousset in that, in certain instances where Jesus found no faith,
he found it impossible to work cures (Mk. 6:5ff.).

There is a special category of Jesus' healings with which Bousset
deals in particular. Those persons who are represented in the
Gospels as demoniacs are in terms of our day the mentally un-
sound. The popular conception of these diseases in Jesus' day,
when disease was not well understood, was to attribute them to
the agency of demons who possessed the afflicted individuals. He
then observes, "Jesus, who was quite a son of his time with regard to these outward ideas, shared their belief."[23] Therefore, some
cures are explained in terms of the departure of demons. Cases
where persons were temporarily relieved and then became worse
are explained as the return of the demon with others worse than
himself (Mt. 12:43-45).

In an attempt to evaluate the importance of the miracles from
Jesus' point of view, Bousset appears to take both a positive and
a negative attitude. On the positive side, he notes the reply of
Jesus to the messengers from John the Baptist (Mt. 11:2ff.). He
also notes that Jesus forecasts woe for the cities of Chorazin and
Bethsaida due to their unbelief in the face of his signs and wonders
(Mt. 11:20ff.). On the negative side he states, "He never regarded
his miracles as anything absolutely unique, or as in themselves
sufficient to confirm him in the eyes of the multitude as the
heaven-sent Messiah."[24] In this connection he notes Jesus' refusal
on occasion to work signs (Mk. 8:11f.).

The miracles of Jesus apart from the healings Bousset puts in a
separate class. "As we know, our Gospel tradition transformed
Jesus into a miracle-worker in the absolute and special sense."[25]
In this class are the raisings from the dead, walking on water,
stilling the storm, feeding the five thousand, etc. As he puts it,
"The devout community traced the simple outline of the human
Jesus upon the gold background of the miraculous."[26] However,
we can still get back to the actual event in many of these cases by
our knowledge of the psychologically possible, and by our ability
to separate the historical from the traditional. "There are in

22 *Ibid.*, pp. 48-49.
23 *Ibid.*, pp. 49-50.
24 *Ibid.*, pp. 51-52.
25 *Ibid.*, p. 53.
26 *Ibid.*

fact but a few stories which record an absolutely miraculous and impossible event, or one for which no analogy can be found. These few must then be cast aside as the mere outgrowths of legend."[27] However, Bousset is convinced that back of most of these miracle-stories lies an historical kernel.

The chief difference in Bousset's approach to miracle from that of the liberal scholars is more one of emphasis than of substance. Bousset does not enter into such a minute analysis and classification of the miracles as do some from the liberal school. Further, while according to Bousset legend plays a rather small part in the miracles of the Gospels, it does at least have some significant place. We shall discuss this further in conjunction with mythology. As a whole, however, there is nothing radically different between the approaches of the two schools.

Bousset dwells more on the death of Jesus than he does on the resurrection. He notes that the church throughout its history has sought to find some special significance in the death of Jesus outside of the fact of the death itself. "In her, that is to say in Paul, whose spirit gave the direction to centuries of development, the Jewish feeling that suffering and defeat were shameful, ignominious, and abhorrent, a problem which demanded special explanation, continued to operate in this one particular."[28]

Bousset makes two primary observations in this regard. In the first place, he thinks it is wrong to seek specialized meaning in Jesus' death. "For us his suffering, crucifixion, and death are the crown and consummation of his life."[29] To him, the supreme meaning of his death is simply that he died. The cross is the element that lifts Jesus above the founders of all other religions. In his death, his uniqueness is revealed.[30]

In the second place, Bousset believes that the resurrection must be treated apart from the study of Jesus' life and personality. This belongs to the early history of the church. "The days of the Passion were followed by Easter in the disciples' hearts, and with the tidings that their Lord had risen again and was alive they founded the first Christian community."[31] Bousset is not primarily interested in the content of those experiences that made up Easter. He feels that they were transient and have no lasting significance. The real significance of the resurrection was that Jesus, whom

[27] *Ibid.*, p. 54.
[28] *Ibid.*, p. 208.
[29] *Ibid.*
[30] *Ibid.*, p. 209.
[31] *Ibid.*, pp. 209-210.

they had come to know so well and love on earth, now appeared to them in a form "freed from all the chances and changes of mortal life." It was this release of Jesus from the temporal and his constant abiding with them that was for them the chief significance of the resurrection.

Once again, we see no significant difference from the liberal lives of the previous chapter. There is less concern here for the precise nature of the resurrection, and with it less concern for its temporal setting, but its meaning is little altered.

When it comes to the question of mythology in the New Testament, there appears to be somewhat of a shift in Bousset from that of the liberal scholars. That shift is to be seen particularly in a greater willingness to consider certain portions of the Gospels as mythological, rather than to equate myth with the denial of the existence of the historical Jesus and thus to dismiss it. We have already noticed that Bousset does feel that a certain amount of material in the miracles of Jesus is a product of legend, small though that amount may be.[32] Of the infancy narratives in Luke, Bousset writes,

> Nor will the first chapters of Luke, with their wonderful poetic beauty, ever cease to be full of meaning and value for us, even though we regard them as pure legend. They bear within themselves their value for all time. They are the glittering halo which the poetic faith of the first community set upon the head of Jesus.[33]

Beginning with this school, the word "myth" has started to lose its bad connotation.

Bousset exhibits much more caution than did the liberal scholars regarding the historical value of John as compared with the Synoptics. It will be recalled that they placed the Synoptics on a definitely higher level than John, even though they said the Synoptics must be used with caution. It appears that Bousset puts all four Gospels about where the liberals placed John. "We know nothing definite as to the duration of Jesus' ministry. The narrative of our first three Evangelists is timeless."[34] He says that even if we were to accept their report as accurate, there is no warrant for concluding from them that because they record only one visit of Jesus to Jerusalem, the ministry of Jesus lasted for only one year. But Bousset shows no more confidence in John's account. "On the other hand, the chronology of the fourth Gospel, with its

---

32 *Ibid.*, p. 54.
33 *Ibid.*, p. 5.
34 *Ibid.*, p. 11.

division of Jesus' life according to the Jewish feasts, is not above suspicion, and cannot be accepted as it stands."[35]

While Bousset apparently has more confidence in the Synoptics than he has in John with respect to historical accuracy, this confidence is slight indeed when compared with the liberal writers. For some incidents he prefers John against the Synoptics. In commenting upon the death of Jesus, he notes that all the Gospels agree that Jesus died on Friday, but that the Synoptics indicate that this was the 15th of Nisan while John makes it the 14th. He notes that there is considerable dispute over this point and then concludes, "But even among those who usually look upon the Johannine tradition with the greatest suspicion, there is now a considerable tendency to give the preference to it in this one instance."[36]

On other points, Bousset prefers the Synoptics over John as historical sources. One instance of this is in connection with the messianic consciousness of Jesus. He accepts the historicity of the event at Caesarea Philippi and holds that this is the first time Jesus has spoken to his disciples about his messiahship. On the other hand, he notes that in our Gospel records the messiahship is spoken of much earlier. Here the Gospel of John is the most noteworthy and gives indication that the Christian community read its own consciousness into the person of Jesus in a way that is unhistorical. "According to the fourth Gospel, John the Baptist is already aware that he is Messiah, as also are the first disciples at their calling."[37]

What is the reason for this apparent lack of historical concern on the part of the Gospel writers? For Bousset, there is evidence that the faith of the community was one thing and the real Jesus as he appeared in the historical situation was another. "We have definite proof that . . . the faith of his followers gilded and coloured the real image of Jesus. For the point of view from which they painted it was throughout that of faith, and not that of historical accuracy."[38] The significance of this observation for the future critical study of the life of Jesus in German scholarship is hard to overestimate.

For the History of Religions school, the real significance of Jesus is found much more in the truth he brought forth than in his person. To be sure, the liberal writers did not attribute to Jesus' person the significance that orthodoxy has given it, but

---

[35] *Ibid.*
[36] *Ibid.,* p. 18.
[37] *Ibid.,* p. 172.
[38] *Ibid.,* p. 167.

nevertheless, they placed much more emphasis on the person
and what he said, did, and meant, than on the principle or timeless truth embodied in it.

Again, however, there is no rigid separation between these
schools of thought, but a difference of degree rather than one of
kind. Two citations should make this clear.

> The evil from which Jesus saves his disciples here and now is,
> above all, the moral evil of sin and debt which each man has
> to bear for himself; and that release is not affected by material
> means, but only by the free and personal will of the living God,
> and by the faith of those whose sins are forgiven them.[39]

In another passage Bousset emphasizes the experience of
Jesus himself as a prelude to his significance.

> Only by walking the appointed path of sorrow in silence and
> simplicity, without pretension and without faltering, in individual
> trust in his heavenly Father, in the unbroken conviction of his
> own divine mission, did he render his highest service. Only so
> did he reveal the new moral world, ennoble suffering and defeat,
> and create the worship of sorrow and the faith in the eternal
> value of martyrdom. Only here did he reach his consummation
> as leader of the ages and nations to God.[40]

Bousset's approach is with reference to history. It would be well
for us to note in addition a theological estimate of the significance
of Jesus, from the point of view of the principal theologian of the
History of Religions school, Ernst Troeltsch.

> The ethic of the Gospel is marked by emphasis on purity of
> intention and a greatly intensified reverence for all moral com-
> mands, without any allowance for conflicting motives or for
> expedience. Above all, it connects this moral conduct with its
> supreme object — a personal relation with God and the supreme
> value of the soul, "for what is a man profited if he shall gain
> the whole world and lose his soul?"[41]

To this point, while we have noticed a considerable difference
between the liberal school and the History of Religions school,
this difference has been confined mainly to the problem of history.
But as we noted at the beginning of this chapter, the History of
Religions school asked another question relative to the relationship of Christianity to other contemporary religious movements.
Perhaps the best way to get at this is to examine the titles applied

---

[39] *Ibid.*, pp. 164-65.

[40]*Ibid.*, p. 209.

[41] Ernst Troeltsch, *The Social Teaching of the Christian Churches,* trans.
Olive Wyon (New York: Macmillan, 1931), p. 52.

to Jesus as Bousset treats them. In the first place, he does feel that in some way Jesus regarded himself as the Messiah. Such things as the return of the disciples to faith after Jesus' death, the record of the trial of Jesus, and the event of Caesarea Philippi, demonstrate that he believed himself to be the Messiah. Yet Bousset sees in Jesus both a reluctance to use the title and a necessity to use the title. The reluctance is seen primarily in the ideas of national fanaticism that had gathered themselves around the title. The necessity to use the title is found in Jesus' desire to look upon his task as more than that of a mere prophet or forerunner, but rather as one who would speak the last, decisive word. Thus Bousset concludes, "The Messianic idea was the only possible form in which Jesus could clothe his inner consciousness, and yet an inadequate form; it was a necessity, but also a heavy burden which he bore in silence almost to the end of his life; it was a conviction which he could never enjoy with a whole heart."[42]

A second designation is that of Son of man. Bousset holds that Jesus also used this of himself. He used it because it could be appropriated as a messianic designation without having all the coarse popular ideas and national ideas that had clustered about the term "messiah" in Jewish life. Yet, it allowed him to designate himself as Messiah in the sense he chose. However, we are not to think that Jesus used this title either early or frequently. "Not until the end of his life, and then only briefly and sparingly, did he adopt the name. Probably he did not speak of his hopes in that respect with any greater certainty, but rather in the same dark, allusive, and foreboding terms as he employed when speaking of his death, his sufferings, or his failure."[43] On the other hand, the Synoptic Gospels put the term into his mouth very frequently. Bousset regards this as unhistorical.[44]

Thus while the Evangelists have greatly expanded their usage of the terms "Messiah" and "Son of Man" in writing the Gospels, these terms were in fact sometimes used by Jesus in reference to himself. This was not the case with a third title, *Kyrios* or "Lord." Bousset discusses this title in his book *Kyrios Christos* (1913). The three central propositions of that book are: (1) The title *Kyrios* was never used by Jesus himself, nor by the early church at Jerusalem to refer to him. (2) However, in the Hellenistic church of Antioch in Syria, he received the designation *Kyrios* as the object of worship of the Christian cult. *Kyrios* was a common

42 *Jesus,* pp. 166-180.
43 *Ibid.,* pp. 181-194.
44 *Ibid.,* p. 193.

designation of the cult-god of the pagan religions there and else-where at that time. (3) Later Paul adopted this name and in-corporated it into his theology.[45] The result of this construction by Bousset was a radical disjunction between the Jesus of history and the Christ of Pauline theology. Along with this there was a loss of interest on the part of the early church in the Jesus of history. Now interest was shifted to the Kyrios. Paul, then, is the real source of the difficulty. As Gunkel puts it, "It is not the Gospel of Jesus that is a syncretistic religion, but the Primitive Christianity of Paul and John."[46] John was later more favorably looked upon by the school, but Paul continued to be regarded as the perverter of the gospel.

William Wrede, another of the members of this school, writes, "Jesus knows nothing of that which for Paul is everything."[47] In reference to Paul he writes, "In comparison with Jesus he is a new phenomenon, as new as is possible with their one great com-mon foundation. He is much further removed from Jesus than Jesus himself is removed from the most noble figures of Jewish piety."[48] As a consequence, the ideas Paul used in the develop-ment of his Christology were derived from the mystery religions and had really no connection with Jesus.[49] Wrede summarizes the position of these scholars quite well:

> This picture of Christ did not develop under the impress of the personality of Jesus. It has often been asserted, but never proved. . . . There remains only one explanation: Paul already believed in such a heavenly being, in a divine Christ before he believed in Jesus. . . . And this view, for Paul the embodiment of religion, the foundation support for his piety, the prop with-out which it would collapse — was this the continuation or the transformation of the Gospel of Jesus? What remains here of the Gospel which Paul is said to have understood? . . . Unless we deny both figures any historicity, it follows that to call Paul a "disciple of Jesus" is quite inappropriate if this is meant to describe his historical relationship to Jesus.[50]

In line with this shocking assertion, Christianity ceased being studied as a theological system in this school, and began to be studied as one of many related religions.

---

[45] Geerhardus Vos, *The Self-Disclosure of Jesus* (Grand Rapids: Eerd-mans, 1953), p. 137.

[46] Quoted in Zahrnt, p. 60.

[47] Quoted in Zahrnt, p. 60.

[48] *Ibid.*, pp. 60-61.

[49] Robinson, p. 81.

[50] Quoted in Zahrnt, p. 61.

AN EVALUATION

As stated in the Introduction, we shall normally not attempt to evaluate the views of the various groups presented here. In part, this shall be done by the writers of the successive approaches as they are presented. In part, the writer hopes to do this in a second volume. Here, however, we make an exception, for two reasons. (1) The movement was neither large enough, nor widespread enough, nor long-lived enough to engage future members of the critical school in serious debate. (2) One of its primary features of importance was the effect some of its tenets had on future critical study. For these reasons we shall briefly evaluate the History of Religions school, first as to its intrinsic worth, and second with regard to its long-range importance.

The great obstacle to the acceptance of the tenets of the History of Religions school is to be found in the survival of the Christian faith as such. If Christianity was only one of a host of religions of syncretistic character that passed through the ancient world, why did it survive? Other religions shared with Christianity a lofty moral idealism or a penetrating mysticism. There were other faiths that worshiped a *Kyrios* who had been born of a virgin, died, and returned to life. Other deities promised redemption and offered the communication of divine life through the sacraments. Why then was it Christianity that survived and not one of the others? The answer appears to be that Christianity is anchored in history. "The basic difference between the Gospels and the cult legends which we find elsewhere in antiquity is their interest in history."[51] The object of the Christian's worship is a man who lived in a precise era of human history. He is not a creation of myth as were the deities of the rival cults of Jesus' day. Furthermore, there were witnesses to the events of his life who were there to contribute their knowledge of this historical personality. Zahrnt has summarized the matter quite well. "Here, then, we have not the eternal event of myth but unique, unrepeatable history; not an idea, but a happening; not a cultic drama, but history in earnest; not metaphysics, but eschatology; not symbol, but word; not an outlook, but faith."[52]

If it had been only from the perspective of its intrinsic worth that we were interested in the History of Religions school, it would have perhaps deserved not more than a glance in our journey through the various phases of the critical evaluation of the Jesus of history; but while the position of the school was

---

[51] Zahrnt, pp. 62-64.
[52] *Ibid.*, pp. 64-65.

very weak in itself, some of the subjects it discussed were much more long-lived. Therefore, in bringing these issues to the surface, it contributed to further investigation. Its principal contribution is in the questions it asked, as noted at the beginning of this chapter. (1) How important is the historical Jesus to Christian faith? The members of the History of Religions school were not the first to ask the question, but they were one group of several who asked the question at about the turn of the century, and their part in keeping this question before the scholarly world was of great importance to what followed. (2) How should the relationship of Christianity to other first-century faiths be evaluated? If we did no more here than mention that Rudolf Bultmann came out of the History of Religions school, we would have said enough. To be sure, Bultmann rejected many of the tenets of that school; but there was also much from it that he carried into his own systematic formulation, as we shall soon see.

CHAPTER FOUR

END OF LIBERAL LIVES IN GERMANY

The destruction of the movement that had produced the liberal lives in Germany was primarily the result of the work of three men. The works of two of these men came out very early in the twentieth century. William Wrede, a member of the History of Religions school, published in 1901 his *Das Messiasgeheimnis in den Evangelien*. His contribution therein to the destruction of the liberal position was not primarily a result of his position in the History of Religions school, but rather lay in a discovery he purportedly made about the construction of Mark's Gospel.

A second work, which appeared in 1906, was Albert Schweitzer's *Quest of the Historical Jesus*. Schweitzer was more thorough in his destruction of the liberal movement; however, after he had completed his demolition of the old school, he proceeded to erect a life of Jesus of his own, using primarily the same technique.

The work of the third appeared before that of either Wrede or Schweitzer and was a much more thorough criticism of the liberal position. In 1892 Martin Kahler published his book now known in English translation as *The So-Called Historical Jesus and the Historic Biblical Christ*.[1] Although this work was much more penetrating in its criticism of the liberal perspective, it did not attract the same attention of the critical school at the time of its issuance as did the works of Wrede and Schweitzer. Consequently, though its long-range effect was greater than either of the other two works, it is only in more recent studies that its real effect has been underscored.

Let us look successively at the works of these three men.

---

[1] Trans. Carl E. Braaten (Philadelphia: Fortress, 1964).

WILLIAM WREDE

In order to understand the real significance of the work of Wrede we must review briefly the view of the Gospels held in the liberal lives. It will be recalled that the liberal scholars were quite agreed that John's Gospel was much inferior as an historical source for the life of Jesus compared with the Synoptics. Also, following the work of Christian Weisse, it was usually felt that of the Synoptics, Mark was the first written. Along with this went the assumption that Mark's Gospel was the primary source for constructing a chronology of Jesus' life.

The place of Matthew and Luke was thus primarily that of supplementing the rather brief account of Mark, or in fewer instances, correcting the account given in Mark.

The work of Wrede directly challenged the validity of this hypothesis. Wrede theorized that there were two positions held in the early church with respect to the messiahship of Jesus. The first and oldest position held that Jesus had neither claimed messiahship nor acted as the Messiah during his life on earth, but that he had become Messiah through his resurrection. Wrede professes to see this indicated at places in the New Testament. One of these instances comes from the speech of Peter in Acts 2:36, "Let all the house of Israel therefore know assuredly that God has made him both Lord and Christ, this Jesus whom you crucified." Another indication of this is found in Rom. 1:4, where Paul writes of Jesus, ". . . designated Son of God in power according to the Spirit of holiness by his resurrection from the dead, Jesus Christ our Lord."

Against this older position there gradually arose an opposing position which insisted that if Jesus was destined to be the Messiah, then he certainly must have given some evidence of this in the days of his flesh. As this train of thought developed, it pushed more and more of the messianic features of Jesus back into the period of his earthly life.[2]

Wrede sees the writer of Mark as being pulled between these two positions. He felt he must ascribe to Jesus messianic traits during his earthly ministry, and yet he must demonstrate that the resurrection had made Jesus the Messiah in a new and more complete sense. Rather than choose either of the alternatives, he adopted a compromise which attempted to do justice to both. Jesus had held a secret messiahship before his resurrection. There are indications of this in Mark's Gospel. In Mk. 1:23-25 and 3:11-12 the demons and demoniacs recognize him as the Mes-

---

[2] Vos, *The Self-Disclosure of Jesus*, pp. 67-68.

siah. In Mk. 3:12 he orders the demons not to make known who he is, and in Mk. 7:36 he gives the same command to people who had witnessed a healing. Furthermore, Jesus holds a number of esoteric conversations with his disciples (e.g., Mk. 4:10-13; 7:17-23; 8:30) in which he gives them instruction concerning the nature of his messiahship and also concerning the need to keep it secret during his life prior to the resurrection. Thus during Jesus' life, his messiahship is known to none except the demons and his chosen disciples.[3]

On the other hand, according to Mark, Jesus held an open and public messiahship after his resurrection. As Wrede came to evaluate this presentation, he concluded that it was a purely dogmatic device on the part of Mark and was devoid of any historical validity. Not only was it dogmatic as far as the device itself was concerned, but the device affected the portrayal of Jesus' life by Mark to such an extent that we are left with a thoroughly unhistorical and unreliable account of the life of Jesus. To be sure, Mark's Gospel is the oldest Gospel that we have, but rather than presenting a simple and unadorned life of Jesus, it has been so affected by this dogmatic device of the "messianic secret" that it is no longer possible for us to obtain from it a real picture of the historical Jesus.[4]

How far this conclusion was from the liberal position should at once be evident. The liberals saw difficulties in places, but were certain that through literary criticism they could arrive at an accurate picture of the historical Jesus. As a result of the work of Wrede, German scholarship became much more skeptical of the possibility of such an achievement.

ALBERT SCHWEITZER

Far more thorough and penetrating in his analysis of the liberal lives of the nineteenth century was Albert Schweitzer. He begins by analyzing the validity of separating the "historical kernel" from the "husk" as the liberal lives had attempted to do. He notes that we have no assurance that such a process is either necessary or possible. He says, for example:

> We may take all that is reported as either historical or unhistorical, but, in respect to the definite prediction of the passion, death, and resurrection, we ought to give up taking the reference to the passion as historical and letting the rest go; we

---

[3] Hugh Anderson, *Jesus and Christian Origins* (New York: Oxford, 1964), p. 31.

[4] Vos, p. 68.

may accept the idea of the atoning death, or we may reject it, but we ought not to ascribe to Jesus a feeble, anemic version of the idea, while setting down to the account of the Pauline theology the interpretation of the passion which we find in Mark.[5]

Schweitzer finds himself in perfect agreement with Wrede in his lack of trust of the historical framework of Mark's Gospel. "The psychological explanation of motive, and the psychological connexion of the events and actions which such critics [the liberals] have proposed to find in Mark, simply do not exist."[6] He sees a need for simplicity in the treatment of Mark's Gospel. By this he means that each pericope must be looked at by itself, and that the scholar must give up concentrating on the connecting links. "The fact is, it is not simply that there is no very obvious psychological connexion between the sections; in almost every case there is a positive break in the connexion. And there is a great deal in the Marcan narrative which is inexplicable and even self-contradictory."[7]

He castigates the methodology of the liberals as they constructed their portraits of Jesus. He notes that each of these scholars approached the Gospels with his own preconception of what was historically possible. Each scholar would then proceed to accept or reject individual items in the historical picture in accordance with their conformity or lack of it with his own particular preconception.[8]

Schweitzer notes the optimism of the liberal movement. It set out to find the "real" Jesus with the confidence that when it had discovered him, it could bring him into its own age as contemporary teacher and savior. In so doing it had in mind the dismantling and dissolution of orthodox dogma which had for centuries made any such study impossible and fruitless.[9] But the liberals had their mind more on the methodology of the orthodox theologians than on their own, for the resultant Jesus of their own formulation was that of a typical contemporary idealist, rationalist, socialist, or romanticist.[10] If the failure of orthodox theology had been in not asking questions about the Jesus of history, the failure of the liberal camp had been in its making of him a perfectly well-adjusted nineteenth-century contemporary in accordance with

---

[5] *Quest of the Historical Jesus*, pp. 332-33.

[6] *Ibid.*, p. 333.

[7] *Ibid.*, pp. 333-34.

[8] *Ibid.*, p. 333.

[9] *Ibid.*, p. 399.

[10] Anderson, p. 19.

the wishes of the particular liberal biographer. Schweitzer summarizes the work of the liberal biographers as follows.

> There is nothing more negative than the result of the critical study of the Life of Jesus.
>
> The Jesus of Nazareth who came forward publicly as the Messiah, who preached the ethic of the Kingdom of God, who founded the Kingdom of Heaven upon earth, and died to give His work its final consecration, never had any existence. He is a figure designed by rationalism, endowed with life by liberalism, and clothed by modern theology in an historical garb.[11]

Against this background, Schweitzer began to construct his positive case. At the outset it should be noted that his objection against the liberal lives was not one of objection against the historical methodology they employed. He shared with them the belief that history was primarily the gathering of facts. He shared with them the confidence that had come about as a result of the striking advances of the natural sciences. Likewise, he was certain that objective analysis of the documents would bring to light the truth. His complaint was neither with the basic method they employed, nor with the result they were trying to achieve, but rather with what he felt to be an insufficient objectivity on their part. They were too anxious to present a docile, meek-mannered Jesus of the Victorian era, "and so gave us a lay figure, too respectable to offend us, too unmysterious to claim our reverence, too diminutive in stature to account for the rise of the Church of Christ."[12]

For this reason Schweitzer sought to portray a Jesus of the first century, removed from us in time and thought though he may be.[13] He notes that up to a point the solution of Wrede and his own solution agree. They both agree that there is a distinct lack of connectedness in the Markan narrative. Similarly, they agree that there is a strong messianic element running through that Gospel. The principal point of difference arises when they try to explain the origin of that messianic element.

> There is, on the one hand, the eschatological solution [Schweitzer's], which at one stroke raises the Marcan account as it stands, with all its disconnectedness and inconsistencies, into genuine history; and there is, on the other hand, the literary solution [Wrede's], which regards the incongruous dogmatic element as interpolated by the earliest Evangelist into the tradition and

---

[11] Schweitzer, p. 398.
[12] Anderson, p. 19.
[13] *Ibid.*

therefore strikes out the Messianic claim altogether from the historical Life of Jesus.[14]

Jesus, then, saw it as his task to bring about the eschatological consummation of history. He had come to release the final woes and to inaugurate the period of conflict and strife that would lead up to his own parousia. In so doing he would bring about the transcendent aspect of the eschatological events. This was the task to which he set himself.[15]

There were then two primary elements in the thought of Jesus as he went about his work. The first was that the end of the world was upon the people of his day. They were living in the very last hours of the present world order. The second element had to do more primarily with the person of Jesus himself and his bringing about that end. He expected in connection with the end of the world his own messianic parousia in the very near future. But in his singular desire to bring history to a close and usher in the kingdom of God he was unsuccessful, and as a result he was put to death by his contemporaries.[16]

While Schweitzer, therefore, was anxious to maintain a closer connection with the historical facts as presented in the Gospels, he was left with another problem. How is it that the almost pathetic personality that he gives us in Jesus can have any real significance for us in the twentieth century? The answer to this is found in the deemphasis of the importance of the historical with reference to the life of Jesus. For Schweitzer the real significance of Jesus lies not in his history but in his spirit.[17] "In reality that which is eternal in the words of Jesus is due to the very fact that they are based on an eschatological world view, and contain the expression of a mind for which the contemporary world with its historical and social circumstances no longer had any existence."[18] This being the case, it is not in the direct application of the words of Jesus to us, but rather in their spirit that we find the real significance of Jesus. We must evaluate our world and not allow it to mold us. We must reach a point of inward freedom as did Jesus. Each man must consequently be "fitted to be, in his own world and in his own time, a simple channel of the power of Jesus."[19]

---

[14] Schweitzer, p. 337.
[15] *Ibid.*, p. 371.
[16] Anderson, p. 20.
[17] *Ibid.*
[18] Schweitzer, p. 402.
[19] *Ibid.*

The closing words of Schweitzer's book have almost a wistful tone to them.

> He comes to us as One unknown, without a name, as of old, by the lake-side, He came to those men who knew Him not. He speaks to us the same word: "Follow thou me!" and sets us to the tasks which He has to fulfil for our time. He commands. And to those who obey Him, whether they be wise or simple, He will reveal Himself in the toils, the conflicts, the sufferings which they shall pass through in His fellowship, and, as an ineffable mystery, they shall learn in their own experience Who He is.[20]

After a period of almost two centuries in which critical scholarship had attempted to produce Jesus of Nazareth as he really was, Schweitzer brought forth the very picture which this liberal approach had been attempting to avoid. Jesus was a fanatical futurist who died in vain for his hope in the parousia. It then became evident in the critical school that faith could not be placed in history. Hugh Anderson has summarized the whole matter appropriately. "Whereas the Liberals, in their search for the truly human lineaments of Jesus, lost the Christ-character or the kerygma-character of his history, Schweitzer, himself no less resolved on scientific objectivity, all but submerged the historical Jesus in the dogmatic 'concept of the Christ.' "[21]

MARTIN KÄHLER

We place the work of Martin Kähler last in this chapter even though his definitive work in this area preceded the work of the other two authors here considered. As mentioned previously, we do so because although currently his work in this area has been far more telling in the critical school, it has been only in comparatively recent years that its true significance has been realized. His work *The So-Called Historical Jesus and the Historic Biblical Christ* first appeared in 1892 in German. It is significant that it is not even mentioned in the work of Schweitzer that appeared fourteen years later. Even more significantly, while the book has enjoyed six printings in German, three of these have come within the last ten years.

We experience some difficulty in attempting to place Kähler in the theological environment of his own day. He was not a member of either the liberal or the History of Religions school. Neither was he a member of any other significant group in the theological milieu of his day. That he was an individualist may

---

[20] *Ibid.,* p. 403.
[21] Anderson, pp. 21-22.

in itself have been a factor contributing to the late recognition
of the significance of his work. Yet his uniqueness was not due
to lack of familiarity with the current theological approaches of
his day.

> Kähler moved in — and out of — the theological schools of
> Tübingen (F. C. Baur) and Erlangen (J. C. K. von Hofmann);
> he was influenced by Hegelians and Ritschlians but refused to
> join their ranks. In a very general way he was counted among
> the biblicists and pietists, yet he rejected verbal inspiration and
> recoiled from pietistic subjectivism.[22]

In the day in which Kähler wrote, the principal task of New
Testament scholarship was to produce from the New Testament
a critically exact life of Jesus. The ways in which the critics went
about their task and the results at which they arrived were various, but their task was the same. Some authors preferred the
presentation of John's Gospel. Others put far more confidence
in the Synoptics and treated John as more of a poetic or philosophical treatise. A larger group than either of the preceding
attempted a synthetic construction involving all four Gospels.
This type of procedure had led to a great variation in the evaluation of the historical sources and to an even greater variation
in the significance attached to Jesus himself. Those of a rationalistic persuasion tended to emphasize Jesus' character and moral
teachings. Orthodoxy saw in him the Christ of the Chalcedonian
formulation. A third school attempted to retain the best from
each of the other two and pictured Jesus in terms of the *kenosis*
Christology.

Philosophy of religion also played its part. Schleiermacher had
emphasized the telling effect of Jesus' God-consciousness. Kant
spoke of him in terms of the ideal — the representative of a humanity pleasing to God. Hegel had emphasized the essential unity
of God and man; and Harnack, as we have already noted, identified Jesus as the preacher of a threefold doctrine of the Father-
hood of God, the brotherhood of man, and the infinite value
of the human soul.[23]

It is against this background that Kähler lifts his battle cry.

> I wish to summarize my cry of warning in a form intentionally
> audacious: *The historical Jesus of modern authors conceals
> from us the living Christ.* The Jesus of the "Life-of-Jesus move-
> ment" is merely a modern example of human creativity, and not

---

[22] Braaten, Introduction to Kähler, p. 2.
[23] Carl E. Braaten, "Martin Kähler on the Historic Biblical Christ,"
The Historical Jesus and the Kerygmatic Christ, trans. and ed. Carl E.
Braaten and Roy A. Harrisville (Nashville: Abingdon, 1964), pp. 81-82.

an iota better than the notorious dogmatic Christ of Byzantine Christology. One is as far removed from the real Christ as is the other.[24]

Kähler goes on to attack the methodology of the life-of-Jesus movement. It was in the first place assumed that it would be possible to go behind the New Testament documents to discover what Jesus was really like. The Fourth Gospel was at once discounted because it pictured Jesus as the eternal Word, and scholars turned their attention to the Synoptic Gospels. But when critical scholarship had made this decision, it found its lot little improved, for it was soon discovered that the Synoptists themselves were more authors than compilers. "That in their Gospels pious legends and involuntary distortions had played a part, the only course remaining was to embark on the quest for the historical Jesus who was faintly discernible behind the primitive Christian reports."[25] Kähler sees as his task "(1) to criticize and reject the wrong aspects of this approach to the life of Jesus and (2) to establish the validity of an alternative approach."[26]

Let us note first the specific reasons for his rejection of the former approach. He begins, "I regard the entire Life-of-Jesus movement as a blind alley."[27] He does acknowledge one virtue of the movement — its setting up of the Bible as superior to abstract dogmatism. However, he goes on to deal with a number of reasons why the Gospels cannot be used as a reliable and sufficient source for a biography of Jesus. There are first of all the historico-scientific reasons. A number of things here call for our attention. (1) In the first place, we are not in possession of any sources for a life of Jesus that would enable us to write a biography of his life. For the believer the Gospels may be adequate, but as sources for contemporary historical science they are of no use. "Our sources, that is, the Gospels, exist in such isolation that without them we would know nothing at all about Jesus, athough the time and setting of his life are otherwise entirely clear to historians. He could be taken for a product of the Church's fantasy around the year 100 A.D."[28]

(2) "These sources cannot be traced with certainty to eyewitnesses."[29] He notes in this connection the very wide disagree-

[24] Kähler, p. 43.
[25] *Ibid.*, p. 44.
[26] *Ibid.*, p. 45.
[27] *Ibid.*, p. 46.
[28] *Ibid.*, p. 48.
[29] *Ibid.*

ment among critics as to what in the Gospels actually goes back to the disciples.

(3) "They tell us only about the shortest and last period of his life."[30] This feature had been noted by others previous to Kähler, but he uses it to demonstrate the unsatisfactory nature of the then popular movement. He calls the Gospels "passion narratives with extended introductions."[31] He notes further that it is not possible to harmonize the accounts even if one were to eliminate the Fourth Gospel.[32]

(4) "These sources appear in two basic forms whose variation must — in view of the proximity of the alleged or probable time of origin of these forms — awaken serious doubt about the faithfulness of the recollections."[33] Here Kähler has in mind the difference between John and the Synoptics. He refuses to take any easy solution to this problem. The sources themselves are thus not adequate to the writing of a biography of Jesus.

Kähler then attacks the psychological approach of many in the life-of-Jesus movement. This he sees in particular in those who have attempted to analyze Jesus' developing consciousness. "The New Testament presentations were not written for the purpose of describing how Jesus developed. They show him manifesting himself and playing an active role, but not making confessions about his inner life, certainly not unpremeditated ones, except perhaps for a few sighs and ejaculations."[34]

His most particular attack upon this psychological analysis is against what he considers to be an unwarranted use of analogy. Analogy is based on a similarity of the two items being compared. But in comparing Jesus with ourselves, that basic similarity is missing. "Will anyone who has had the impression of being encountered by that unique sinless person, that unique Son of Adam endowed with a vigorous consciousness of God, still venture to use the principle of analogy here once he has thoroughly assessed the situation?"[35] At this point Kähler attacks the position of the liberals as he writes, "The distinction between Jesus Christ and ourselves is not one of degree but of kind."[36] This being the case, Kähler illustrates the inappropriateness of psychological analysis.

---

30 *Ibid.*, pp. 48-49.
31 *Ibid.*, p. 80.
32 *Ibid.*, p. 49.
33 *Ibid.*
34 *Ibid.*, p. 51.
35 *Ibid.*, p. 53.
36 *Ibid.*

"The inner development of a sinless person is as inconceivable to us as life on the Sandwich Islands is to a Laplander."[37]

We anticipate here somewhat the further development of Kähler in his book, but in so doing we set in view the particular nature of the Gospels from his point of view. He says the Gospels "are not the reports of impartial observers who have been alerted to his presence, but, rather, the *testimonies* and *confessions* of believers in Christ."[38]

If then it is impossible for us to arrive at a true biographical picture of Jesus, where shall we find help?

> Where do we come to know Jesus? Only a few can carry on the work of historical science, and only a few are sufficiently trained to evaluate such work. To be sure, such work would relieve us of the authority of the Bible, but it would in turn subject us to the authority, not of an empirical science, but of the alleged results produced by this science.[39]

If this be the case, then Christ is accessible to us only through the work of scholars — if there. He therefore surmises, "There must be another way to reach the historic Christ than that of the scientific reconstructions which employ source criticism and historical analogy."[40]

At this point, Kähler asks two questions which for him are determinative of the course he will follow. "What is a truly 'historic figure,' that is, a person who has been influential in molding posterity, as measured by his contribution to history? Is it not the person who originates and bequeaths a permanent influence?"[41] He then develops this thought. The person who is remembered in history is the one who has accomplished something significant. He is remembered for his work or for his words or for his personal characteristics. The effect, therefore, of a man is to be measured in terms of the people on whom he has left an impression and in terms of the environment that he has been able to affect. "Thus, from a purely historical point of view the truly historic element in any great figure is the discernible personal influence which he exercises upon later generations."[42]

The next task then is to apply this evidence to Jesus. What was it in Jesus that had a permanent influence on posterity? "According to the Bible and Church history it consisted in noth-

---

[37] *Ibid.*
[38] *Ibid.*, p. 92.
[39] *Ibid.*, pp. 61-62.
[40] *Ibid.*, p. 63.
[41] *Ibid.*
[42] *Ibid.*

ing else but the faith of his disciples, their conviction that in Jesus they had found the conqueror of guilt, sin, temptation, and death."[43] This conviction of the disciples is all important. It is summed up in the New Testament confession, "Christ is Lord."

If this be the case, it is very easy to see why Kähler had so little interest in history as it had been conceived in the life-of-Jesus movement. At this point we see the beginning of the distinction between the Jesus of history and the Christ of faith which was to exert such a decisive influence on all future critical study of the life of Jesus. "The risen Lord is not the historical Jesus *behind* the Gospels, but the Christ of the apostolic preaching, of the *whole* New Testament."[44]

Kähler puts it another way. The Jesus of history has to do with the temporal, the transient, and the earthly. The historic Christ has to do with the suprahistorical significance of Jesus and his worth to all humanity. He notes in this connection how little really significant influence the Jesus of history had in the New Testament. He was only able to win from the disciples a very shaky loyalty. They were only loosely attached to him at best, and when the moment of trial came they were quick to desert him. It was only after the resurrection, when they were enabled to grasp with the help of the Holy Spirit what Jesus had told them before his death, that his significance as the historic Christ came into view. Thus Jesus' earthly, historical existence ceased to have primary effect on the disciples.[45] This, for example, is what Paul refers to when he writes to the Corinthians, "Though we once regarded Christ from a human point of view, we regard him thus no longer" (II Cor. 5:16).

It may not be obvious to the English reader of Kähler's book what is self-evident in German. Centrally involved in his argument is the distinction between two German words for "history." These words are usually used by Kähler in their adjectival form. The first, *historisch,* is translated "historical." The second, *geschichtlich,* is translated "historic." This in itself gives little help to the English reader unless he goes back of these terms to get at their differentiated meaning. Various attempts have been made to distinguish these terms from one another. Historical *(historisch)* has often been equated with objective history, outer history, or writing history. It is the kind of thing with which the liberal life-of-Jesus movement was primarily concerned. Historic *(geschichtlich)* has often been equated with existential history, inner history,

---

43 *Ibid.*
44 *Ibid.,* p. 65.
45 *Ibid.,* pp. 65-66.

or making history. This was what primarily interested Kähler. Braaten has pointed out the distinction very clearly. "A historic event has great significance for the future and is remembered by posterity as determinative in the continuous life of people. A historical fact may be completely insignificant to anyone and registered as a mere disconnected joint in an ancient chronicle."[46]

The first and primary significance of Jesus for the disciples was consequently that he evoked faith in his disciples. But a second factor is of equal importance, namely, that faith was confessed by the disciples. "The real Christ, that is, the Christ who has exercised an influence in history, . . . *this real Christ is the Christ who is preached*. The Christ who is preached, however, is precisely the Christ of faith."[47]

The different manner in which Kähler goes about obtaining his information about the historic Christ also sets him apart from the liberal movement. The Gospels are of course his source as they were for the life-of-Jesus movement. One must not center his attention on the individual incidents in the Gospels. These, of course, would have no primary significance for him even if they could be proved. The totality of the biblical message is what is of significance to him. "In this whole discussion we are trying to explain how inadvisable and indeed impossible it is to reach a Christian understanding of Jesus when one deviates from the *total* biblical proclamation about him — his life as well as its significance."[48]

Kähler next takes up a discussion of the foundation of this faith in Christ. He begins by asserting that the relationship to Christ in whom the Christian believes must be as possible for the lay Christian as it is to the most learned theologian. Here he is very critical of the life-of-Jesus movement. For him, this movement has become one in which the priest is the saint. He draws an historical analogy. "As the simple scriptural theology of Pietism once deposed the dogmaticians from their papacy of learning, so today it is the task of the dogmatician, in defense of the plain Christian faith, to set limits to the learned pontificating of the historians."[49]

He sees as impossible any reconciliation between the need to establish facts by scientific devices on the one hand, and the need to experience faith on the other. "Therefore, Christian faith and a history of Jesus repel each other like oil and water as soon as

---

[46] *Ibid.*, pp. 21-22.
[47] *Ibid.*, p. 66.
[48] *Ibid.*, p. 68.
[49] *Ibid.*, p. 73.

the magic spell of an enthusiastic and enrapturing description loses its power."[50]

What is it that we have in the Gospels, then, if it is not a narration of the events of Jesus' life? For Kähler we have more of a picture of Jesus than a narrative. "The purpose is to report not so much *what* happened as *who* acted and *how*."[51] Our need is not so much to believe in the facts as to believe in a person who is revealed to us in the facts. "If this is true, then all the worries about chronology and pragmatism, about development of consciousness and ascertainable progress, lose their urgency."[52]

This biblical picture of Christ has two very important aspects to it. In the first place, it is a picture that must come from the whole Bible. In the second place, it is a picture and not a table of events. Let us first notice briefly the biblical aspect. The Old Testament contributes its share to the picture of the biblical Christ. The general background of the Old Testament and its effect upon his life are of great importance. Subsequently, every part of Scripture contributes to this picture. It is never possible to separate Christ from the Bible.[53]

However, the facts of the Bible do not determine the picture. The picture rather is created by the writers' use of the facts. "Nowhere in the Gospels do we detect a rigorous striving for accuracy of observation or for preservation of detail; everywhere we see that the evangelist's purposes have determined how the materials at his disposal are to be employed."[54] It simply is not possible for us to know the details of the tradition. Scientific research cannot take us back to the first witnesses who gave us the tradition. Furthermore, Kähler has much less confidence in stating the relationship of the Gospels to one another than did those in the life-of-Jesus movement. The priority of Mark, or the superiority of the Synoptics to John, are not established theses for him.[55]

The details of the apostolic memory of Jesus have been preserved for their religious significance, not their historical significance. "They [the Gospels] are not the reports of impartial observers who have been alerted to his presence, but, rather, the *testimonies* and *confessions* of believers in Christ."[56] If then the

---

50 *Ibid.*, p. 74.
51 *Ibid.*, p. 81.
52 *Ibid.*
53 *Ibid.*, p. 86.
54 *Ibid.*, p. 89.
55 *Ibid.*, p. 90.
56 *Ibid.*, p. 92.

purpose of the Gospels be to proclaim a message in order to establish faith, it should be self-evident that they would have little interest in some of the details of Jesus' life, for example the period of his youth and his preparation for the public ministry. Kähler notes the radical difference of this approach from that of the biographers of his day. "Without a doubt the Gospels are the complete opposite of the embellishing, rationalizing, and psychologizing rhetoric of the recent biographies of Jesus."[57]

Here, once again, we see the adumbration of existentialism in the work of Kähler. The Jesus of history would not concern the contemporary Christian in the least if there were not something analogous in the time of Jesus with what exists today. "We need no source-documents to record these facts, that is, their essential meaning and abiding worth cannot be established by historical documents at all; only the witness and the faith of Christians can do that."[58]

From all that has preceded, it should be evident that Kähler's view of biblical authority has both a positive and a negative element in it. The negative element is seen in his denial of verbal inspiration, however defined. He agrees that to a certain extent the books of the Bible must be regarded as a collection of historical documents whose value must be established by scientific research. But for Kähler this is not the most important consideration. It is more important to ask, Can we do justice to the Bible when we view it from an historical perspective?[59] At this point his positive attitude toward the Bible comes in.

> I deny that the purpose of the Gospels is to serve as documents for a *scientifically reconstructed biography* of Jesus. . . . Their purpose is to awaken faith in Jesus through a clear proclamation of his saving activity. When measured by this purpose I regard them as completely perfect, whereas I deny that when used as biographical sources they are somehow made more perfect through the fact that they are our only available sources for this kind of research.[60]

It is thus in the kerygmatic feature of the New Testament books that we find their real significance. The reader must be encountered by the Word, and must grant to the Word authority over his mind and will.[61] "As we concern ourselves with this sharply etched history, we find that the great deeds of God and the per-

---

[57] *Ibid.*, pp. 93-94.
[58] *Ibid.*, p. 96.
[59] *Ibid.*, p. 124.
[60] *Ibid.*, p. 127.
[61] *Ibid.*, p. 134.

son of his Christ become contemporary for each one of us, making of us first hearers, then learners, and finally believers."[62]

The influence of Kähler on the modern critical school would be hard to overestimate. From our perspective his influence on Bultmann is doubtless the most important. But that is the case chiefly because we are concerning ourselves with historical study. His influence in the area of theology has been equally significant. He was a prolific writer; a complete list of his works includes 165 titles most of which deal in some manner with theological controversies of his day.[63] Among the theologians he specifically influenced are Karl Barth, Emil Brunner, and Paul Tillich. Furthermore, Kähler has sometimes been called the father of form criticism. This can easily be overstated, but if by this one means that Kähler held some of the basic assumptions that were later developed by the form critics, it may be granted.

But Kähler has also come under the criticism of contemporary scholarship. The criticism most often leveled at him is that he completely abandons history in favor of the kerygma.

> The consequence of this view is that faith does not need to rely upon a certain verifiable minimum of solid historical facts which have been laid bare by a process of historico-critical exfoliation. The preaching of the biblical Christ creates faith, and the assurance of the essential historicity of this Christ is given as an essential and ineradicable element of that faith itself. Without this statement the historicity of the picture would have to be established some other way. By Kähler's refusal to gain the assurance of the historicity of the Christ from any other source outside the preaching from faith unto faith, he has directed us exclusively to the kerygmatic Christ who must authenticate his reality and meaning in the encounter with men.[64]

This feature of Kähler's work has left modern critical scholarship with an uneasy feeling as is witnessed by the recurrent recent attempts to find a certain minimal historical core in the Gospels. We shall investigate this further in subsequent chapters.

While all three men considered in this chapter made a contribution to the end of liberal lives of Jesus, the work of the first two was more negative than it was positive. Furthermore, Wrede and Schweitzer belong to two of the schools already studied. Thus the six questions at the end of Chapter One need be asked only with respect to the views of Kähler.

Regarding the possibility of writing a biography or history of

---

[62] *Ibid.*, p. 136.
[63] Cf. *ibid.*, p. 7.
[64] Braaten, in Braaten and Harrisville, pp. 99-100.

Jesus, Kähler is completely negative. The nature of the documents does not permit us to do so. They are isolated. They cannot be traced to eyewitnesses. They tell of only a small fragment of Jesus' life, and they appear in two irreconcilable forms.[65] Furthermore, what is historically impossible is theologically irrelevant. Faith must not be made dependent upon the oscillating opinions of historical research. "If faith is made dependent upon the methods or results of historical scholarship, then the historian becomes the priest of Protestantism."[66] However, the believer does have available to him the historic Christ, who is encountered not via historical research, but in the Bible as witnessed to by the Holy Spirit.

Kähler does not deal with the subject of miracles. This is perhaps partly due to his concern for the kerygma and partly due to his seeing in them no such problem as do the naturalistic scholars we have encountered to this point. In the case of a sinless being, as Kähler pictures the historic Christ to be, the ability to work miracles would be self-evident.

While Kähler does not deal with the subject of the resurrection in the portion of his book that we have in English translation, he does in chapters three and four of the first German edition. In these chapters he is debating with his critics, of whom Wilhelm Hermann is the chief. Hermann, much like the liberal scholars we have studied, identified the resurrection of Jesus as *Glaubensgedanke,* "a concept of faith," which gives the meaning of Jesus' inner life for the believer. Kähler pointed out that this made the resurrection dependent on faith rather than what should be the case — faith dependent on the resurrection. Thus Hermann dissolved the objective reality of the resurrection in the subjectivity of faith. In contrast, for Kähler "The Resurrection experience of Jesus is regarded as an essential part of the historic Christ."[67]

Regarding the place of mythology in the New Testament, Kähler, like the others we have studied to date, has very little to say. He recognizes that pious legends had a part in the construction of the Gospels.[68] In another place he says that "there is no sharp conceptual difference between oral tradition and legend." He indicates their value in connection with the authority of the Bible. "Once the infallibility of our biblical records is no longer demanded, then their comparatively remarkable trustworthiness will again

[65] Kähler, pp. 48-49.
[66] *Ibid.,* p. 26.
[67] Braaten, pp. 97-98.
[68] Kähler, p. 44.

be appreciated, even the trustworthiness of the legends, so far as this is conceivable."[69]

Kähler refuses to take the easy way out of the problem of the comparative historical value of John and the Synoptic Gospels. "If the author of the Fourth Gospel openly professes to be a preacher (John 20:31), the others are basically no less the same."[70] One cannot solve the problem of differences by attributing to the Synoptics historical accuracy and using John to varying degrees as a supplement to their account. There is a certain respect in which the accounts in the Synoptics are one-sided. But while the selection of either the Synoptics or John is not nearly as clear to Kähler as it has been to some of the other critics, the difficulty presented by this phenomenon is much less intense. For neither the Synoptics nor John is primarily a description of the historical Jesus, but rather a description of the historic Christ.

Kähler's estimate of the significance of Jesus is best seen in his own statement:

> Why, in the final analysis, do we commune with the Jesus of our Gospels? What does he offer us? "In him we have redemption through his blood, the forgiveness of our trespasses" (Eph. 1:7). Do I really need to know more of him than Paul "delivered to [the Corinthians] as of first importance, what [he] also received, that Christ died for our sins in accordance with the Scriptures, that he was buried, that he was raised on the third day in accordance with the Scriptures, and that he appeared" (I Cor. 15:3f.)? This is the good news brought in the name of God (I Cor. 15:12f.; Rom. 1:1f.; II Cor. 5:18f.; Gal. 1:6f.). This is the witness and confession of faith which has overcome the world (I John 5:4). If I have all this I do not need additional information on the precise details of Jesus' life and death.
>
> . . . .
>
> Therefore, the reason we commune with the Jesus of our Gospels is because it is through them that we learn to know that same Jesus whom, with the eyes of faith and in our prayers, we meet at the right hand of God, because we know, with Luther, that God cannot be found except in his beloved Son, because he is God's revelation to us, or, more accurately and specifically, because he who once walked on earth and now is exalted is the incarnate Word of God, the image of the invisible God — because he is for us God revealed. "That is what the believer seeks. That is what the church celebrates."[71]

---

[69] *Ibid.*, pp. 141-42.
[70] *Ibid.*, p. 81.
[71] *Ibid.*, pp. 59-61.

CHAPTER FIVE

FORM CRITICISM AND BULTMANN

THE APPROACH OF THE FORM CRITICS

There were many contributors to the birth of the form-critical approach to the New Testament, some of whom we have already mentioned. If it were necessary to point to one individual as the most significant predecessor to the form-critical approach to the New Testament, it would doubtless be Hermann Gunkel. He was the first to apply the method of form criticism to the Old Testament. His point of departure was the assertion that the writers of the Old Testament were not professional researchers in any sense of the word, but were rather compilers of traditional material. This literary tradition was preserved in a great many literary types, called in German *Gattungen*. It was therefore the task of the Old Testament critic to sort out and separate each type and study it as a unit, paying particular attention to such things as form, content, style, and structure. Gunkel then went further to inquire about the *Sitz im Leben* (life situation) in which each of these forms had arisen. Gunkel continued to develop his theories for several decades, but the technique itself was demonstrated in his commentary on Genesis in 1901.[1] The profound effect of his analysis on New Testament scholarship is seen in Vincent Taylor's claim that form criticism is "the child of Gunkel's spirit."[2]

All three of the scholars studied in the previous chapter also contributed to the historical climate that produced form criticism. Wrede pointed out to his own satisfaction, and that of many

---

[1] Cf. Hugh Anderson, *Jesus and Christian Origins*, p. 30.
[2] Vincent Taylor, *The Formation of the Gospel Tradition* (New York: Macmillan, 1933), p. 11.

others, the dogmatic construction of the Gospel of Mark, and thus had destroyed one of the cherished fortresses of liberal life-of-Jesus research. Schweitzer demonstrated the lack of connection between the sections of the Markan narrative and said that emphasis must be laid on the analysis of the sections themselves, not on their connections. Kähler in his approach to the Gospels employed a number of techniques that have earned for him in at least some meaningful sense the title, "father of form criticism."

In addition to the observations of these three men, Julius Wellhausen sought to demonstrate the influence of the theology of the primitive Christian community on the resultant form of the narratives about Jesus and the form of his sayings, and J. Weiss attempted to discover from the tradition by a process of selection the "oldest Gospel."[3] It was inevitable that before long, some of these methods should be applied more systematically and thoroughly to the Gospels.

The method that developed along these lines came to be known by the German word *Formgeschichte*, "form history," or as it is better known in English, "form criticism." Before we look more closely at the work of one of the principal form critics, let us look at some of the broad principles of the school and trace briefly its development.

There were, it seems, two very broad principles behind the work of the form critics even though they differed greatly in the development of their methodology. While most of the attention of Gospel criticism had previously been directed toward source criticism of the Gospels, now attention was directed to the period between the death and resurrection of Jesus and the composition of the first Gospel, Mark. Thus they attempted to discover laws governing the formation and transmission of the oral tradition behind the Gospels. One of the consequences of this investigation was their conclusion that the early tradition of the church circulated initially as isolated fragments. The joining of these fragments together in the form of a narrative occurred much later — either at a later stage of the oral period, or when the tradition was first committed to writing. K. L. Schmidt was one of the first to emphasize this disconnected nature of the units that we have in our Gospels. "The net result of this standpoint was a decline of interest in the problems that had occupied the older positivistic historical criticism, the question of the external framework of the life of Jesus and the considerations of context."[4]

---

[3] *Ibid.*
[4] Anderson, pp. 30-31.

Not only was the transmission of the tradition considered important, but also the origin of that tradition. Form critics became convinced that the collective consciousness of the early church lay behind the tradition. They came more and more to feel that the Christian community created much of the tradition and transformed the rest. Wrede had demonstrated to the satisfaction of the critics that Mark's Gospel lacked historical dependability. He had traced this lack of dependability to theological reasons on the part of its author. Form critics picked up Wrede's basic criticism; however, they attributed the lack of historical accuracy not to the theological predisposition of the writer, but rather to the fact that the Christian community preserved and transformed traditions which fulfilled its needs for cult practice, missionary expansion, and apologetic.[5]

The form-critical method was first given a systematic treatment in a book by Martin Dibelius which appeared in 1919. This work has since become known to English readers under the title *From Tradition to Gospel*.[6] The position of Dibelius was rather conservative as compared to later members of the school. He found the origin of the tradition connected primarily with the kinds of people that had preserved it. Thus various elements could be traced back to preachers, teachers, or missionaries. He felt that under the hands of these people the tradition had undergone considerable change; however, the possibility that some tradition went back to Jesus he did not deny.[7]

A far more radical approach was taken by Rudolf Bultmann. His principal work on form criticism appeared in 1921 and has since been translated under the title, *The History of the Synoptic Tradition*.[8] He combined his form-critical approach with a later, more fully developed existentialist philosophical approach, and eventually denied that the Gospel writers had any kind of historical objective in writing.[9]

M. Albertz took a more conservative approach to the Gospels. He agreed that the early church adapted the tradition to its use, but felt that back of that tradition lay the historical situation in the ministry of Jesus. Joachim Jeremias applied the methodology of form criticism with special reference to the parables of Jesus. He attempted to separate from the parables the interpretive and didactic additions of the early church. This more conservative

---

[5] *Ibid.*, pp. 31-32.
[6] Trans. Bertram Lee Woolf (New York: Scribner, 1935).
[7] Cf. Anderson, p. 32.
[8] Trans. John Marsh (New York: Harper, 1963).
[9] Cf. Anderson, p. 32.

approach of the form critics has prevailed alongside the school
of Bultmann, where the more skeptical approach has continued.[10]

RUDOLF BULTMANN

We have chosen to focus our attention on Bultmann in this
chapter, for three reasons. In the first place, along with Dibelius
he is one of the two chief form critics. In the second place, he
combines with that form-critical approach an existentialist philosophical approach which has had far-reaching results in his
treatment of the subject of the Jesus of history. Our third reason
is a very practical one. His treatment has profoundly influenced
the critical approach to the life of Jesus. As will be seen in the
three following chapters, subsequent writers in the critical school
are generally classified on the basis of their position with respect
to Bultmann.

In a relatively brief essay, in a condensation of his methodology,
Bultmann notes two characteristics of contemporary research.
One he designates as "the new religious-historical point of
view."[11] By this, Bultmann makes primary reference to the
work of Bousset and Heitmüller and the History of Religions
school. Their work had made it clear, according to Bultmann, that
there were two distinct groups of Christians in the early history
of the church. One group was primarily Palestinian and conceived
of Jesus as the Messiah who was soon to return as the Son of
man. The other group was primarily Hellenistic, and while its
members shared hope in the end of the world, they placed their
primary emphasis on the present, exalted Lord. Our Gospels
came primarily from this second group. He goes on to say, however, that the matter is not as simple as this, for Hellenistic influence has been found even in Palestine. One of these Hellenisti-
cally influenced groups he finds to be the followers of John the
Baptist. He believes that the controversy between the disciples
of John and those of Jesus had its effect upon the formation of
the Gospels and as a result it is possible that "many a word is
attributed to him [Jesus] which he did not utter." He feels that
this whole situation is filled with possibilities and contingencies
and that as a result, "One can only emphasize the uncertainty
of our knowledge of the person and work of the historical Jesus
and likewise of the origin of Christianity."[12]

---

[10] *Ibid.*, pp. 32-33.
[11] Rudolf Bultmann, "The Study of the Synoptic Gospels," in R. Bultmann
and Karl Kundsin, *Form Criticism,* trans. Frederick C. Grant (New York:
Harper, 1934), p. 17.
[12] *Ibid.*, pp. 17-20.

A second characteristic of contemporary research Bultmann designates as "the new literary-historical method of approach which has come to be known as Form criticism."[13] This, of course, is the primary concern of his essay. He notes that the generation of such scholars as H. J. Holtzmann, Adolf Jülicher, and Johannes Weiss assumed that they could extract the history of Jesus' life as well as his sayings by an analysis of Mark and Q.[14]

But the turning point had come with the work of Wrede. Bultmann considers Wrede's work and theory of the messianic secret to be the most important Gospel research in the generation preceding his own writing. He goes on to describe how Wrede's work destroyed faith in the historical credibility of Mark's Gospel, in showing how Mark had manipulated the material he had at hand in accordance with his theological and dogmatic purpose, so that "One can not make out from his narrative either the development of the Messianic consciousness and claim of Jesus or the course of his activity, nor the reasons for his failure and death."[15]

Wellhausen did much the same to Q that Wrede had done to Mark. According to Bultmann, Wellhausen had demonstrated that this sayings source was influenced by primitive church theology. "It grew out of the primitive community and is steeped in its views and interests, and therefore gives us no infallible reflection of the preaching of Jesus."[16]

With this background he begins his discussion of form criticism. At the outset, one must distinguish between the traditional material which the Gospel writers had at hand and the editorial additions with which they wove them together. That this is what really occurred is demonstrated to Bultmann's satisfaction by a comparison of Matthew and Luke with Mark. The results of this comparison make several things obvious to him. He feels it shows that the original tradition about Jesus was made up almost completely of small, detached units. These units were in the form both of sayings and of narrative. Furthermore, references to time and place were totally lacking in these units, and are as a consequence the editorial additions of the Evangelists.[17]

The point of departure for such an investigation must be centered on the Gospel of Mark. Mark's technique is quite simple as

[13] *Ibid.*, p. 20.

[14] *Ibid.*, p. 21. Q, for German *Quelle*, refers to a hypothetical early source, mostly of the sayings of Jesus, distinct from Mark but common to Matthew and Luke.

[15] *Ibid.*, p. 22.

[16] *Ibid.*

[17] *Ibid.*, p. 25.

compared to the other Synoptic Gospels. The chief problem of
these writers was to localize the sayings of Jesus, which had been
collected without any reference to the time or place of their
original occurrence. In their handling of this problem Matthew
and Luke proceeded in different ways. Matthew left the narrative
framework of Mark the way he found it, but introduced appropriate sayings from the Q source into the framework where they
fit best.

Luke, on the other hand, created new scenes for the sayings.
The observation of this process was relatively easy in the cases
of Matthew and Luke, but what about Mark? Bultmann was confident that the principles learned from observing what Matthew
and Luke did with Mark could be applied to an investigation of
the construction of the Gospel of Mark.[18] What is the result of
this technique?

> The result is primarily negative, and we conclude that the
> whole framework of the history of Jesus must be viewed as
> an editorial construction, and that therewith a whole series of
> typical scenes, which because of their ecclesiastical use and their
> poetic and artistic associations we had looked upon as scenes
> in the life of Jesus, must be viewed as creations of the evan-
> gelists. On the other hand, it is certainly a positive gain that
> we may now recognize which parts of the gospels are derived
> from older traditional material.[19]

But this is not the end of the problem, for there are two attendant problems with which we must deal. What certainty do we
have that the traditional materials themselves have not been
worked over by the Evangelists? According to Bultmann there is
no such certainty, but once again there are certain devices at our
command to distinguish the primary from the secondary. He
notes that primitive literature makes use of certain more or less
fixed forms which are governed by their own laws of style. He
points out that the existence of these forms has long been recognized in the Old Testament. This is also the case in the Gospels.
This is important, because these forms show a certain resistance
to change.

As a consequence, when one examines the various individual
sections in the Gospels, he may observe whether the form of
expression has been preserved or whether it has been revised,
and as a consequence he will be able to determine the age of the
tradition contained in it. Furthermore, we may be able in at least

---

18 *Ibid.*, pp. 26-27.
19 *Ibid.*, p. 28.

some sense to discover the laws or principles by which the development takes place.

There are available to us certain aids in the discovery of these laws. First of all, by observing Matthew and Luke in their use of Mark, we may gain some idea of how development takes place. Secondly, while we do not have the Q document, by observing the ways in which Matthew and Luke have edited it we may gain more insight into these laws. Finally, "If we are able to deduce a certain regularity in this procedure, then we may certainly assume that the laws held good even earlier, and we may draw conclusions as to the state of the tradition prior to Mark and Q."[20]

Bultmann concedes that this is a very difficult process and that one must proceed with great caution; however, there are certain helps to the Gospel critic. He may observe how gospel material was transmitted in the later church in such compositions as the apocryphal gospels. Furthermore, a study of contemporary Jewish literature will give some help inasmuch as their forms were very similar to those of the Gospels. "Accordingly, the study of Jewish literature helps us to recognize the characteristic forms of the evangelic literature and the laws of style which govern them."[21]

The second attendant problem is even greater. Once we have discovered the traditional material that lay before the Evangelists, what assurance do we have that these traditions are historical narratives?[22] The above processes will help somewhat here, but they will not make historical certainty possible.

Bultmann then proceeds to describe some of the laws governing the formation of the tradition. He notes in the first place "that the narrators do not give us long, unified accounts but rather small single pictures." This terminology, it will be observed, is reminiscent of that of Kähler. The simplicity and brevity of the scenes is emphasized. Apart from the passion narrative, no event is given us that covered a period of more than two days. The number of speaking characters in any individual scene is very limited. There are, as a rule, no more than three, and usually only two. When crowds are involved in an incident, they are customarily treated as a unit.[23]

As these stories are passed on from person to person, their substance remains the same, but there is great variation in detail. Bultmann gives us some examples. In Mk. 9:17 we are told of a

20 *Ibid.*, pp. 28-29.
21 *Ibid.*, pp. 29-30.
22 *Ibid.*, p. 28.
23 *Ibid.*, p. 32.

father who brought his demoniac son to Jesus. Luke adds that it was his only son (9:38). In Mk. 3:1 we are told of the palsied hand that was healed. Lk. 6:6 tells us that it was the right hand. Mk. 14:47 says that the ear of the high priest's servant was struck off. Lk. 22:50 says it was the right ear. Jn. 18:10 elaborates further by giving the name of the servant and the name of the disciple who struck it off. This supplying of names, which is typical of the apocryphal gospels, can be seen already at work in the canonical Gospels. This causes Bultmann to be skeptical even of names given in Mark.[24]

Bultmann notes two other characteristics of the narratives. In the first place, he demonstrates the tendency of Matthew and Luke to put into direct discourse what is indirect in Mark. Second, there is "the inclination to impose a schematic idea on the course of Jesus' activity."[25] An example of this may be seen in the way the scribes and the Pharisees appear regularly interrogating Jesus and seeking to trip him up in his speech.

Bultmann now brings us to an analysis of the forms themselves. He begins by asserting that forms of particular literary types are included in the material. He further asserts that each of these forms has its own distinct characteristics. The first of these forms he designates as miracle stories.[26] He sees in the miracle stories of the Gospels a strong resemblance to similar narratives in Hellenistic sources. Thus he feels we may use these Hellenistic narratives to throw light on those contained in the Gospels.[27]

Bultmann finds the possible source of the nature miracles in a number of things. In some cases Old Testament models have made a contribution. In other cases celebrations of the early church have had an effect on them, e.g., the Easter story on the transfiguration and on Peter's confession, or the celebration of the Eucharist on the feeding of the five thousand. In still other cases miracle stories grew from sayings, e.g., the story of the miraculous catch of fish in Lk. 5:1-11 from Jesus' saying about "fishers of men." He concludes, "In general the stylistic characteristics of the Synoptic miracle stories we have considered show that these stories have grown up in the same atmosphere as the Jewish and Hellenistic miracle stories."[28] His comments on these nature miracles are very similar to those we saw in the liberal lives of Jesus.

The most evident feature of the miracle stories that contain

24 *Ibid.*, pp. 32-33.
25 *Ibid.*, p. 34.
26 *Ibid.*, p. 36.
27 *Ibid.*, pp. 36-37.
28 *History of the Synoptic Tradition*, pp. 230-31.

healings is that they very regularly occur consisting of three parts. In the first part we are given a description of the condition of the patient. Two things are regularly emphasized in this section. First, the gravity of the illness and its long duration are underscored. Second, we are told of the futility of all attempts to heal the illness and of the scorn of the people at the very thought of an attempted healing.[29]

In the second part of the narrative we are told of the healing itself. Bultmann notices a significant difference here between the Hellenistic narratives and those of the Gospels, in that the Gospel narratives are marked by the comparative simplicity of the methodology employed. Another characteristic of this second section is that very often no one but the subject was present at the time of the performance of the miracle itself.

The third part of the narrative is usually characterized by two features. In the first place, we are told of expressions of wonder and awe on the part of those who have witnessed the miracle. Second, the subject of the healing usually gives a very evident sign that the healing has been accomplished; for example, the lame man takes up his bed and walks.[30]

The second of the forms with which Bultmann deals he designates as apothegms. These are sayings that are transmitted in connection with a minor narrative framework. He calls them apothegms after similar narratives of that name in Greek literature. In this form the narrative framework is secondary and serves merely as a scene for the saying, which is of primary importance.

Bultmann notices some differences in the apothegm as it appears in Jewish literature from that found in Greek writings. In the Jewish apothegm, the saying of the hero, which usually comes in response to a question, characteristically appears as either a counterquestion, a short parable, or both. He gives examples from the Talmud and the Gospels, and says that when they are characterized by these features we may safely conclude that they originated in a Jewish environment.

The Greek apothegm, on the other hand, is introduced by characteristic formulas such as, "When he was asked by," or "Once when he observed how." Where this is the case in the apothegms of Jesus, it may be concluded that they originated in the Hellenistic church. A further task in these instances is to distinguish in which cases the saying and narrative framework

---

[29] *Form Criticism,* p. 37.
[30] *Ibid.,* pp. 37-39.

are so closely attached that the one loses its meaning without the other, and in which cases the narrative framework has been artificially supplied. One particular area in which these apothegms were used by the early Christian church was in its attempt to defend itself for having broken with the customs of the past, by an appeal to a saying of Jesus. In some cases Bultmann feels that such apothegms may be original with Jesus, but in other cases he sees them as having originated in the primitive Christian community.

Some apothegms that he claims are not original with Jesus are those which are biographical in character. These stories tend to express "what Christians had experienced of their master or what he had experienced at the hands of his people."[31]

The third form that Bultmann distinguishes in the Gospels is comprised of the sayings of Jesus. These sayings he distinguishes from the conflict and didactic sayings, which he discusses under the apothegms. Bultmann asserts that "we must give up the historicity of many of these narratives," but that in some cases we may have an historical saying of Jesus. How then are we to distinguish the historical from the nonhistorical? The chief means at our disposal is the context in which the saying occurs. If the saying derives its meaning from the context, we may be more certain that we have the original sense of the words. On other occasions, the context in which a saying is put is not meaningful, and in these cases we must use a great deal more caution in evaluating its historicity and original meaning.[32]

These sayings Bultmann divides into five types. (1) We have first the wisdom words, or *Logia*. This is the kind of thing we have in the proverbs of the Old Testament as well as in the proverbial literature of all ancient people.[33] Bultmann observes that the majority of the sayings of Jesus have parallels in the Jewish wisdom literature. In fact he quotes Gerhard Kittel, who said that "Not one of the ethical precepts of Jesus was, or needed to be, entirely unique."[34]

He then takes up the possibilities with respect to the origin of the wisdom sayings found in the Gospels. He says it is possible that Jesus may have been the source of some of the sayings attributed to him. It is also likely that Jesus may occasionally have drawn on a store of proverbs in use at his time. But Bultmann puts the origin of a majority of these sayings in a third

[31] *Ibid.*, pp. 39-46.
[32] *Ibid.*, pp. 46-47.
[33] *History of the Synoptic Tradition*, p. 69.
[34] *Form Criticism*, p. 55.

category. "It is quite clear that we must reckon with the possibility that the primitive community placed in his mouth many a beautiful saying that was really derived from the treasure of Jewish proverbial lore."[35] He notes that many of these sayings meet the needs of the Christian community after Jesus' time, and he concludes, "These wisdom-sayings . . . are least guaranteed to be authentic words of Jesus; and they are likewise the least characteristic and significant for historical interpretation."[36]

(2) Another class is designated as prophetic and apocalyptic sayings. In these, "Jesus proclaimed the arrival of the Reign of God and preached the call to repentance, promising salvation for those who were prepared and threatening woes upon the unrepentant." These sayings are characterized by their brevity and vigor and are patterned after the style of ancient prophecy rather than contemporary apocalyptic. Here, as in the first class, one may find some authentic words of Jesus; but also here, according to Bultmann, we may see the Christian community at work. Three particular kinds of supplementation are evident. Some of these sayings have been taken over from Christian prophets and put into Jesus' mouth. In other cases, an original statement of Jesus has been supplemented by the Christian community. And finally, some of these sayings have been taken over from non-Christian Jewish sources and attributed to Jesus.[37]

(3) A third group of sayings is concerned with the Law. These are similarly traced by Bultmann. These sayings are concerned with the regulations of the community and with such subjects as divorce, alms-giving, fasting, etc. Due to their diametrical opposition to legalistic piety, they could not have originated in contemporary Judaism. Bultmann feels that most of these that are antilegalistic in tone go back to Jesus himself. The exact formulation in some instances may belong to the community, but the work of Jesus at minimum lies back of them. There are here, however, as in the other sayings, certain ones that belong to the community rather than to Jesus. Included in this group are sayings that bear on the mission of the church and its discipline. Also included among the nonoriginal sayings are those "in which the church expressed its faith in Jesus, his work, his destiny, and his person."[38] The passion predictions, for example, must be included in this category.

---

[35] *Ibid.*
[36] *Ibid.*
[37] *Ibid.*, pp. 56-58.
[38] *Ibid.*, p. 59.

(4) Another group is called the I-sayings of Jesus. These are sayings in which Jesus speaks in the first person regarding the significance of his person and work.[39] Here very frequently the reference to Jesus in the saying is a secondary introduction. Many of these I-sayings have been modified by the church in its formulation of the tradition. Some have been put into the mouth of Jesus even though they were spoken first by other Jewish teachers, and some arose in the Christian community and were subsequently put into Jesus' mouth.[40] Bultmann feels that these I-sayings were primarily the work of the Hellenistic church.[41]

(5) In a final class are the similitudes and other forms related to them. Best known in this group are the similitudes themselves, or as they are more commonly known, parables — although Bultmann distinguishes between the two.[42] These are characterized by many well-known literary devices, chief of which are hyperbole, paradox, and metaphor. Here once again Bultmann sees the Christian community at work. Often the Christian community has misinterpreted the parables. Very frequently this misinterpretation takes the form of turning the parables into allegories. The impression that in some cases Jesus used parables to conceal the truth is attributed to the work of the Evangelists. Most particularly the interpretation of the parables as predictive allegories is rejected. Bultmann's frequent assertion of community formation and tailoring is present here as it has been elsewhere.[43] His lack of confidence in this mass of material is well summarized as he writes,

> We can only count on possessing a genuine similitude of Jesus where, on the one hand, expression is given to the contrast between Jewish morality and piety and the distinctive eschatological temper which characterized the preaching of Jesus; and where on the other hand we find no specifically Christian features.[44]

After discussing these five types of sayings, he once again deals with the subject of authenticity from an overall perspective. He states, "The investigation of the sayings of Jesus leads to a considerable uncertainty, but it does not end finally in complete scepticism."[45] He emphasizes the care with which one must remove the secondary layers of the tradition, and insists that complete

---

39 *History of the Synoptic Tradition*, p. 130.
40 *Form Criticism*, p. 52.
41 *History*, p. 163.
42 *Ibid.*, p. 174.
43 *Form Criticism*, pp. 48-49.
44 *History*, p. 205.
45 *Form Criticism*, p. 60.

skepticism will not be the end result. He writes, "On one point one must rest content: The *character* of Jesus, the vivid picture of his personality and his life, cannot now be clearly made out; but, what is more important, the content of his message is or will be ever more clearly recognizable."[46] We do not, however, possess any assured historical evidence for any sayings of Jesus. We must be content with his message. "Though one may admit the fact that for no single word of Jesus is it possible to produce positive evidence of its authenticity, still one may point to a whole series of words found in the oldest stratum of tradition which give us a consistent representation of the historical message of Jesus."[47] Bultmann then proceeds in no more than two pages to list a few passages which he regards as bearing the content of Jesus' message.[48]

The fourth basic form that Bultmann identifies in the Gospels he calls historical stories and legends. He does not separate the two, because he feels that the historical stories are so dominated by legend that it is only possible to treat them together. He defines legends in such a way as to distinguish them from miracle stories. "I would describe legends as those parts of the tradition which are not miracle stories in the proper sense, but instead of being historical in character are religious and edifying."[49] He admits that most of them contain something miraculous, but that this is not necessarily the case, as for example in the instance of the Last Supper. The chief differentiating feature of these legends in comparison with the miracle stories is that they gain their meaning from the context in which they appear. They cannot be treated as independent units as can the miracle stories. The context might be the life of a religious hero, in which case the legend is biographical. The context might be "the faith and cult of the community," in which case the legend is cultic. He admits that the boundaries between historical stories, legends, miracle stories, and biographical apothegms are difficult to draw.[50]

The concluding portion of Bultmann's essay is concerned with the results of the foregoing on our evaluation of the Gospels and our knowledge of the life of Jesus. According to Bultmann, it was not any historical concern that gave us the Gospels, but rather the needs of the early Christian community. To be more definite, the specific needs of that community which gave rise to the

[46] *Ibid.*, p. 61.
[47] *Ibid.*
[48] *Ibid.*, pp. 61-63.
[49] *History*, pp. 244-45.
[50] *Ibid.*, p. 245.

Gospels were the cultic, or the needs of worship. As the Christians proclaimed the Gospel in the Hellenistic world, they dwelt on the death and resurrection of Jesus, which was for them the decisive event for the salvation of men. As a result, earliest attention was paid to the passion narrative, and consequently it is quite probable that the tradition concerning it was handed down as a sequence of events at a very early date. But we are not to suppose thereby that the narrative is historical or that an interest in the historical was primary in its formulation. It is more accurately described as being edificatory in purpose. "The whole narrative has been composed from the point of view of faith and worship: it was as the Messiah, the Son of God, that Jesus suffered and died. . . . It is equally clear that the Resurrection Narrative has been composed in the interest of faith and under the influence of devout imagination."[51]

As a result of this meaning which Jesus came to have for the early church, many "cult-legends" were formed to trace specific items in the cult to the time of the life of Jesus himself. This was a common practice in other religions of the day. The only significant difference was that Jesus was a real person, while the other cult-deities were purely mythical. Among these legends were such things as the transfiguration, the birth of Jesus, his temptation, Peter's confession, Jesus' entry into Jerusalem, Peter's miraculous draught of fish.[52]

As far as the actual composition of the Gospels is concerned, Mark was the first to write and likely created the gospel as a literary type. Matthew and Luke as they wrote modified Mark in their attempt to include as much of the traditional material that they had at hand as possible. This is seen, for example, in their inclusion of Q, in their emphasis on Jesus as a teacher, in their greater emphasis on the miraculous in the life of Jesus, in Matthew's use of numerous Old Testament citations to prove that Jesus was the Messiah, and in attempts to universalize the message of the gospel. In the case of John the development is even more full, in that while he uses the tradition, the Jesus whom he portrays is the result of faith.[53]

Bultmann concludes,

> All this goes to show that the interest of the gospels is absolutely different from that of the modern historian. The historian can make progress toward the recovery of the life of Jesus only through the process of critical analysis. The gospels, on the

---

51 *Form Criticism*, pp. 64-66.
52 *Ibid.*, pp. 67-69.
53 *Ibid.*, pp. 69-70.

other hand, proclaim Jesus Christ, and were meant to be read as proclamations.[54]

What is the result of all this on our knowledge of the Jesus of history? Bultmann is very brief here, obviously because he lacks confidence in our ability to know very much about Jesus at all. He does not feel we can say anything definite about Jesus' developing messianic consciousness. As a matter of fact, he says it must be left an open question whether or not Jesus ever regarded himself as the Messiah. It is likely that Jesus "first became the Messiah in the faith of the community."[55] Be that as it may, he agrees that the movement Jesus started was a messianic movement as is indicated by his followers.

To those outside the circle of Jesus' followers, the movement around Jesus looked like any of numerous such movements that captivated segments of the Jewish population and led ultimately to the war against Rome and the destruction of Jerusalem in A.D. 70. At any rate, when he came to Jerusalem he was put to death by the Roman procurator as politically dangerous. Bultmann says we cannot be certain about the part of the Jewish authorities in the death of Jesus, since the passion narrative is "too thickly overgrown with legend." He believes the artificial opposition of the scribes and Pharisees has had its effect on the Gospels[56] here as elsewhere.

Regarding the content of Jesus' teaching, he holds that both the ethical and the eschatological played an important part. He does not think we are justified in accepting the one as primary and discarding the other as secondary. He redefines eschatology in terms of the present. "Only the future, which is God's, can bring salvation to man; and this future still faces man, in the present, and requires of him the decision for the world or for God."[57] He summarizes his view of the significance of Jesus very well in the final paragraph.

> Jesus sets forth neither an individual nor a social ethics; that is, he measured the deeds of men neither according to an ideal conception of human personality nor of human society, but he taught men that the present instant is the moment of decision, in which it is possible to yield up every claim of one's own and submit obediently to the will of God.[58]

---

[54] *Ibid.*, p. 70.
[55] *Ibid.*, p. 71.
[56] *Ibid.*, pp. 71-72.
[57] *Ibid.*, p. 73.
[58] *Ibid.*, pp. 73-74.

COMPARISON WITH DIBELIUS

While we have concerned ourselves primarily with Bultmann in our study of form criticism, it would be of value to us to compare him briefly with Martin Dibelius, the other principal form critic. We do so mainly in connection with their classification of forms. The forms that Bultmann calls apothegms, Dibelius calls paradigms, because he believes their primary object was to serve as examples for Christian preaching.[59]

There are two further differences in the analysis of this form by the two authors. Bultmann, as we have seen, regards it as one of the two principal classes of Jesus' sayings. Dibelius, on the other hand, classifies it as narrative material.[60] As to the relative historicity of this form, both authors are cautious. Bultmann at times goes so far as to assert that the story was invented by the church as a setting for the saying.[61] Dibelius feels that the need of the paradigm to serve as support for the message of the preacher was primary, and that historical accuracy was secondary.[62]

To the form called by Bultmann miracle stories, Dibelius gives the name "tale" *(Novelle).*[63] This is apparently an attempt to emphasize the form rather than the content, which Bultmann's characterization does more obviously. The change in name, however, does not obscure that this is primarily a designation of content.

What Bultmann designates as sayings and subdivides into five classes, Dibelius calls exhortations. The treatment of Dibelius here is much less detailed than that of Bultmann. He sees them, as the name he gives them implies, as having been collected for hortatory purposes, "to give the churches advice, help, and commandment by means of the Master's words."[64]

Dibelius divides the legends of Bultmann into two classes: legends, which refer primarily to human persons,[65] and myths, which refer primarily to divine persons.[66] Furthermore, this combination occupies a much smaller place in the thought of Dibelius than it does in that of Bultmann: "Pure personal Legends only occupy a relatively small space in the material of the synoptic Gospels."[67] "Only to the smallest extent is the tradition assembled

---

[59] Dibelius, p. 58.

[60] *Ibid.,* pp. 40ff.

[61] *Form Criticism,* p. 45.

[62] Dibelius, pp. 62ff.

[63] *Ibid.,* p. 71.

[64] *Ibid.,* p. 246.

[65] *Ibid.,* p. 105.

[66] *Ibid.,* p. 266.

[67] *Ibid.,* p. 105.

in the Gospel [Mark] of a mythological character and this is confined to the epiphany narratives and a few Tales."[68]

Finally, both critics agree that the passion narrative was the
first section of the gospel story to receive a connected sequence.
This, of course, is to say nothing about the historicity of the
details contained therein.

AN EVALUATION

Since the form-critical method reached its apex in the early
twentieth century, it has steadily lost the interest of historical
investigators. There have been several reasons for this. In the first
place, it was recognized that the method could be variously used.
It did not dictate to what conclusion a particular scholar would
come in his investigation of the Gospels. Rather, one's theological
point of departure would largely determine the conclusions to
which he came.[69]

Second, it became increasingly obvious that much of the material in the Gospels did not have the distinctness of form that the
form critics attributed to it.[70]

Finally, great difficulty was experienced when the form critics
attempted to correlate the various forms with their settings in
the life situations of the church.[71]

We shall forego a detailed analysis and evaluation of the methods
of form criticism. This has been done by others and we need not
restate the arguments. One of several helpful books in this area
is that by E. Basil Redlich.[72] The negative conclusions of his
book are more useful than are the positive ones. He points out a
number of very telling limitations of the form-critical method.
What we say here, briefly, is intended as a supplement to his
treatment. Not only are the miracle stories a class that is more
concerned with content than form, but also the question must be
asked if in the healing miracles form takes any very important
place at all. The form critics here emphasize that these healings
are usually narrated in three parts, and in this way they are
similar to the Jewish and Hellenistic stories of the same era. But
upon reflection it becomes clear that it would be very difficult to
tell of a cure, whether miraculous or natural, in any other way.[73]

---

[68] *Ibid.*, p. 279.
[69] Cf. James M. Robinson, *A New Quest*, pp. 36-37.
[70] Anderson, p. 33.
[71] *Ibid.*, p. 36.
[72] E. Basil Redlich, *Form Criticism* (London: Duckworth, 1939).
[73] Alan Richardson, *The Miracle-Stories of the Gospels* (London: S.C.M., 1941), p. 28.

In the second place, it seems that the needs of the primitive Christian church are too much emphasized by the form critics. The probabilities are that (1) statements by Jesus were created by the early church in order to deal with problems that arose in the fellowship, or (2) statements by Jesus were preserved by the early church that dealt with problems that arose in its fellowship. Either of these would be possible, but which was the more likely to have happened? The observation of Everett Harrison is to the point:

> Form criticism either forgets or minimizes the regulating influence of the apostles and other witnesses of the life of Jesus. In their desire to honor the Lord, these leaders would not be a party to the habit of ascribing to Jesus what in fact did not originate with him at all. The presence of hundreds of people in the early church who had known and followed our Lord in the days of his flesh must have had a powerful effect in keeping the tradition true to the facts.[74]

The application of sayings of Jesus to the needs of the early church does not by virtue of that fact alone take them out of the possibility of having been historical utterances of Jesus previous to his death.[75]

A third question that should be considered is, What is the relationship of form to historical trustworthiness? One of the underlying assumptions of the form critics appeared to be that if a given passage had a specific form it thereby was not historical. Considered from another perspective, is not the very converse of this true? "The forms of the Gospel tradition afford no proof that it is not historical, and we may go further. The form is a guarantee of the contents and was imposed for that very purpose."[76]

We make here one final observation. If the Gospel narratives were to such an extent as the form critics claim the product of the primitive Christian community, that community did a remarkably poor job of creating sayings on the part of Jesus to deal with its vexing problems. Why were not statements created by the early church to deal with such questions as the necessity of the cross, the mission to the Gentiles, and the polity of the early church?[77] Or why was there not developed a statement on the part of the

---

[74] Everett F. Harrison, *Introduction to the New Testament* (Grand Rapids: Eerdmans, 1964), p. 150.

[75] F. F. Bruce, "Form Criticism," *Baker's Dictionary of Theology,* ed. Everett F. Harrison (Grand Rapids: Baker, 1960), p. 228.

[76] Ernest Findlay Scott, *The Validity of the Gospel Record* (New York: Scribner, 1938), p. 140.

[77] Taylor, p. 86.

early church to deal with the question of circumcision which continued to vex the church of the New Testament era?[78] To questions like these the form critics give us no ready answer.

While form criticism itself failed to continue to exert as strong an influence as it did in the early twentieth century, many of the basic assumptions of the movement had continued significance particularly in German scholarship under the leadership of Bultmann and his successors. The result was a decrease in the interest of critical scholarship in the life of the historical Jesus and an increased emphasis on the church in the New Testament era.[79]

BULTMANN AND MYTHOLOGY

Far more exceptional in its nature than his work on form criticism, and arousing far more activity in the critical school, was Bultmann's essay, "New Testament and Mythology." It would appear that the type of thought expressed therein had a profound influence on him in his earlier form-critical analysis. In order to understand Bultmann's position, we must examine this. essay with some thoroughness.

He begins by noting what for him is the mythological cosmology of the New Testament. The world there presented is three-storied. At the center of this structure is the earth, with heaven above and hell beneath. In heaven abides God with his angels. In hell there is the place of torment. The earth between is the scene of both natural and supernatural events. The supernatural events are the result of the intervention of God and his angels on the one hand, and Satan and his demons on the other. For this reason, miracles are of very regular occurrence.[80]

In such a cosmology, man is not in control of his life. He may be possessed by evil spirits and captivated by Satan, or God may give guidance to his thought and grant to him special powers. The present age is held captive by Satan, but its end will be soon. This end will be climactic and will be brought about via a cosmic catastrophe. In connection with this climax, there will be the resurrection of the dead, the last judgment, and the assignment of men to either heaven or hell.[81] Bultmann concludes, "This then is the mythical view of the world which the New Testament

---

[78] Bruce, p. 228.

[79] Anderson, p. 33.

[80] Rudolf Bultmann, "New Testament and Mythology," *Kerygma and Myth*, I, ed. Hans Werner Bartsch, trans. Reginald H. Fuller (London: S.P.C.K., 1964), p. 1.

[81] *Ibid.*, pp. 1-2.

presupposes when it presents the event of redemption which is
the subject of its preaching."[82]

This event of redemption is pictured in terms of God sending
his pre-existent Son to this earth as a man. Through his death and
resurrection, death, which had resulted from Adam's sin, is
abolished and the demonic forces have lost their power. From his
place of exaltation, Christ will soon return. Following his return,
there will occur the resurrection and the judgment of men and
suffering and death will cease.[83]

Paul and the other New Testament writers expect this to happen
very soon, and are attempting to win many to faith in Christ to
assure their resurrection and prepare many others for Christ's
return.[84]

Bultmann feels that all of the above is the language of mythology and finds its source in Jewish apocalyptic writings of the
day and in the redemption myths of gnosticism. "To this extent the
kerygma is incredible to modern man, for he is convinced that the
mythical view of the world is obsolete."[85]

He finds the incredibility and the unacceptability of this aspect
of the New Testament primarily in two particulars. In the first
place, it is against everything we know about modern science.
He says it is senseless to expect the Christian to accept the
cosmology of the New Testament, because there is nothing particularly Christian about that cosmology. He further notes that it
would be impossible for modern man to accept that cosmology
even if he wanted to, because a man's world view is determined
by the particular place in history in which he finds himself. To
be sure, he can alter that world view, and contribute to its change,
but only when he is confronted with a new and compelling set of
facts which force him to do so. At any rate, he cannot go back
to an outmoded concept. "All our thinking today is shaped
irrevocably by modern science."[86] To ask modern man to accept
New Testament mythology as an article of faith would, in the
opinion of Bultmann, reduce faith to works.

He then goes on to illustrate in what particulars the world view
of the New Testament is unacceptable. He discusses, for example,
the idea of heaven and hell presented in the New Testament. The
idea that one can ascend into a local heaven or descend into a
local hell are to him absurd. They are tenets of a cosmology

---

82 *Ibid.,* p. 2.
83 *Ibid.*
84 *Ibid.*
85 *Ibid.,* p. 3.
86 *Ibid.*

that believes in a three-storied world. "No one who is old enough to think for himself supposes that God lives in a local heaven."[87]

The idea of the return of the Son of man on the clouds of heaven and the meeting with him in the air expressed in I Thess. 4:15ff. can no longer be expected. He feels that the entire eschatology of the New Testament must be given up as mythological inasmuch as Christ never returned as the writers of the New Testament expected. "Even if we believe that the world as we know it will come to an end in time, we expect the end to take the form of a natural catastrophe, not of a mythical event such as the New Testament expects."[88]

He notes two other particulars of the New Testament as completely unacceptable to modern science. In the first place, now that we have become acquainted with the forces and laws of nature, it is no longer possible for us to accept belief in the real existence of spirits whether they be good or evil. In the second place, the miracles of the New Testament can no longer be defended as miraculous. He regards it as indefensible to support their historicity by assigning them to nervous disorders or hypnotic effects. He admits that our physiological and psychological knowledge is incomplete, but we still assign maladies to causes and are attempting to find those causes, unintelligible though they may be. "It is impossible to use electric light and the wireless and to avail ourselves of modern medical and surgical discoveries, and at the same time to believe in the New Testament world of spirits and miracles."[89] The unacceptable nature of the New Testament world view from the perspective of modern science is summarized as follows. "Man's knowledge and mastery of the world have advanced to such an extent through science and technology that it is no longer possible for anyone seriously to hold the New Testament view of the world — in fact, there is no one who does."[90]

But there is a second reason for the rejection of the New Testament world view in addition to the scientific one. That is found in modern man's understanding of himself. Modern man, according to Bultmann, regards himself as an essential unity. He may regard himself as pure nature or pure spirit, yet he is a unity. Modern man refuses to regard himself as "the victim of a strange dichotomy" over part of which he has control and part of which

---

[87] *Ibid.*, p. 4.
[88] *Ibid.*, pp. 4-5.
[89] *Ibid.*
[90] *Ibid.*, p. 4.

is subject to the control of external powers. He is aware of such maladies as schizophrenia, but this is not attributed to either divine or demonic agency. Further, "he finds *what the New Testament has to say about the 'Spirit'* . . . *and the sacraments utterly strange and incomprehensible."*[91] How a supernatural agency can enter into man's natural powers and have effect upon him is incomprehensible, since he is conscious of his own moral responsibility. How baptism in water can have such a profound effect on man's future, or how material food can convey spiritual strength, is equally difficult for him to understand.

He goes on to analyze some other biblical doctrines and reject them on the basis of their unacceptability to modern man. For example, the idea that death is the punishment for sin is abhorrent to modern man regardless of his philosophical or religious position. While the idea of death may present more of a problem to the idealist than to the naturalist, they both regard it as the necessary process of nature. "And to attribute human mortality to the fall of Adam is sheer nonsense, for guilt implies personal responsibility, and the idea of original sin as an inherited infection is subethical, irrational, and absurd."[92]

The doctrine of the atonement is equally unacceptable. How could the death of a sinless man (which itself is difficult for Bultmann to conceive of) have effect on the guilt of another? "What a primitive mythology it is, that a divine Being should become incarnate, and atone for the sins of men through his own blood!"[93]

The idea of the resurrection of Jesus is just as difficult for Bultmann. The biologist does not regard death as a problem, and the idealist "could not believe that such a life is made available by the resuscitation of a dead person." That God should make life available to man on the basis of a nature miracle is unthinkable. That such an event could be an act of God in the first place, and that it could have any effect upon his life in the second place, is incredible.[94]

The ideas of the death and resurrection of Jesus, and that of his being the God-man, Bultmann traces to gnostic influence. "As for the pre-existence of Christ, with its corollary of man's translation into a celestial realm of light, and the clothing of the human personality in heavenly robes and a spiritual body — all this is not only irrational but utterly meaningless." Why salvation should

---

91 *Ibid.,* p. 6. Italics in original.
92 *Ibid.,* p. 7.
93 *Ibid.*
94 *Ibid.,* p. 8.

be accomplished in this way or why man's end should take this form is inexplicable.[95]

Bultmann has now reached a crucial point in his discussion as he asks the question, "Does this drastic criticism of the New Testament mythology mean the complete elimination of the kerygma?"[96] He rejects any process of selection that accepts some of the features of the kerygma and rejects others, for this only reduces the quantity of mythology. The more fundamental question is "whether the New Testament consists exclusively of mythology, or whether it actually demands the elimination of myth if it is to be understood as it is meant to be."[97]

Bultmann feels that before this question can be answered, the nature of myth must be understood. Here Bultmann reaches the most critical point in his interpretation. He does not feel that myth should be interpreted cosmologically, which according to him is most likely the way it has been interpreted throughout the greater part of the church's history, but rather anthropologically, or more particularly existentially. Myth, according to Bultmann, is an attempt by man to find the origin of the world and a purpose for its existence beyond the world itself. Myth also is an indication of man's feeling of dependence. "The real purpose of myth is to speak of a transcendent power which controls the world and man, but the purpose is impeded and obscured by the terms in which it is expressed."[98] He therefore concludes, "Hence the importance of New Testament mythology lies not in its imagery but in the understanding of existence which it enshrines. The real question is whether this understanding of existence is true. Faith claims that it is, and faith ought not to be tied down to the imagery of New Testament mythology."[99]

Bultmann then goes on to apply his criticism to the New Testament itself. He says that the New Testament contains rough edges and contradictions which must be removed.[100] Next he notes the previous attempts at demythologizing. Here he has in mind primarily the liberals and the History of Religions school. He mentions in passing the allegorical method of dealing with mythology. "This method spiritualizes the mythical events so that they become symbols of processes going on in the soul." He notes that this

[95] *Ibid.*
[96] *Ibid.*, p. 9.
[97] *Ibid.*, p. 10.
[98] *Ibid.*, pp. 10-11.
[99] *Ibid.*, p. 11.
[100] *Ibid.*, pp. 11-12.

is a very comfortable solution to the problem, but one that avoids the necessity of criticism.[101]

The older liberal theologians regarded the mythological as only temporary and relative. For this reason they felt they could dispense with it "and retain only the broad, basic principles of religion and ethics." The idea of a decisive act of God in history is given up. The most fundamental truths of religion are eternal, although they are only realized in human history. The acceptance of these principles does not include the acceptance of the age or of the person who was the first to discover them. Bultmann finds himself very much opposed to this position.

> The New Testament speaks of an *event* through which God has wrought man's redemption. . . . [Jesus'] person is just what the New Testament proclaims as the decisive event of redemption. It speaks of this person in mythological terms, but does this mean that we can reject the kerygma altogether on the ground that it is nothing more than mythology?[102]

For Bultmann the answer is obviously No.

He next notices the approach of the History of Religions school to mythology. For them the importance of the New Testament lay not in its instruction about religion and ethics, as with the liberals, but rather in actual religion and piety. "The essence of the New Testament lay in the religious life it portrayed; its highwatermark was the experience of mystical union with Christ, in whom God took symbolic form." Bultmann agrees with the advocates of this school that the essence of religion means a detachment from the world, but disagrees as to the nature of that detachment. For the History of Religions school it is essentially mystical; for Bultmann it is essentially eschatological. But finally, this school comes under the same criticism as did that of the liberals, for "like the liberals, they are silent about a decisive act of God in Christ proclaimed as the event of redemption."[103] So for them as for the liberals the basic question still remains, Can the kerygma of the New Testament be separated from the mythological terms that surround it without ceasing to be kerygma?

For Bultmann the only solution to the problem of demythologizing the New Testament is the existentialist one. "The mythology of the New Testament is in essence that of Jewish apocalyptic and the Gnostic redemption myths." Both of these systems have at their base a dualistic conception of the world. The only

---

101 *Ibid.*, p. 13.
102 *Ibid.*, pp. 13-14.
103 *Ibid.*, pp. 14-15.

way man can be redeemed from this dualism is by divine intervention. Both these systems expect such an intervention. According to Jewish apocalyptic the present age will soon end and will
be followed by another brought in by the coming of the Messiah.
According to gnosticism a Son of God will be sent to earth in
the form of man to teach the elect and to show them how they
may reach their heavenly home.[104] For Bultmann the significance
of these mythological types is not to be found in their imagery,
but in their conception of human existence; and it is to this subject that he next turns his attention.[105]

In his discussion of the Christian interpretation of being, he
discusses first human existence apart from faith. He notes first of
all the basic difference between the New Testament and gnosticism.
In gnosticism matter is the source of evil. The soul of man is
imprisoned in an evil, material body. In the New Testament, on
the other hand, sin rather than matter is the cause of corruption
and death. "The Gnostic conception of the soul as a pure, celestial element imprisoned by some tragic fate in a material body
is entirely absent."[106] Paul does indeed use the term "flesh" repeatedly in connection with sin, but by this he means not the
body or the physical side of man, "but the sphere of visible, concrete, tangible, and measurable reality, which as such is also the
sphere of corruption and death." Living according to the flesh
from Paul's point of view covers a host of things. The life of crude
indulgence and the boastful achievement of one who feels he
has fulfilled the requirements of the law are both included. "It
includes every passive quality and every advantage a man can
have, in the sphere of visible tangible reality."[107] The real slavery
of man comes about when he bases his life on the transitory,
visible, tangible sphere of things. The man trying thus to secure
himself comes inevitably into conflict with other men. In so doing
he may give vent to feelings of anger, envy and jealousy, or he
may seek to bargain or compromise to increase his security. "Thus
man becomes the slave of anxiety. . . . Everybody tries to hold
fast to his own life and property, because he has a secret feeling
that it is slipping away from him."[108]

Over against this life apart from faith, Bultmann opposes the
life of faith. "The authentic life, on the other hand, would be
a life based on unseen, intangible realities." It is a life that gives

---

[104] *Ibid.*, pp. 15-16.
[105] *Ibid.*, p. 16.
[106] *Ibid.*, p. 17.
[107] *Ibid.*, p. 18.
[108] *Ibid.*, p. 19.

up all "self-contrived security." This life must be experienced as
a result of "faith in the grace of God." This grace of God gives
us forgiveness of sin. To him sin is that desire for security based
on tangible realities in our past. In opening our hearts to God
we are released from the past and enabled "to open ourselves
freely to the future." But the one requirement of such faith is
that we abandon all attempts at self-erected security and commit
ourselves wholly to God.[109]

The kind of detachment of which Bultmann is here speaking
is different from that of asceticism. It means keeping the world
at a distance, or of dealing with it "as if not." At this point he
cites a number of passages from Paul which demonstrate to
him that "everything in the world has become indifferent and
unimportant."[110]

This is what Bultmann means when he refers to "eschatological
existence." He believes that he has freed the eschatology of
gnosticism and Jewish apocalyptic from its accompanying mythology. That is, "The age of salvation has already dawned for the
believer and the life of the future has become a present reality."
He feels that the Gospel of John has carried the process of demythologizing the farthest in that it has completely eliminated
apocalyptic eschatology. But this life of faith is not a possession
to be guarded with rigorousness, which might lead to asceticism.
Nor is it an assured possession, which might lead to the other
extreme of libertinism. It is a life that needs constant decision
and renewal. "To believe means not to have apprehended but
to have been apprehended. It means always to be travelling along
the road between the 'already' and the 'not yet,' always to be
pursuing a goal."[111]

For the Christian the essential character of faith is not a possession of transcendent realities, but the faith itself. By "Spirit"
Paul means "the possibility of a new life which is opened up by
faith." The Spirit is neither a supernatural force nor a present
possession of the believer. "It is the possibility of a new life which
must be appropriated by a deliberate resolve."[112]

Paul further shows how the person who is freed from the
anxiety and frustration of clinging to tangible security is freed
to live and enjoy fellowship with others. This is the kind of thing
Paul refers to in Gal. 5:22.[113]

---

109 *Ibid.*, pp. 19-20.
110 *Ibid.*, p. 20.
111 *Ibid.*, pp. 20-21.
112 *Ibid.*, pp. 21-22.
113 *Ibid.*, p. 22.

After concluding his discussion of the Christian interpretation of being, Bultmann takes up his second main concern — its relation to the New Testament and the event of redemption. He discusses first, at considerable length, the possibility of attaining the life of faith apart from Christ. The New Testament, he says, "claims that faith only became possible at a definite point in history in consequence of an *event* — viz., the event of Christ. Faith in the sense of obedient self-commitment and inward detachment from the world is only possible when it is faith in Jesus Christ."[114] But then the question arises, Is this self-understanding necessarily to be linked to Christ at all? Is it not possible to have a Christian self-understanding without Christ? Is not theology itself a precursor of existentialism, and is not this theology itself in need of demythologizing further until Christ is completely removed from it? He notes, for example, the approach of such secular philosophers as Heidegger and Jaspers, which apparently brings them to the same place as Bultmann. Some have accused Bultmann of borrowing categories from these men and forcing them on the New Testament, but he replies, ". . . One should rather be startled that philosophy is saying the same thing as the New Testament and saying it quite independently."[115]

For Bultmann there are really two questions here. The first is, Can the nature of man be *discovered* apart from the New Testament? To this he replies, "As a matter of fact it has not been discovered without the aid of the New Testament, for modern philosophy is indebted both to it and to Luther and Kierkegaard."[116] The far more important question for Bultmann is, Is the "nature" of man realizable apart from Christ? Here he parts company with the philosophers, for they assume that all that needs to be done is to inform man about his "nature" and he will be able to realize it. In contrast, Bultmann notes that the New Testament "affirms the total incapacity of man to release himself from his fallen state."[117]

As a consequence, the New Testament goes on to say something that secular existentialist philosophy would never say. The saving act of God is that which enables man to live authentically.[118]

The point of departure of the existentialist philosopher and the Christian is quite similar. Both agree that man can be only what

---

[114] *Ibid.*
[115] *Ibid.,* pp. 22-25.
[116] *Ibid.,* p. 26.
[117] *Ibid.,* p. 27.
[118] *Ibid.*

he already is. Both agree that authentic existence "is possible only because in some sense it is already a present possession." But in speaking this way the New Testament addresses only Christians, "those who have opened their hearts to the redemptive action of God. It never speaks thus to natural man, for he does not possess life, and his plight is one of despair." The reason for this plight from Bultmann's point of view is that natural man can only become what he already is. The New Testament "sees that natural man, man apart from Christ, is not as he ought to be — he is not alive, but dead."[119]

Thus the primary difference here between Bultmann and philosophy is in the concept of the fall. Philosophical existentialism feels that all that is needed is for man to be shown his fallen plight, and that then he will be able to escape from it. The New Testament, on the other hand, regards the fall of man as total.

Bultmann makes his position quite clear.

> As a result of his self-assertion man is a totally fallen being. He is capable of knowing that his authentic life consists in self-commitment, but is incapable of realizing it because however hard he tries he still remains what he is, self-assertive man. So in practice authentic life becomes possible only when man is delivered from himself. It is the claim of the New Testament that this is exactly what has happened. This is precisely the meaning of that which was brought in Christ. At the very point where man can do nothing, God steps in and acts — indeed he has acted already — on man's behalf.[120]

Thus through Christ man receives the forgiveness of sins, but this is not to be understood in a judicial sense of the remission of punishment. It rather means that man is now free to obey. "The New Testament speaks and faith knows of an act of God through which man becomes capable of self-commitment, capable of faith and love, of his authentic life."[121]

In coming more specifically to the life of Christ, Bultmann states that we have here a series of events that is neither purely mythological nor purely historical. Such things as the pre-existence of Christ, his being a Son of God, his virgin birth, are definitely mythological for him. On the other hand, Jesus of Nazareth is a concrete figure of history. How little interested Bultmann is, however, in the events of Jesus' life is seen in the fact that he spends less than two pages on the subject and then concludes, "We shall not, however, pursue the examination of the particular incidents

119 *Ibid.,* p. 28.
120 *Ibid.,* p. 31.
121 *Ibid.,* pp. 32-33.

of his life any further. In the end the crux of the matter lies
in the cross and resurrection."[122]

He then proceeds to a discussion of the cross. He notes first
of all that there is much mythological interpretation that has grown
up around it. The ideas of Jesus' pre-existence, his being the incarnate Son of God, his sinlessness, his blood atonement, his vi-
carious bearing of the sin of the world, his enduring the punishment for sin on our behalf in order to deliver us from death —
"This mythological interpretation is a mixture of sacrificial and
judicial analogies, which have ceased to be tenable for us
today."[123]

The significance of the cross is not that it brings about the
forgiveness of all past and future sins of mankind. Its meaning
is found in that it delivers man from the power of sin, and as
such it takes on cosmic dimensions.

> By giving up Jesus to be crucified, God has set up the cross for
> us. To believe in the cross of Christ does not mean to concern
> ourselves with a mythical process outside of us and our world,
> with an objective event turned by God to our advantage, but
> rather to make the cross of Christ our own, to undergo cruci-
> fixion with him. The cross in its redemptive aspect is not an
> isolated incident which befell a mythical personage, but an event
> whose meaning has "cosmic" importance. Its decisive, revolu-
> tionary significance is brought out by the eschatological frame-
> work in which it is set. In other words, the cross is not just an
> event of the past which can be contemplated, but is the escha-
> tological event in and beyond time, in so far as it (understood
> in its significance, that is, for faith) is an ever-present reality.[124]

Therefore, for Bultmann, the cross and the passion of Jesus
are ever present realities and are not to be confined to the events
of the first century.[125]

Bultmann in coming to grips with the problem of history employs Kähler's distinction between the two German words: "In
its redemptive aspect the cross of Christ is no mere mythical
event, but a historic *(geschichtlich)* fact originating in the historical
(historisch) event which is the crucifixion of Jesus."[126] Then the
question arises, If we are to be able to discover the real meaning of the cross must we understand it as the cross of Jesus, a
figure of past history? Here Bultmann draws a distinction between

---

122 *Ibid.*, pp. 34-35.
123 *Ibid.*, p. 35.
124 *Ibid.*, p. 36.
125 *Ibid.*, p. 37.
126 *Ibid.*

ourselves and the first preachers of the gospel. For them it was the cross of the one whom they had lived with and seen die. But not so with us. "The meaning of the cross is not disclosed from the life of Jesus as a figure of past history, a life which needs to be reproduced by historical research. On the contrary, Jesus is not proclaimed merely as the crucified; he is also risen from the dead. The cross and the Resurrection form an inseparable unity."[127]

The unity of the significance of the cross and of the resurrection is much emphasized by Bultmann. It is "a single, indivisible cosmic event which brings judgment to the world and opens up for men the possibility of authentic life."[128] However, Bultmann goes on to deny the significance of the resurrection as a miraculous proof sufficient to convince the unbeliever. He admits that it is often used as such in the New Testament, "But these are most certainly later embellishments of the primitive tradition."[129] Moreover, "An historical fact which involves a resurrection from the dead is utterly inconceivable!"[130]

That the resurrection could not be a miraculous proof sufficient to convince the skeptic is seen not merely in "The incredibility of a mythical event like the resuscitation of a dead person," nor in the impossibility of verifying its historicity, but in that the resurrection is itself an article of faith,

> And you cannot establish one article of faith by invoking another. You cannot prove the redemptive efficacy of the cross by invok-, ing the resurrection. For the resurrection is an article of faith because it is far more than the resuscitation of a corpse — it is the eschatological event. And so it cannot be a miraculous proof. For, quite apart from its credibility, the bare miracle tells us nothing about the eschatological fact of the destruction of death. Moreover, such a miracle is not otherwise unknown to mythology.[131]

The present significance of the resurrection is really the important factor. It is not a miraculous proof from the past, but an article of faith from the present. "Indeed, faith in the resurrection is really the same thing as faith in the saving efficacy of the cross."[132]

The next question then is, How does one come to believe in the

---

127 *Ibid.*, p. 38.
128 *Ibid.*, p. 39.
129 *Ibid.*
130 *Ibid.*
131 *Ibid.*, pp. 39-40.
132 *Ibid.*, p. 41.

saving efficacy of the cross? For Bultmann the answer is very clear. "Christ meets us in the word of preaching as one crucified and risen. He meets us in the word of preaching and nowhere else. The faith of Easter is just this — faith in the word of preaching."[133] At this point Bultmann puts this preaching or kerygma in radical opposition to the historical Jesus. "It would be wrong at this point to raise again the problem of how this preaching arose historically, as though that could vindicate its truth. That would be to tie our faith in the word of God to the results of historical research. The word of preaching confronts us as the word of God. It is not for us to question its credentials."[134] In accepting this word of preaching, we are given an opportunity of understanding ourselves. Thus,

> The resurrection itself is not an event of past history. All that historical criticism can establish is the fact that the first disciples came to believe in the resurrection. The historian can perhaps to some extent account for that faith from the personal intimacy which the disciples had enjoyed with Jesus during his earthly life, and so reduce the resurrection appearances to a series of subjective visions. But the historical problem is not of interest to Christian belief in the resurrection.[135]

Bultmann owes a great deal to the work of Martin Kähler. There are three basic points that he takes over from Kähler. (1) He agrees with Kähler that there is a distinction between the historical Jesus and the historic Christ. (2) He also accepts the conclusion of Kähler that it is the historic Christ who is presented in the kerygma and not the historical Jesus who is the object of the Christian faith. (3) He also accepts Kähler's judgment that the Gospels cannot be used as sources for the life of Jesus. They supply us rather with the kerygma of the early church.[136] Bultmann of course gave all of these points significant development, but he began basically where Kähler had finished.

ANSWERS TO THE SIX QUESTIONS

On the possibility of writing either a biography or a history of Jesus, Bultmann is the most negative of all the critics we have encountered to date. His research as a form critic demonstrated to him that a quest of the historical Jesus was impossible. Although he claims not to deny the possibility of any knowledge

---

[133] *Ibid.*
[134] *Ibid.*
[135] *Ibid.*, p. 42.
[136] Norman Perrin, "The Challenge of New Testament Theology Today," *Criterion*, IV (Spring 1965), 26-27.

at all of the historical Jesus, his resultant position is on the very fringes of total skepticism. "I do indeed think that we can know almost nothing concerning the life and personality of Jesus since the early Christian sources show no interest in either, are moreover fragmentary and often legendary; and other sources about Jesus do not exist."[137]

Furthermore, what his research as a form critic demonstrated as impossible, his position as an existentialist regarded as illegitimate. Biblical interest must be centered on the kerygma and one's response to it, not on the historical Jesus. Even the attempt to establish the legitimacy of the kerygma by means of historical research must be ruled out. We are not able to go beyond the "that" of Jesus' history into the "what" and "how."[138]

> The attempt to demonstrate the legitimacy of the kerygma by scientific research serves a modern interest, for it puts to the kerygma a question with which it is not at all concerned. The kerygma is not interested in the "objective historicity" beyond the "that," but requires faith in the crucified and risen Christ, and on this basis interprets the history of Jesus — in so far as the kerygma has any interest in that history at all, which of course is not the case in Paul and John, but only in the Synoptic Gospels.[139]

Concerning the miraculous in the life of Jesus, Bultmann is completely negative. He will not even be party to the rationalizations of the liberal theologians. "The miracles of the New Testament have ceased to be miraculous, and to defend their historicity by recourse to nervous disorders or hypnotic effects only serves to underline the fact."[140]

His thoroughgoing rationalism is never more evident than it is in the following passage:

> Modern man understands the motion of the universe as a motion which obeys a cosmic law, a law of nature which human reason can discover. Therefore, modern man acknowledges as reality only such phenomena or events as are comprehensible within the framework of the rational order of the universe. He does not acknowledge miracles because they do not fit into this lawful order.[141]

---

[137] *Jesus and the Word,* trans. L. P. Smith and E. H. Lantero (New York: Scribner, 1958), p. 8.

[138] Bultmann, "The Primitive Christian Kerygma and the Historical Jesus," *The Historical Jesus and the Kerygmatic Christ,* ed. and trans. Braaten and Harrisville, pp. 20ff.

[139] *Ibid.,* p. 25.

[140] "New Testament and Mythology," p. 5.

[141] *Jesus Christ and Mythology* (New York: Scribner, 1958), pp. 37-38.

His feeling regarding the resurrection of Jesus is akin to his attitude toward miracles. The historical validity of the resurrection is "utterly inconceivable." Furthermore, the resurrection is an article of faith; it has in Bultmann's terminology "eschatological" significance. An attempt to establish its objective reality is an attempt to establish a guarantee for faith. It is not possible to demonstrate the efficacy of the cross by appeal to the resurrection. Finally, he notes that such an event is well known in mythology, and therefore the resurrection of Jesus cannot possibly claim our acceptance any more than do these other mythological accounts.

For Bultmann myth plays an all-important place in the New Testament. One could derive this merely from the title of the second essay we considered, to say nothing of the extended treatment it receives in that work. The real purpose of the mythology is to be found in its existential significance. "The real purpose of myth is not to present an objective picture of the world as it is, but to express man's understanding of himself in the world in which he lives."[142]

He tells us more particularly how myth accomplishes this. "It may be said that myths give to the transcendent reality an immanent, this-worldly objectivity. Myths give worldly objectivity to that which is unworldly."[143]

Regarding the comparative historical value of John as against the Synoptics, Bultmann would doubtless prefer that we ask the question in another way. What is John's interest in history as compared with the Synoptics? His answer to this question would be forthright. John has no interest in history. The Synoptics have little interest in history. In other words, Bultmann discounts both the historical value and the importance of finding such value in all of the Gospels. This seems to be underscored in that if Bultmann has any preference among the Gospels, it is for the one that he says shows no interest in history — John. The reason for this is in what Bultmann regards as the beginning of the process of demythologizing in John. This sets it apart as superior to the Synoptics.[144]

The significance of Jesus is that man sees in him the love of God revealed. In this revelation of the love of God man is enabled to understand himself, enabled to be free. Fallen, self-assertive man may know of his needs, but he is incapable of

---

[142] "New Testament and Mythology," p. 10.
[143] *Jesus Christ and Mythology,* p. 19.
[144] *Ibid.,* pp. 32-34.

realizing them apart from the event of Christ. "The event of Jesus Christ is therefore the revelation of the love of God. It makes a man free from himself and free to be himself, free to live a life of self-commitment in faith and love."[145] By his response to this event, man becomes capable of living an authentic life.

---

[145] "New Testament and Mythology," p. 32.

CHAPTER SIX

CRITICS TO THE RIGHT OF BULTMANN

INTRODUCTION

That Bultmann is generally considered very much to the "left" theologically should give us an indication of the wide spectrum of theological thought with which we will deal in this chapter on critics to the "right" of Bultmann. They range all the way from the most conservative theologians to those who maintain the tenets of the currently much less popular old liberalism. There is, however, with all the critics to his right a feeling that Bultmann has not done justice to the question of history as it relates to the Christian faith. They believe the events that occurred in the years around A.D. 30 must be investigated from the perspective of history to a much more thorough extent than Bultmann finds necessary. They see much more of importance in the ministry of Jesus than the cross, and the knowledge of these events they consider a necessary and legitimate concern of the Christian faith.[1]

We are nevertheless confronted with a great problem in any kind of attempt to summarize works of so disparate a character as these. A lengthy treatment would be highly preferable to a short one, but within the confines of our treatment this is not a possibility; thus what we present here is very much of a sketch. There do appear, however, to be two chief kinds of treatment among this group of critics; one traces an independent course and takes little or no notice of Bultmann, and a second is so completely involved in a direct refutation of Bultmann that its

---

[1] Perrin, "The Challenge of New Testament Theology Today," *Criterion,* IV (Spring 1965), 28.

every statement is made with the consciousness that it is doing battle with him.

ETHELBERT STAUFFER

An especially fitting representative of the first kind of treatment is Ethelbert Stauffer. If anyone should have come from such a national and theological environment as would make him willing to engage Bultmann in debate, that would have been Stauffer. As professor of New Testament at the University of Erlangen, he comes from the milieu of German biblical criticism toward which most of our investigation in this book has been directed, and from which, of course, Bultmann himself came. It is therefore somewhat surprising that he takes as little notice of Bultmann and the Bultmannians as he does. This is no doubt part of the reason for their extreme irritation with him.

Again, we will summarize his thought in terms of the six questions at the end of Chapter One. As to the possibility of knowing the historical Jesus, he acknowledges the contention of the critical school that there is back of the Gospels a "theological and church-oriented bias" that is much earlier than the time of the writing of the Gospels themselves.[2] The important question, consequently, for Stauffer is how one may separate the historical elements in the Gospels from the dogmatic elements. He does not find the solution in precisely the same place that others have, but concentrates his attention on what he calls new sources. By a comparison of the statements of these new sources with the Gospels, we are able to arrive at what is historical and what is not.

Of these new sources there are, according to Stauffer, three kinds. The first are what he calls "indirect" sources. These are, in the main, sources that tell of the environment and life of first-century Palestine. These sources can throw light on "conditions, events, and personalities" that are in some way related to the life of Jesus.[3] These documents are free of the dogmatic bias of the Gospels, for with very few exceptions their authors know nothing of the existence of Jesus. Stauffer uses these sources along with the Gospels to construct his chronology of the life of Jesus. This first kind of source is particularly useful to Stauffer in two areas. (1) While our knowledge of the childhood and youth of Jesus is practically nil, these sources can at any rate give us some indication of the kind of environment in which Jesus spent the earlier

---

[2] Ethelbert Stauffer, *Jesus and His Story,* trans. Richard and Clara Winston (New York: Knopf, 1960), p. vii.

[3] *Ibid.,* p. viii.

years of his life.[4] (2) Much more importantly, we get from these sources a better picture of the legal situation in first-century Palestine. Stauffer regards this as very helpful, for the treatment given this in the Gospels in connection with the trial of Jesus is vague. When, however, we combine what we find in the Gospels with what we find in Jewish legal history, we come up with a much clearer picture.[5]

The second kind of new source available to us is the direct statement about Jesus in ancient Jewish documents. He has reference here to documents in which Jesus is identified by name. Most of these sources are the work of Jewish rabbinical authorities. Stauffer notes that these have been known for some time, but that the prejudicial attitude toward them as sources for the life of Jesus has prevented their proper use. These sources may, however, be used for purposes of checking, clarifying, and evaluating what we find in the Gospel accounts. It must be realized that we have in these accounts the reverse of the prejudice found in the Gospels. That is, while the Gospel writers tend to put Jesus in a wholly favorable light, those of the rabbis put him in a completely unfavorable one. They give indication of the campaign that was launched against Jesus in his life by the Jews, resulting in his condemnation and crucifixion.[6]

How can these documents be of any value to us in our attempt to construct a chronology of Jesus' life? They possess, says Stauffer, both a positive and a negative value. Positively, when we find in them basic agreement with the Gospels, we are in possession of evidence that was accepted by both sides and we likely have reliable historical facts. Negatively, when these sources disagree with what we find in our Gospels, we are dealing with an area that has been distorted by one or both of the sources. In this case it becomes the work of the historian to investigate the origin of the bias that has distorted the tradition.[7]

The third kind of new source available to us is found in the late Jewish apocalyptic writings. The bearing of these documents is not primarily upon the life of Jesus but rather upon his message. Stauffer notes that the general public has sometimes been led to believe that everything Jesus said is contained in the scrolls of the Qumran community, which of course is not true; but he does think the various Jewish apocalyptic writings reveal that some of the sayings of Jesus that have been regarded as authentic

---

[4] *Ibid.*
[5] *Ibid.*, pp. viii-ix.
[6] *Ibid.*, p. ix.
[7] *Ibid.*, p. x.

until now are to be found in the traditions of an era before the time of Jesus, and that certain other sayings coming from a period after Jesus have been read back into his life; but the net result of all this has been to demonstrate the uniqueness of Jesus rather than to demonstrate that Jesus was merely a product of the traditions and thought of his time.[8]

With this background, Stauffer addresses himself to the question of the possibility of a biography of Jesus. Our hope for any real understanding must be based on our knowledge of the nature of the sources. "We shall come to understand the Christian Gospels and the Jewish texts on Jesus as documents in a passionate controversy centering around the interpretation and the meaning of Jesus."[9] Here Stauffer differs somewhat from other critics we have discussed, for he finds the origin of the Gospels not primarily in their use for teaching, preaching, liturgy, or missionary work, although all of these played a part. Rather they are fundamentally polemical. What is involved here primarily is the struggle of the early church against Judaism. "Out of these struggles emerged the Gospels and the rabbinical or Baptistic documents concerning Jesus."[10] Both the Gospels and the Jewish documents must be understood in this polemical sense.

Stauffer in only three sentences dismisses the possibility of such biographies as those of the nineteenth century. But while he feels that any attempt at biography is impossible, he does not hold the same skepticism for what he calls "a history of Jesus." We should explain briefly what he means by such a history. In the first place, he has in mind something far less inclusive than the nineteenth-century liberals attempted to produce.

> I mean a strict clarification of those facts which can be ascertained, possibly of a certain series of events, perhaps too of a number of causal relationships. I shall proceed along pragmatic lines, refraining from any psychologizing. Chronology will be my guide. I shall synchronize but not invent or speculate. This is what I mean by a historical viewpoint.[11]

Stauffer makes one other prefatory remark before he begins his treatment. He will not interpret what he finds. He bans the Evangelists' interpretation of the life of Jesus, the interpretations offered by "the dogmas of the church," and even his own personal interpretations of Jesus. The one place where he allows interpretation to enter is in connection with Jesus' interpretation of him-

---

8 *Ibid.*, pp. x–xi.
9 *Ibid.*, p. xii.
10 *Ibid.*
11 *Ibid.*, p. xiii.

self. Even here, however, he disavows any attempt of an historian to investigate Jesus' mental processes. He feels that he must confine himself to "the authentic self-affirmations of Jesus" in the Gospels.[12]

Stauffer refuses to let presuppositions, whether they be positive or negative, be the determining factor in evaluating the place of miracles in the life of Jesus. He is emphatic here that one's guide must be source criticism. He notes the significant place miracles play in the Gospel accounts, and along with this points to certain important attendant features: (1) Jesus' desire to have his miracles checked by outsiders and opponents; (2) the acknowledgment of his miracles even by his opponents; (3) indications that Jesus was condemned and put to death in part because he deceived people with his miracles.[13]

He acknowledges that this is all New Testament evidence, but goes on to point out that there is evidence of this, both early and plentiful, in Jewish sources. He next attacks the thesis that they may be accounted for on the basis of the credulity of the Jewish people in Jesus' time. "The Jews of antiquity were extremely realistic in regard to miracles, and at least the opponents of Jesus among them were highly critical. Had that not been so, the miracles of Jesus would not have been so vehemently discussed and so gravely misinterpreted."[14]

Stauffer also discounts the theory that accounts for the miraculous as a common commodity attributed to all religious founders. The Mandaeans, for example, acclaimed John the Baptist as a savior; but they did not attribute miracles to him even though they did to Jesus. The same is true of Islam. Even though Muhammad is held in higher regard than Jesus, no miracles are attributed to Muhammad while many are attributed to Jesus.[15] Also, the miracles of Jesus differ from contemporary accounts of the miraculous. "They are unique and differ sharply from the prestidigitation and wonder-working, the magic tricks, and the tales of demonic vengeance characterizing the other miracles that figure in contemporary accounts."[16] They differ too from the miracles that are attributed to Jesus in the postapostolic writings.

Finally, Stauffer writes briefly about the significance of the miracles. They must not be regarded as "proofs," but rather as "signs." The interpretation of these signs was diverse. By Jesus'

---

12 *Ibid.*
13 *Ibid.*, p. 9.
14 *Ibid.*, p. 10.
15 *Ibid.*, pp. 10-11.
16 *Ibid.*, p. 11.

enemies they were looked upon as offensive and blasphemous. By Jesus' friends they were looked upon as evidence that he was from God.[17]

Stauffer observes that all early Christian tradition places emphasis on the empty tomb. There are evidences in Paul's letters, for example, that point out that the ideas of the resurrection and the empty tomb were older than the time of his writing. Furthermore, as was the case in connection with the miracles, further weight is given to the truth of the resurrection by the reluctant witness of Jesus' opponents that the tomb was found empty.[18] He goes on to note that the various Gospel records give divergent accounts of the appearances of Jesus, but back of them all there was a desire by the Evangelists to convey three facts. (1) "The risen Christ was a vital personality who acted according to a definite plan, bearing witness to himself by appearing whenever, wherever, however, and before whomever he pleased."[19] (2) "The risen Christ existed in a new form of existence whose character was neither spiritualistic nor materialistic."[20] He continued in some of the activities that he participated in previous to his death. He was still flesh and blood and partook of food. On the other hand, he was not limited physically as he had been before his passion. For example, he could pass through closed doors. (3) "The Evangelists and their authorities could not explain this; they could only state it as a fact, only 'testify' to it."[21]

Stauffer concludes his discussion of the appearances by noting that the opponents of Jesus gave their own explanations of the empty tomb and the appearances, but that even in the New Testament itself we have attempts to refute these negative conclusions.[22]

The position of Stauffer with respect to the place of mythology in the New Testament can be deduced from the nature of his treatment. He attempts to make an historical reconstruction, which he feels is possible, and for that reason he does not even talk about mythology. Doubtless he would say there are legendary elements in the New Testament, but their importance to him would be of relatively minor significance.

Stauffer presents some new insights in his comparison of the Gospel of John with the Synoptics. The Synoptics are to be

---

17 *Ibid.*, pp. 11-12.
18 *Ibid.*, pp. 143-44.
19 *Ibid.*, pp. 151-52.
20 *Ibid.*, p. 152.
21 *Ibid.*
22 *Ibid.*, pp. 152-53.

preferred for their preservation of the speech of Jesus, but the Gospel of John clarifies the chronology of Jesus' life.[23] This characterization of John, it should be recognized, is counter to most estimates of that book we have encountered so far. He notes that it is not possible to fit the chronology of John into the Synoptics, but that the converse is perfectly possible. This he regards as important evidence that the Johannine chronology is correct. He goes so far as to suggest that the Fourth Gospel is a corrector and integrator of the accounts given in the Synoptics. This Gospel then gives us a picture of the entire period of Jesus' ministry beginning with the ministry of John the Baptist and carrying it through the events of the passion and resurrection.[24] On the basis of the synchronization of the data in the Synoptics and John, Stauffer arrives at the years A.D. 28 to 32 for the public ministry of Jesus. "Within this period there is room for all the feasts and dates mentioned in the Gospel of John, and for the dates fixed by the Synoptics as well, without any necessity for arbitrary arrangements."[25]

In the book to which we have given our primary attention, Stauffer deliberately excludes his own interpretation of Jesus. He does, however, give us Jesus' interpretation of himself, and in another writing we shall find Stauffer's own view. The clue to Jesus' self-understanding is to be found in the Aramaic statement *Ani hu,* "I am he." Stauffer goes to great length to trace the development and meaning of this statement in the Old Testament and then relates this term as Jesus applied it to himself.

> Judging by the linguistic form, the earlier history, and the content of the *Ani hu* formula, there can no longer be any doubt of what Jesus meant when he used it. He was in all deliberation using the Old Testament and liturgical formula of God's self-revelation. He wished to convey that in his life the historical epiphany of God was taking place.[26]

Stauffer's further development of this self-estimate of Jesus is significant.

> It was the boldest declaration. "I am He" — this meant: where I am, there God is, there God lives and speaks, calls, asks, acts, decides, loves, chooses, forgives, rejects, suffers, and dies. Nothing bolder can be said, or imagined.
>
> It was the profoundest declaration. The historical epiphany of

[23] *Ibid.,* p. 4.
[24] *Ibid.,* p. 7.
[25] *Ibid.,* p. 8.
[26] *Ibid.,* pp. 192-93.

God was fulfilled in the form of a man, not only of a fallible, suffering, mortal man, but of a human man; in the form of a new humanity and brotherhood, in the forward-looking form of a wholly new *humanitas*. God himself had become man, more human than any other man in the wide expanse of history.[27]

Stauffer gives his own view of Jesus' significance more fully elsewhere:

> Jesus is the revealer of God. This is precisely the meaning of the authoritative claim with which Jesus entered into history. Jesus did not want to be regarded either as the Messiah or as a prophet, and still less as a teacher of the law. In word and deed he claimed for himself the authority of God. He made his claim to authority without any metaphysical deduction or theoretical explanation. "No one knows the Son except the Father" (Matt. 11:27). But he has left no doubt that all things have been delivered to him (Matt. 11:27). He forgave sins and nullified paragraphs in the Torah. The Mosaic law is only relatively valid; the word of Jesus is absolute. "Heaven and earth will pass away, but my words will not pass away" (Matt. 24:35). The carpenter from Nazareth spoke the formula *Ani hu* and was therefore condemned to death as a blasphemer of God.[28]

As a result of this, Stauffer regards Jesus as primarily "the founder of a new humanity."[29] "Jesus is the epiphany of a humanity which is not of this world. Therefore he is more human than any other man in this world."[30] It is up to us by our study of Jesus in his relationship to the people of his day to come to realize what this humanity means to us.[31]

It should be no surprise that Stauffer has come under the severe criticism both of the members of Bultmann's school of interpretation and of those who have become known as the "new quest" school. That criticism will be noted in Chapter Eight.

CRITICS OF BULTMANN

Obviously the second group of critics in this chapter, those who write in conscious opposition to Bultmann, cannot be treated as Stauffer has been. They deal with the subject only on the points at which they find themselves in opposition to Bultmann. Furthermore, deep-seated and fundamental though their opposition is, they do not oppose him on every single point. In summar-

---

[27] *Ibid.,* pp. 194-95.
[28] Stauffer, "The Relevance of the Historical Jesus," *The Historical Jesus and the Kerygmatic Christ,* ed. and trans. Braaten and Harrisville, pp. 51-52.
[29] *Ibid.,* p. 52.
[30] *Ibid.,* p. 53.
[31] *Ibid.*

izing the views of this group we shall concentrate on four promi-
nent representatives. The first is Joachim Jeremias, who has been
characterized as one who neither wants to abandon the quest
of the historical Jesus nor wants to join the "new quest," but
would rather like to see the original quest continued.[32] This is
not to say that he can appropriately be placed with the liberals
of the original quest, because he is aware of the basic faults in
their method of investigation. Ernst Kinder and Walter Künneth
can best be identified as adherents of Lutheran theology, though
one would not be justified in classifying the works by them to
which we refer in this chapter as the official German Lutheran
orthodox position. They are rather writing as individuals within
that tradition.[33] The fourth representative is the neo-orthodox
giant, Karl Barth.

Probably the most important work relating to the possibility of
writing a biography or history of Jesus is an essay by Jeremias.[34]
He says it is impossible to write a biography of Jesus. "Without
a doubt it is true to say that the dream of ever writing a biography
of Jesus is over."[35] He refers here to the kind of biography that
bases itself on the Gospels without paying attention to the results
of higher criticism. However, for Jeremias, this does not mean
we should give up the quest for the historical Jesus and Jesus'
message; it means we must pursue our task cognizant of the
work of criticism.[36]

Jeremias is aware, however, of what had happened in the
nineteenth-century quest. He is aware of the modernization of
Jesus that occurred in that quest and admits that we are running
the same risk when we attempt in the twentieth century to get
back to the historical Jesus. Furthermore, he admits that the
historian cannot possibly free his research from his own personality; but in spite of this he believes we are better equipped to
engage in such a pursuit today than were the scholars of the
nineteenth century. In the first place, we have learned from the
excesses and the mistakes of the original quest. Also, we have
learned that we must expect less from such a quest than did
the nineteenth century. He then goes on to describe five "bul-
warks which will protect us from arbitrary modernizations of

---

[32] Joachim Jeremias, *The Problem of the Historical Jesus,* trans. Norman
Perrin (Philadelphia: Fortress, 1964), p. xviii.
[33] Braaten and Harrisville, *Kerygma and History,* p. 12.
[34] Jeremias, p. xviii.
[35] *Ibid.,* p. 12.
[36] *Ibid.*

Jesus," which make our investigation today more realistic and more possible than was that of the nineteenth century.[37]

(1) The development and refinement of literary criticism itself has been a great aid, from Jeremias' point of view. The discovery of "sources" in the Gospels, or as he puts it more cautiously, "strands of tradition," has been a great help. But the investigation of the oral period antedating the writing of the Gospels has been an even greater aid. By these devices we have been able to trace the sources of our Gospels back into their preliterary stage and to recognize what comes to us from the tradition and what is the editorial work of the Evangelists. (2) Form criticism has attempted to discover the laws that operated in determining what was included in the tradition. It has further enabled us to separate the Hellenistic additions to the early Palestinian tradition. (3) Studies of the life and environment of Palestine in Jesus' day have made a further contribution to our knowledge. Three kinds of literature have been especially helpful. The rabbinical literature, Jewish apocalyptic, and Qumran (Dead Sea) scrolls have all made their contribution. Through this we have come to see the customs of first-century Palestine, the religious climate of Judaism, and more particularly Jesus' uniqueness in comparison with what we find in first-century Palestinian Judaism. (4) We have been further aided by the beginnings of the study of Jesus' mother tongue, Aramaic. This kind of study has further illustrated the exceptional character of some of Jesus' utterances. (5) Finally, we have been aided by the discovery of the nature of Jesus' eschatological message. Here, once again, it has become clear how Jesus' message in this regard differed from the contemporary ideas of Jewish apocalyptic. He must in light of this no longer be regarded as a Jewish rabbi, wisdom teacher, or prophet. He rather preached a message of hope to the religious and social outcasts which ran counter to everything we find in Judaism.[38]

Jeremias at once comes into conflict with the ideas of Bultmann as he discusses the relation of kerygma to history in the Gospels. He feels strongly that we cannot confine our interest to the kerygma in the Gospels. This is true for two basic reasons. In the first place, the sources themselves do not permit such a position.

> Every verse of the gospels tells us that the origin of Christianity lies not in the kerygma, not in the resurrection experiences of the disciples, not in a "Christ-idea." Every verse tells us, rather,

37 *Ibid.*, pp. 15-16.
38 *Ibid.*, pp. 16-19.

that the origin of Christianity lies in the appearance of the man who was crucified under Pontius Pilate, Jesus of Nazareth, and in his message.[39]

Jeremias believes that the influence of the faith of the primitive Christian community on the Gospels has been greatly exaggerated. He holds that the message of Jesus is perfectly accessible to us from the Gospels and that the "Christological overlay" plays a relatively small part in the Gospels as we have them.[40]

A second reason why we may not content ourselves with interest solely in the kerygma is because "the kerygma refers to an historical event."[41] The kerygma is an interpretation of that event. To put it precisely, the kerygma is always an interpretation of historical events. The kerygma is not the creator of an historical tradition. "Whatever statements of the kerygma we may care to examine, their origins are always to be found in the message of Jesus."[42] But not only does the kerygma permit historical investigation, it demands it. "The incarnation implies that the story of Jesus is not only a possible subject for historical research, study, and criticism, but demands all of these."[43] Jeremias concludes that it is now generally acknowledged in contemporary New Testament scholarship that the study of the historical Jesus must be undertaken and that one must not rest content with the kerygma.[44]

While it is true from Jeremias' point of view that history must be regarded as primary in the Gospel accounts and kerygma must be regarded as secondary, one must not push this to the point of placing the two in opposition to one another. That is, apart from the faith of the church the gospel would be only dead history. On the other hand, the kerygma would be the mere proclamation of an idea apart from the historical Jesus. "To isolate the message of Jesus leads to Ebionitism; to isolate the kerygma of the early church leads to Docetism."[45]

But while we must say that kerygma and history cannot be separated, we are not saying thereby that they both stand on the same level. The two rather stand in the relationship of call to response. "The life, acts, and death of Jesus, . . . is the call of God. The early church's witness of faith, . . . is the response to

---

[39] *Ibid.,* p. 12.
[40] *Ibid.,* p. 13.
[41] *Ibid.*
[42] *Ibid.,* p. 14.
[43] *Ibid.,* pp. 14-15.
[44] *Ibid.,* p. 15.
[45] *Ibid.,* p. 22.

God's call."[46] Considered from this point of view, the call is primary and the response is secondary. The preaching of the early church must not be equated with the revelation of God. The revelation of God is Jesus, while the preaching of the primitive church is a witness to that revelation. "The historical Jesus and his message are not *one* presupposition among many for the kerygma, but the *sole* presupposition of the kerygma."[47]

In his assertion of the primary place of history, Jeremias is joined by two of the authors under consideration here. Karl Barth comments on Bultmann's treatment of the cross and resurrection of Jesus:

> Apparently the kerygma must suppress or even deny the fact that the cross and resurrection of Jesus Christ, the total Christ event, is the event of our redemption, that it possessed an intrinsic significance of its own, and that only because it has that primary significance has it a derived significance here and now. Yet this event is the ground of our faith and of the kerygma, and faith and kerygma are only second to it and derivative from it.[48]

Ernst Kinder joins in affirming the primacy of history. "Theology and preaching will be able to be promising, procreative, and constructive with respect to kerygmatic power and existential effect only when they devoutly let the supernatural facts of saving history stand in their transubjective actuality."[49]

This leads naturally to another concern of these writers. What is the relationship of the objective to the subjective in one's response to the gospel? Here Kinder is the most outspoken. He accuses Bultmann of refusing to accept the New Testament witness because his approach is preconditioned by "the so-called modern picture of the world."[50] A more logical approach would be to accept the witness of the New Testament rather than come to it with a priori suspicions of it, or of the witness of church tradition contained in it.[51]

Kinder will not allow faith to precede facts. "Faith knows that as faith it is created, supported, and fulfilled by facts."[52] Facts are

---

[46] *Ibid.*, p. 23.

[47] *Ibid.*, pp. 23-24.

[48] Karl Barth, "Rudolf Bultmann—An Attempt to Understand Him," *Kerygma and Myth*, II, ed. Hans Werner Bartsch, p. 110.

[49] Ernst Kinder, "Historical Criticism and Demythologizing," *Kerygma and History*, ed. and trans. Braaten and Harrisville, p. 84.

[50] *Ibid.*, p. 83.

[51] *Ibid.*

[52] *Ibid.*, p. 75.

not only necessary to faith, but they are necessary to guard against importing into the Christian faith some concept of science that is alien to it and antagonistic to it, as has been the case with Bultmann.[53]

It should be noted here that Kinder's basic argument is not with an existential approach to New Testament interpretation, but rather with what precedes that approach. The interpretation of the New Testament must be done on the basis of its factual content. In the kind of existential interpretation proposed by Bultmann, the subject takes precedence over the object. Truths are thought of first of all in terms of their "kerygmatic impact" and then of their "existential significance."[54] This results in what Kinder considers to be an unhappy state of affairs. "In this way its important concern becomes a half-truth resulting in this disastrous and false alternative: Not objectively factual, but kerygmatically potent and existentially significant; not the fact, but the act; not ontical, but ontological, et cetera."[55] As he puts it elsewhere, "When the objective factuality is denied, ultimately the kerygmatic power and existential significance no longer exist."[56] The concern here is that we begin with the subject matter of the New Testament and not with the hearer of its message.[57]

Kinder also finds a subtle shift in the theology of Bultmann wherein the term "nonhistorical," which is meant to convey the idea of something that cannot be established by historical investigation, is transformed to mean something that did not happen at all. This being the case, there is a complete loss of interest in history, and these realities are subsequently judged only in terms of their kerygmatic power and existential significance.[58]

Walter Künneth joins Kinder on many of these points. He feels that Bultmann's theology threatens to rob the Christ-revelation of its "once-for-allness" and to place it in the consciousness of the individual. As he puts it, "Subjective validity and interpretation take the place of the actual reality."[59] Bultmann goes to the opposite extreme of some of the members of the original quest. For them revelation was only history. Bultmann runs the danger of eliminating history. "Bultmann misses altogether the essence and

---

[53] *Ibid.*
[54] *Ibid.*, p. 79.
[55] *Ibid.*, pp. 79-80.
[56] *Ibid.*, p. 83.
[57] *Ibid.*, p. 85.
[58] *Ibid.*, p. 73.
[59] Walter Künneth, "Bultmann's Philosophy and the Reality of Salvation," *Kerygma and History,* ed. and trans. Braaten and Harrisville, p. 106.

uniqueness of biblical Christian faith by relativizing history. He is
not able to recognize the foundation of faith; namely, the revelation which is bound to history."[60]

From the perspective of these scholars, Bultmann's neglect of
history has produced the fear that Christianity under this kind of
treatment may become docetic. "I am most embarrassed: much as
I am loath to charge Bultmann with heresy, I cannot deny that
his demythologized New Testament looks suspiciously like docetism."[61] As another has expressed it, "I can see very grave dangers
in this position. . . . We are in danger of Docetism, where Christ
becomes an idea; we are in danger of putting the proclamation
of the apostle Paul in the place of the good tidings of Jesus."[62]

These critics of Bultmann are less concerned about the questions of miracles and the resurrection than they are about some
other features of Bultmann's theology. Furthermore, the diversity
of the critics to the right of Bultmann on these questions is very
great. What we say here briefly is only representative of some
members of this theological camp and should not be considered
to be typical. Barth speaks critically of Bultmann's interpretation
of the resurrection. " 'On the third day he rose again' does not
appear to be the basic fact of Christianity, but only an explanation
of the kerygma and of faith, and one which could be dispensed
with if necessary. . . . He seems to think that in the kerygma Jesus
Christ is on his way to rising in us."[63]

Künneth criticizes Bultmann's relegation of the resurrection to
a point of subsequent interpretation of faith: his insistence that it
stands as a means of interpreting the significance of the cross.
Künneth presents his own interpretation of the resurrection in
opposition.

> It is a hidden turning point of the world, a break-through of a
> second creation and the beginning of a genuine and real
> eschatology. From this perspective it also becomes self-evident
> that miracles, angels, and demons are not fanciful mythological
> notions, but rather new illuminating realities in which the true
> being of the cosmos and of man is unveiled in its "authen-
> ticity."[64]

In another context Künneth charges Bultmann with holding
an obsolete view of the possibility of miracles, for modern scientific spirit has long since gone beyond the idea of a closed uni-

---

60 *Ibid.,* p. 108.
61 Barth, p. 111.
62 Jeremias, p. 11.
63 Barth, p. 101.
64 Künneth, p. 117.

verse under the dominion of natural law which lies at the base of Bultmann's ideas.[65]

Kinder joins Künneth in his criticism of Bultmann at these points. His denial of the miraculous and the resurrection is only a part of his neglect of the objectively factual elements of the Christian faith.[66]

Along with the question of history, that of mythology occupies the greatest attention of these critics of Bultmann. They criticize him here at several points. There is in the criticism of some of these writers the denial that mythology really plays any important part in the New Testament. This denial is grounded in several particulars. Künneth feels that Bultmann has made the error of confusing a "world picture" with a "world view." A world picture, he says, comes out of a specific situation. This is dependent upon the facts that are available at any time in the history of the world. A world view, on the other hand, "has to do with the interpretation or the specific understanding of the world picture."[67] This being the case, a given world picture may be interpreted in terms of a number of world views. This is so regardless of the particular world picture that happens to be in vogue at any given time. Thus the same world picture may equally lead to the interpretation of a world view of atheistic materialism, heathen mythology, biblical faith, or a number of other world views. "Faith or the interpretation of the events of nature is therefore in principle independent of the nature and structure of the world picture."[68] Bultmann has unjustifiably assumed that the world picture of the New Testament presupposes a single world view.

Künneth goes on to challenge the "world view" that Bultmann claims is at the base of the New Testament. He notes how Schniewind has demonstrated that even in the Old Testament there are numerous exceptions to Bultmann's concept of the world picture of the Bible as that of a three-storied world with a localized God in heaven. If this be the case even in the Old Testament, it certainly cannot be maintained that Bultmann's neat picture of the New Testament is true. Furthermore, the pervasive biblical doctrines of the attributes of God, for example his omnipotence, omnipresence, and eternity, run counter to the idea of the world picture that Bultmann supposes is at the base of the New Testament.[69]

---

[65] *Ibid.*, p. 104.
[66] Kinder, p. 71.
[67] Künneth, p. 103.
[68] *Ibid.*
[69] *Ibid.*

Barth seems to be referring to the same problem when he says that what is needed first is that we understand the message of the New Testament before we become bogged down in such matters as its thought forms, etc. "The task of translation is a secondary concern, and it can only be done well if both reader and exegete take in hand the primary task first" — namely, the understanding of its message.[70]

In connection with this Barth also accuses Bultmann of bringing to the New Testament preconceived notions about what he expects to find there. "Is it possible to understand any text, be it ancient or modern, if we approach it with preconceived notions about the extent and limit to which it can be understood? Is it not preferable to come to it with an open mind, and patiently follow what it has to say?"[71] But with Bultmann the concept of myth as he understands it has become the infallible criterion guiding his hermeneutics; and what is even more significant, that concept of myth is completely alien to the New Testament itself. Barth puts his charge in the form of a question. "To what is he [the exegete] responsible, the presuppositions of his own thought and of the contemporary world, and to a principle of understanding determined by that thought, or to the actual text he is trying to understand, and to the criterion to be derived from its spirit, content and aim?"[72]

Barth also brings up another question in his attempt to discount the importance of the place of mythology in the New Testament. To support his contention that mythology in the New Testament has basic reference to thought forms rather than content Bultmann would have to demonstrate that the New Testament writers had deliberately chosen such a device to reveal their message, but such a demonstration is impossible and as a matter of fact unthinkable. "However much the New Testament writers borrowed their imagery and language from the surrounding world, it could hardly have occurred to them to produce their message as the proclamation of general cosmic truths disguised as a tale about the gods and their doings."[73]

Künneth emphasizes that to whatever extent mythology has played a part in the New Testament, it is mythology that has already been demythologized in the New Testament itself. Thus, whenever the New Testament borrows terms or concepts from the contemporary world, it pours into them a new content so that it

---

[70] Barth, pp. 87-88.
[71] *Ibid.*, p. 108.
[72] *Ibid.*
[73] *Ibid.*, p. 109.

is made perfectly clear what a given term means in its New Testament setting. Two primary examples of this are the words *Kyrios* and *Logos* as they are used in the New Testament. Both terms were also used in the pagan contemporary society, but the content of these words in the New Testament is unique.[74]

Not only do some of these authors accuse Bultmann of coming to the New Testament with preconceived notions as he attempts to demythologize it, but they go even further than this, and locate the source of these preconceptions. They arise from his acceptance of the philosophy of Heidegger. Barth in particular points this out. Thus Bultmann comes to the New Testament with an already developed system and attempts to force the message of the New Testament into the mold of that system. This in itself should explain why Bultmann adopted the hermeneutical device of demythologizing. It was necessary to use such an extreme device to make the New Testament speak in Heideggerian terms. The question then becomes, How much worth can we attribute to that particular philosophical system? Does it contain eternal truth that mankind has never realized before? Or is it only one of the many philosophical systems that have arisen during the history of mankind? Barth's answer is of interest. "Neither Heidegger today nor Bultmann thinks that the Heidegger of 1927 has *the* philosophy, or that it dropped from heaven, as people used to think Aristotelianism had, or as Hegel used to boast of his own system."[75]

Finally, Kinder severely criticizes Bultmann for his approach to the New Testament from what we may call a nonchurch or even antichurch point of view. It is not a question of coming to the New Testament with no presuppositions. It is a question of which presuppositions one brings with him. "If we do not approach the Bible from the standpoint of the church, we do so from the standpoint of some world view. There is no third possibility such as neutrality without presuppositions."[76]

This position results in the converse of the situation that gave rise to the original quest. There church dogma was attacked. Here antichurch dogma is attacked. "When historical and literary methods are posited as primary and absolute norms they are no longer merely methods; they have become 'isms,' and they possess the content of a definite philosophy, though such be unintentional."[77]

---

[74] Künneth, p. 114.
[75] Barth, pp. 114-15.
[76] Kinder, pp. 66-67.
[77] *Ibid.*, p. 68.

Künneth has summarized what to him appears to be the result of demythologizing. "There cannot have been such a revelation of God as the primitive church handed down to us judged by the standard of reason of the modern man. The belief that the crucified historical Jesus is at the same time world-transcending Lord cannot be demanded of our thought, cannot be the real content of faith."[78]

We may pass over the question of the comparative historical value of John and the Synoptics in these writers, for this is once again an area in which they do not wish to do battle with Bultmann. Doubtless, the variation here among biblical critics to the right of Bultmann would be manifold. We would find no consensus here.

With regard to the significance of Jesus, our task is even greater. We shall not attempt to develop at length the position of any of these critics. We shall merely intimate what the position of each of them is.

Barth denies that the significance of Jesus, and therefore of the New Testament, is to show man his plight and to give him the power to extricate *himself* from that state. Bultmann's major emphasis is on man's subjective experience. Barth holds that the New Testament, in contrast, speaks of the work of Jesus in an objective way. "The New Testament asserts that in faith the believer attaches himself to something which is wholly and entirely outside himself, something without him and in spite of him, something which took place for him on God's initiative in the death of Jesus Christ."[79]

Jeremias puts a great deal of emphasis on the message of Jesus, who claimed to deliver to man a message from God.

> If with utmost discipline and conscientiousness we apply the critical resources at our disposal to the study of the historical Jesus, the final result is always the same: we find ourselves confronted with God himself. That is the fact to which the sources bear witness: a man appeared, and those who received his message were certain that they had heard the word of God.[80]

We may put Kinder and Künneth together here, for they represent as we have already noted the position of Lutheran orthodoxy. Künneth summarizes their position. "According to the New Testament, . . . the authentic scandal is the paradoxical event

---

[78] Künneth, p. 118.
[79] Barth, p. 99.
[80] Jeremias, p. 21.

of revelation that the crucified man Jesus of Nazareth is the Redeemer and Ruler of the world."[81]

The controversy between the Bultmannians and the critics to the right of him has been intense. An examination and evaluation of the charges and countercharges would carry us far beyond the scope of our treatment here. We note simply the tone of the dispute. The most violent subsequent contention from the point of view of the critics to Bultmann's right is that Bultmann is guilty of heresy. Bultmann and his defenders come back with the charge that the critics to his right have betrayed the Reformation. For they contend that Bultmann has merely carried out to its logical conclusion the Reformation doctrine of justification by faith, and has not allowed historical research to become a work of man upon which he bases his faith.[82]

---

[81] Künneth, p. 118.

[82] Reginald H. Fuller, *The New Testament in Current Study* (London: S.C.M., 1963), p. 25.

CHAPTER SEVEN

CRITICS TO THE LEFT OF BULTMANN

Introduction

The number and variety of critics with whom we could deal in this chapter is not nearly as great as in the previous chapter. We noted in that chapter that Bultmann was considerably "left of center" on the theological spectrum. This in part accounts for the reduction. Furthermore, there are a number of writers to the left of those we shall consider in this chapter. Such atheistic existentialists as Kamlah and Sartre could be included here. But since our study deals only with the critical movement as it is expressed by those who claim some connection with the Christian faith, we shall omit these scholars from our treatment.

We shall deal here principally with two of what might be considered to be the three chief representatives of this movement. Karl Jaspers is really somewhat on the borderline between the theistic and atheistic thinkers. He has been described as an agnostic and humanistic thinker,[1] although the first of those two terms is perhaps too strong. He enters the discussion with somewhat of an apology, inasmuch as he does not believe it is the business of the philosopher to interfere with the minister or theologian; however, he feels that due to the philosophical nature of much of Bultmann's work, he must discuss it from the point of view of a philosopher.[2] Moreover, Jaspers does classify himself as a liberal, although we shall soon see that this term does not carry the same meaning as it did in the case of the liberal lives of Jesus.

---

[1] Reginald H. Fuller, *The New Testament in Current Study,* p. 27.

[2] Karl Jaspers, "Myth and Religion," in Karl Jaspers and Rudolf Bultmann, *Myth and Christianity* (New York: Noonday, 1958), pp. 3-4.

A second representative of this school is the American, Schubert Ogden. He too identifies himself with this new liberal theological movement. "We have aligned ourselves with the 'liberal' tradition in Protestant Christianity that counts among the great names in its history those of Schleiermacher, Ritschl, Herrmann, Harnack, and Troeltsch, and more recently, Schweitzer and the early Barth and, in part at least, Bultmann."[3]

Neither Ogden nor Jaspers, however, would want to be classified with this group without further clarification. Ogden in particular notes what he calls a "growing appreciation for liberal theology's achievements"[4] since the Second World War, and while he admits that the old liberal position has had to be reappraised, he contends that this reappraisal has not had an effect on either its historical-critical method or its realization that prescientific thought must be evaluated in terms of modern knowledge of the world.[5]

But while these theologians find themselves in basic agreement with the earlier liberals in these respects, there are other respects in which they are basically at odds with them. The chief difference here appears to be in the philosophical base from which they start.

> Although we agree with the liberal theologians that the only "objectivity" about Jesus of which the New Testament itself intends to speak is one that has its basis in the word he proclaims and is, we want to make much clearer than they generally did that his proclamation is not a body of timeless truths, but an *existentiell* communication demanding decision.[6]

The third thinker in this school, the Swiss theologian Fritz Buri, we shall not consider as thoroughly since his position is very close to that of Ogden.

ANSWERS TO THE SIX QUESTIONS

It will be recalled that in Chapter Five we asserted that Bultmann's conclusion with respect to the historical Jesus and the possibility of writing a biography of his life was almost completely negative. He reached this conclusion largely on the basis of two lines of evidence. In the first place, he did not believe that the sources available to us sufficed for that purpose; and in the second place, his existentialist point of departure was such that he felt the only necessary element to posit with respect to the Jesus of

---

[3] Schubert M. Ogden, *Christ Without Myth* (New York: Harper, 1961), p. 131.   [4] *Ibid.*, p. 16.   [5] *Ibid.*

[6] *Ibid.*, p. 162. *Existentiell* denotes "that which has to do with the individual's own unique situation and responsibility" (S. M. Ogden, in Preface to R. Bultmann, *Existence and Faith,* London, 1964, p. 7).

history was the mere "that" of his historicity. Thus, while movements to the right of Bultmann talk about Christ in terms of
events, Bultmann himself speaks in terms of *the event* of Christ.

The critics to the left of Bultmann criticize him for his insistence
on this event. The question they ask is, Why must faith of necessity
be based on the historical event of Jesus of Nazareth? There is
perhaps one overriding reason for the contempt with which these
scholars address themselves to the question of history. They are
more "orthodox" existentialists than is Bultmann. That is, they are
more completely immersed in the philosophical disciplines of
this school of thought, and insist on what they would call logical
consistency as against what they regard as logical inconsistency
in Bultmann. Jaspers, for example, is quick to assert that true
faith cannot depend on objective guarantees in the external world
that are universally valid.[7] Jaspers admits that the Bible has had
great significance for the Western world for these past 1500 years,
but he denies that its significance lies in the history it portrays.
Its real import is to be found in "the spirit of the faith."[8] What
then is the place of the Bible for contemporaries? "The only
essential thing is to speak in such a way that, with the help of
a text, a present content of faith should be disclosed, and be
shared in communication."[9]

Ogden concurs with Jaspers in his disregard for the historically
arrived at objective events. For him too, the fulfilment of one's
life as a person is dependent on individual decision regarding self-
understanding, and it must be left to the responsibility of the individual to seek this fulfilment.[10]

How then should what appears to be historical in the Gospels
be regarded? It must be regarded mythologically. Jaspers states
this most precisely. "While liberalism repudiates an objective
redemptive history conceived as an absolute event and as a
prerequisite of salvation for all men, it accepts this history as a
myth."[11]

It is at this point that these scholars find their most fundamental
disagreement with Bultmann. Ogden in particular, following Buri,
points to what he regards as a fundamental contradiction in the
thought of Bultmann. On the one hand Bultmann insists that one
would be in error if he attempted to ground confidence in the
Scriptures via historical investigation. With this, Ogden finds him-

---

[7] Jaspers, p. 47.
[8] Jaspers, "The Issues Clarified," in Jaspers and Bultmann, p. 103.
[9] *Ibid.*
[10] Ogden, p. 136.
[11] Jaspers, "Myth and Religion," p. 47.

self in complete agreement. But then Bultmann also insists that the kerygma originated in an historical event and that the New Testament is "simply the proclamation of the person and destiny of Jesus of Nazareth in their significance as the history of salvation." Here Ogden is in complete disagreement,[12] for he finds that the two statements above involve a necessary contradiction, which we must notice more carefully.

Bultmann's thought, according to Ogden, may be summarized in two propositions. (1) "Christian faith is to be interpreted exhaustively and without remainder as man's original possibility of authentic historical *(geschichtlich)* existence as this is more or less adequately clarified and conceptualized by an appropriate philosophical analysis."[13] The reasons why Bultmann adopts this position are mainly two. In the first place, it is the only way possible to approach contemporary man with what he regards as an inescapable demand for a demythologized New Testament. In the second place, it is the only way one may arrive at an adequate expression of the Christian faith.[14]

The problem, however, arises when Bultmann tries to combine with this proposition a second which Ogden summarizes as follows. (2) "Christian faith is actually realizable or is a 'possibility in fact,' only because of the particular historical *(historisch)* event Jesus of Nazareth, which is the originative event of the church and its distinctive word and sacraments."[15] The contradiction arises, according to Ogden, because the first proposition is a completely existential one, that is, its conception of the Christian faith is to be thought of in terms of one's possibility of authentic self-understanding. Thus it must not be connected to any particular historical occurrence. The second proposition, however, is one that places emphasis on history. But if the historical event of Jesus Christ is necessarily connected with faith, then clearly that faith cannot be conceived of in existential terms.[16]

Inasmuch as these authors think of faith in these terms, it should be no surprise that they show almost no interest in any kind of an attempt to write a biography or history of the life of Jesus. Jaspers expresses their lack of confidence in the Gospel sources as he writes, "Stories based on the reports of contradictory

---

12 Ogden, p. 109.
13 *Ibid.*, p. 112.
14 *Ibid.*, p. 115.
15 *Ibid.*, p. 112.
16 *Ibid.*, p. 117.

witnesses and containing scanty data cannot be regarded as historical facts."[17]

We shall once again deal with the questions of miracles and the resurrection together, since these writers have the same view of these matters as Bultmann, and so give them very little attention.

Jaspers first mentions the resurrection in connection with his analysis of modern science. He points out as Bultmann failed to do that the resurrection was no more plausible to the people of Jesus' day than it is to us, but he uses this not as a proof that the resurrection may have happened, but rather as a demonstration that the differences of the modern age from the first century are often overdrawn.[18] When dealing with the resurrection as a tangible reality he merely states, "A corpse cannot come to life and rise from the grave."[19]

Ogden is outspoken in his criticism of those who are to the right of Bultmann.

> The only way one can conceivably establish such mythical events as the virgin birth or the resurrection as objective historical events is by illicitly assuming that because they are possible they are also actual (as Karl Barth has rightly been accused of doing) or by simply begging the question and smuggling a presumption as to their historicity into the premises of the demonstration (as is done by Macquarrie). In both cases, logic is sacrificed to some special interest by the adoption of a mode of argument any unbiased mind would regard as indefensible.[20]

The basic agreement of these scholars with Bultmann is no more evident than when Bultmann himself, in reply to the criticism of Jaspers, points out that on the issues of the possibility of a corpse coming to life again, and of what he calls a "magic causality," he and Jaspers are in agreement.[21]

Furthermore, these writers agree with Bultmann as to how these features of the Gospels should be interpreted. They must be interpreted as myths; and provided that they are not misunderstood as empirical realities, they may be used to point out some existential truth.[22]

While the two authors under primary consideration here both deal extensively with the question of mythology, and come out

---

17 "Myth and Religion," p. 17.
18 *Ibid.,* p. 5.
19 *Ibid.,* p. 17.
20 Ogden, pp. 135-36.
21 Rudolf Bultmann, "The Case for Demythologization," in Jaspers and Bultmann, p. 60.
22 "The Issues Clarified," p. 104.

largely at the same place, their approach to the subject is quite different due to their point of departure. Jaspers approaches the subject as a philosopher, Ogden as a theologian. Jaspers finds two fundamental errors in Bultmann's demythologizing. The first of these errors is in his conception of modern science and the modern world view. According to Jaspers, Bultmann has in mind three particular things here. He first of all thinks of the world as a closed causal system which will tolerate nothing of the miraculous. Second, he views man as a unity with no possibility of being interfered with by gods or demons. Finally, he refers primarily to the scientific method with its characteristic features of testing and verification.[23] Jaspers directs his criticism principally at Bultmann's contention that there is *a* total world view. Modern science, to the contrary, disavows such a notion. As a matter of fact, the primary effect of science has been that of destroying such world views. Furthermore, in questions relative to faith, the ability of modern science to disintegrate faith is no more real than that of previous rational systems. Jaspers concludes, "Bultmann's statement, 'The unity of the world in scientific thinking is matched by the unity of scientific thinking itself' is completely false. The opposite is true."[24]

Bultmann's error with respect to his view of modern science is matched by an equally erroneous view of a scientific philosophy, according to Jaspers. The difficulty here is that Bultmann confines his philosophy to a single book by Heidegger, *Sein und Zeit,* and misunderstands that book.[25] In his emphasis on what Jaspers would call the scientific and objective aspects of that book, Bultmann leaves behind him the one factor that Jaspers sees as the unifying factor in all modern thought that goes by the name "existentialism."

> If the various attempts at philosophizing which are today lumped together as Existentialism have anything in common despite their differences of tendency, form, and content, it is, negatively, the rejection of so-called scientific philosophy, and, positively, the affirmation of a moral earnestness foreign to mere knowing.[26]

Bultmann's fundamental error, on the basis of his conception of modern science and a scientific philosophy, according to Jaspers, is that he assumes that mythology has to do only with form and

---

23 "Myth and Religion," pp. 4-5.
24 *Ibid.,* pp. 6-7.
25 *Ibid.,* p. 8.
26 *Ibid.,* p. 9.

not with the content of the New Testament message. In assuming that the mythological form may be disposed of he is mistaken. "Mythological thinking is not a thing of the past, but characterizes man in any epoch."[27]

Jaspers lists what he considers to be the three basic elements of the word "myth."

> (1) The myth tells a story and expresses intuitive insights rather than universal concepts. . . .
> (2) The myth deals with sacred stories and visions, with stories about gods rather than with empirical realities.
> (3) The myth is a carrier of meanings which can be expressed only in the language of myth.[28]

Jaspers is quick to admit that mythological thinking is subject to abuse. But this is the case primarily when its symbols are interpreted literally and materially and not as a code. The language of myths does speak of a reality, but that reality is not empirical; rather it is existential. If one grasps its existential character one may appropriate it as an effective element in one's life provided he keeps in mind two critical ideas. (1) "Whereas mythical language is historical, and hence its truth can lay no claim to the universal validity of knowledge, it is precisely by virtue of this quality that it can lend the historical *Existenz* something of the unconditional."[29] (2) "All mythical images are ambiguous."[30] However, when mythology is improperly used, an undesirable situation arises:

> Some pious people conceive of this tangible presence as an empirical reality. True piety, as a matter of course, eliminates the materialistic, magical, and utilitarian misuse of literal interpetation. There is also an impious, materialistic conception of the myth as tangible reality, which no longer regards the myth as a cipher, and which leads to superstition.[31]

One must use mythical thinking as an avenue to faith. This means that some myths will be more meaningful to some people than others. It even means that certain myths will be rejected by some. But in rejecting a particular myth, one must not insist that others reject it also. The goal must remain the perception of the existential truth contained in the myth, and one must remember

---

27 *Ibid.*, p. 15.
28 *Ibid.*, pp. 15-16.
29 *Ibid.*, p. 18.
30 *Ibid.*
31 *Ibid.*, p. 19.

that existential truth is spiritually effective only in such mythical thinking.[32]

The fault of Bultmann, therefore, from Jaspers' point of view is not that he recognizes myth in the New Testament; the fault lies in what he does with that myth. One does not attain the language of faith by putting myths into nonmythological terms. One must realize, as Bultmann fails to do, that there is in myth a truth that cannot be translated. The task of the minister, therefore, as Jaspers sees it, is that he must attempt to understand his mythological language, or language of transcendence, and then to lead his people into the same discovery.[33]

Jaspers' entire conception of myth is well summarized in the following words.

> The whole of mythical, as well as speculative, thinking is transcended in the inexorable commandment: "Thou shalt not make unto thee any graven image or any likeness." Since, as finite sensory rational beings we cannot think otherwise than in terms of objects and guided by our senses, the commandment can only mean that we are not to posit as absolute any idea, any mythical figure, any representation of events or entities. It is always the language of transcendence, limitlessly rich, that clarifies meaning at all levels; it is never the transcendence itself.[34]

At first glance the position of Ogden may appear to be in direct opposition to that of Jaspers, for while Jaspers maintains that myth must be retained, Ogden demands that demythologizing must be carried out to an even greater degree than Bultmann has done it. The difference between the two, however, appears to be mainly semantic.

Ogden believes that the demand Bultmann makes for demythologization must be accepted without reservation. He takes serious issue with the claim frequently made that God is independent of his world and has no need of men to fulfil his work. God does need men, and the church does need the abilities of capable men. Yet when the church insists on presenting the gospel "in a form that makes it incredible and irrelevant to cultured men," she runs the risk of losing the abilities of these men she so desperately needs.[35]

The fault with Bultmann is not in his demand that the New Testament must be demythologized, but that he stops his demy-

---

[32] *Ibid.,* pp. 19-20.
[33] *Ibid.,* pp. 33-35.
[34] "The Issues Clarified," p. 89.
[35] Ogden, p. 130.

thologizing at a certain point. When he appeals to the "unique event of Jesus Christ" he is, as Ogden agrees with Buri, " 'falling back into mythology.' "[36] The stance of Ogden here is very closely related to his attitude toward history, which we have already discussed. Ogden therefore concludes that in relation to the question of mythology, only the positions of Barth and Buri are self-consistent. Either all mythology must be accepted (in the sense of the objective, not in the sense Jaspers gives to it) as with Barth, or it must all be rejected as with Buri.[37]

But what does the rejection of myth mean to Ogden? Here the difference of Ogden's position from that of Jaspers is of no significance at all, because demythologization to him does not mean that the use of myth must be completely banned, but that it must not be considered the only means whereby the Christian understanding of existence may be presented. "Mythological concepts may by all means still be used, but they can be used responsibly only as 'symbols' or 'ciphers,' that is, only if they are constantly *interpreted* in nonmythological (or existential) terms."[38]

Ogden describes what is necessary for the contemporary Christian in terms of what he calls "dekerygmatization." That is, the proclamation of God's act in Jesus Christ is merely a symbol of one's transition from inauthentic existence to authentic existence. This transition is achieved simply by human decision. He therefore concludes, "The only tenable alternative to Bultmann's position, therefore, is to reject his appeal to a mythological saving-event as incompatible with modern man's picture of himself and his world and, in so doing, to carry to its logical conclusion, to the point of 'dekerygmatization,' the program of demythologization he proposes."[39]

Their lack of interest in history as event should forwarn us that these authors are not very much interested in the question of the comparative historical value of John as against the Synoptics. Ogden does not even raise the issue, and Jaspers makes only a few brief comments on the subject. Jaspers appears to be somewhat surprised that Bultmann's primary interest is in the Gospel of John, even though the reason Bultmann finds it of value is not due primarily to its historical correctness. Jaspers finds the Synoptics to be of much more value than John. "The spiritualized Christ of the Gospel according to St. John, though noble and

---

[36] *Ibid.,* p. 107.
[37] *Ibid.,* p. 134.
[38] *Ibid.,* p. 128.
[39] *Ibid.,* p. 110.

captivating as a fairy tale hero, seems to us far less significant than the living figure of Jesus in the Synoptics."[40] He goes on to point out that in addition to its lack of historical accuracy, the Gospel of John as against the Synoptics and Paul gives the first tacit approval to Christian anti-Semitism.[41]

He refers again to this question in connection with a comparison he makes of a philosopher's approach to Jesus with that of a theologian. He points out at considerable length that the philosopher must approach him as a man in an historical setting who is confronted with all the problems and decisions of any other man. He then concludes, "This conception of Jesus is that of the Synoptics (prior to the later additions); it is not that of the Gospel according to St. John."[42] From this it may be concluded that Jaspers feels we are closer to history in the Synoptics than we are in John, though we must use even them with great care. On the other hand, John cannot possibly claim our acceptance as an historical source.

It would be well for us to begin our examination of the significance of Jesus for these authors by comparing them with two previous points of view we have studied. Though the word "liberal" has been used on occasion in this chapter, there is a fundamental difference in the way these authors approach the significance of Jesus from the way the liberals did in an earlier chapter. Ogden makes this most explicit. He is willing to accept their contention that one must find the significance of Jesus in his proclamation, but while they found the importance of that proclamation to be a body of timeless truths, for Ogden it is to be found in "an *existentiell* communication demanding decision."[43] As a consequence, the difference in the way these authors see Jesus' significance from that of the older liberals is to be found primarily in the philosophical point of departure of the two schools of thought.

While these authors point out their differences with the liberals, they also go to great lengths to clarify their differences with Bultmann. Their great and fundamental difference with Bultmann is their contention that he is in error in his claim to exclusiveness for the event of Christ, or, to put it in other words, his claim that the event of Christ is that which makes authentic existence possible. Ogden confronts Bultmann's position most directly. He

---

[40] "Myth and Religion," p. 21.
[41] *Ibid.*
[42] "The Issues Clarified," p. 82.
[43] Ogden, p. 162.

begins by describing Bultmann's position in opposition to the approach of philosophy in three propositions. (1) Philosophy claims that authentic existence is always a real possibility for man apart from any external help. (2) The reason philosophy claims this, according to Bultmann, is that it fails to see man as a completely fallen being. (3) As against this, Bultmann claims that man is completely fallen, and as a result, that authentic existence is only realizable in Jesus Christ.[44]

Against these propositions Ogden raises his argument. In the first place, he is not willing to accept Bultmann's conclusion that because man is completely fallen, authentic existence is not possible for him apart from Christ. Thus, while Ogden is willing to accept Bultmann's judgment that man is completely fallen, which Bultmann claims philosophy is unwilling to do, Ogden will not go on to assert that the event of Christ is necessary for man's rescue. He writes, "It is at least conceivable that what makes authentic existence everywhere factually possible is not that man is not completely fallen, but that, in spite of his fallenness, he is everlastingly the object of God's love which is omnipresently efficacious as a redemptive possibility."[45]

As a consequence, while Bultmann would insist on *the* event of Christ as a prerequisite to authentic self-understanding, Ogden would insist only on *some* event in which God's grace becomes evident and to which man may respond.[46] That the event of Jesus Christ may have this meaning Ogden does not dispute; that only in this event is such meaning to be found he does dispute. This would make faith entirely dependent upon one historical event, something Ogden is not willing to accept.[47] Jaspers says that Bultmann's insistence on *the* event gives his theological thought a flavor of orthodoxy.[48]

Before we can meaningfully explain the significance of Jesus from the point of view of these two authors, we need to consider two other matters of importance with which they deal. First, what part does the Bible or the New Testament play in the discovery of authentic existence; and second, what is the place of man in this discovery? Jaspers states his position in regard to the Bible most precisely. "For us, the Bible is the favorite arena of spiritual contest; another one is provided by the Greek epic poems and

---

44 *Ibid.*, p. 120.
45 *Ibid.*, p. 121.
46 *Ibid.*, p. 123.
47 *Ibid.*, p. 124.
48 "Myth and Religion," pp. 49-50.

tragedies, and still another by the sacred books of Asia."[49] He is quick to admit that historical sources of spiritual life are important, and that for the Western world the Bible is of primary importance; but he emphatically denies that the Bible has any exclusive claims in this regard. Consequently, the Asian can find his way to God without Christ and without the Bible.[50] Jaspers is even critical of Bultmann's attempt to narrow down the event within the scope of the Western Judeo-Christian tradition. He admits that Jesus poses "the question of moral decision in relation to God" with extraordinary clarity and force, but he goes on to note that the question has been raised by those both before and after Jesus. Thus we see substantially the same thing in the prophets of the Old Testament and in the philosophers. To narrow the issue down as Bultmann attempts to do is from Jaspers' perspective to give exclusiveness to the utterances of primitive Christians.[51]

Ogden does not put his argument so much in terms of opposing the Bible to the sacred books of other religions, but with Jaspers he considers the whole of the Bible as well as other sources outside the Bible. He asserts that authentic existence was a possibility before the coming of Christ and that this is made abundantly evident in the way God dealt with Israel. He is further certain that for the church the decisive word was spoken in the person of Jesus of Nazareth. But, he concludes, "The point of this claim is not that the Christ is manifest only in Jesus and nowhere else, but that the word addressed to man *everywhere,* in all events of their lives, is none other than the word spoken in Jesus and in the preaching and sacraments of the church."[52]

The clue to the lack of emphasis by these scholars on any single source is to be seen in their analysis of modern man in his relationship to God. Ogden puts it this way: "All that is required of one who would take seriously the demand for demythologization and existential interpretation is that he take with equal seriousness the freedom and transcendence of God and the freedom and responsibility of man."[53] God's redemptive grace is always given to man and the responsibility of man is to accept it.[54]

Jaspers joins in this assertion of the freedom of man. "In liberalism everything is centered on the responsibility of man

---

49 *Ibid.,* p. 20.
50 *Ibid.,* p. 46.
51 "The Issues Clarified," pp. 100-01.
52 Ogden, pp. 155-56.
53 *Ibid.,* p. 141.
54 *Ibid.*

thrown back on himself. It is through freedom, and only through freedom, that he experiences how he is given to himself by transcendence in freedom — not by freedom."[55] In another context he is attempting to refute what he regards as an error in thinking of man as radically sinful and as a consequence thinking of the biblical account in terms of a necessary rescue of man from his sinful nature. At this point he has an even more optimistic view of man's ability than has Ogden. In this context he writes, "We find in the biblical faith itself an entirely different conception of man — namely the conception of man's God-created inborn ability, *nobilitas ingenita,* as the Pelagians called it."[56] As a result, man, from Jaspers' point of view, has the confidence that he will be able to fulfil God's will through resources in his own personality and that God himself will aid man in that achievement "in an incomprehensible and unpredictable way."[57] How profound is Jaspers' confidence in the freedom and ability of man is made very clear in another context when he takes direct issue with Bultmann on the doctrine of justification by faith.[58]

Given their confidence in the ability of man, it should be no surprise that these writers, even to a greater extent than those we have encountered in previous chapters, find little place for special revelation. Jaspers poses the question in a very honest fashion. "Is man with his reason master and judge of everything that is, can be, and should be [liberalism] or must he listen to God [orthodoxy]?"[59] His reply to this is direct. While God certainly can act in his transcendence, the only way those actions become meaningful to man is through the experiences of man. If this is the case, one may not give obedience to a sacred text or to an ecclesiastical official, for each man must himself be meaningfully related to God. As he puts it, "Speaking in mythical terms, we may say: liberal faith opposes the assertion of a direct revelation, not out of a will to employ freedom, but out of its idea of God as actualized in mankind's relations with the hidden, all-guiding transcendence."[60]

On the basis of their conception of the freedom of man and the nature of revelation, these critics draw their conclusions as to the message of the New Testament. Here we shall present the case from Ogden's point of view, which he summarizes in the

55 "Myth and Religion," p. 38.
56 *Ibid.,* p. 50.
57 *Ibid.,* p. 51.
58 "The Issues Clarified," pp. 74-75.
59 "Myth and Religion," p. 42.
60 *Ibid.,* pp. 42-43.

form of three propositions. (1) "The New Testament never doubts for an instant that before God each individual is entirely and radically responsible for his final destiny."[61] (2) "The only basis of man's salvation the New Testament knows anything about is the everlasting love of God that is primordially active in the mighty works of creation, preservation, and redemption."[62] What Ogden omits in this second proposition is as important as what he includes. He here actively opposes Bultmann's contention that the New Testament is Christocentric in favor of what he regards as a more adequate theocentric emphasis.[63] (3) "The only final condition for sharing in authentic life that the New Testament lays down is a condition that can be formulated in complete abstraction from the event Jesus of Nazareth and all that it specifically imports."[64]

Jaspers speaks of the significance of Jesus from the purely philosophical point of view.

> The philosopher, as opposed to the critical-historical skeptic, regards Jesus as a historical figure, and sees in Jesus' faith the same calm determination which the philosopher seeks, and the same uncertainty with respect to God's will, which the philosopher experiences. To him, Jesus, a man, represents questioning of God, obedience to God, search for God — i.e., to know God's intentions — a search he carries on although he is already secure in God. To him Jesus represents the overcoming of all human rigidities and presumptions, a breakthrough to truthfulness and love that knew no bounds, one of the great men who have been crucial in determining the course of philosophy.[65]

While Ogden puts it in more conventional theological terms, he says much the same thing. "The New Testament does *not* affirm that in Christ our salvation 'becomes possible.' It affirms, rather, that in him what has always been possible now 'becomes manifest,' in the sense of being decisively presented in human witness."[66] In another passage, Ogden is more censorious.

> To be sure, the deepest conviction of Christian faith is that God's saving action has been decisively disclosed in the event Jesus of Nazareth; and, in this sense, Jesus is indeed God's "work" of salvation. But when this conviction is so expressed that the event of Jesus becomes a condition apart from which

[61] Ogden, p. 141.
[62] *Ibid.*, p. 142.
[63] *Ibid.*, p. 143.
[64] *Ibid.*
[65] "The Issues Clarified," p. 82.
[66] Ogden, p. 143.

God is not free to be a gracious God, the heretical doctrine
of works-righteousness achieves its final and most dangerous
triumph.[67]

With this background, Ogden is concerned "that the event of
Jesus in its parts and as a whole" be "a 'historical' *(geschichtlich)*
event in the sense clarified by Bultmann."[68] His feeling here is
that Bultmann is too selective in what he allows from Jesus' life
as giving man the possibility of self-understanding.[69]

Thus Jaspers sees Jesus as one of several examples of authentic
existence in the history of mankind that may and should be imi-
tated. Ogden looks upon Jesus as an event to be encountered
as a means of encountering God's love, in which one may realize
authentic existence. Neither of these critics looks upon Jesus as
being the only way to that goal.

We shall not go into any of the subsequent argumentation
among the critics to the left of Bultmann, Bultmann, and the
critics to his right. The critics to the right of Bultmann have the
same general objection to this school as they have to Bultmann.
Bultmann's reaction to this school has not been developed to any
length. In the first place, Bultmann has found himself embroiled
more with the critics to the right, and in the second place, there
appears to be no basis for discussion. Bultmann stands by the
necessity of the Christ-event. The critics to the left deny its necessity. A gap like this cannot be bridged.

---

[67] *Ibid.,* p. 145.
[68] *Ibid.,* p. 159.
[69] *Ibid.*

CHAPTER EIGHT

CRITICS WITHIN THE CIRCLE OF BULTMANN: THE NEW QUEST

POINT OF DEPARTURE

Within the past dozen years there has arisen a new school of thought in critical scholarship regarding the question of the Jesus of history. This school has come to be designated as the "new quest of the historical Jesus." This phrase was coined by James M. Robinson and used as the title of his book. The rise of the movement, however, was not with Robinson, whose book was published in 1959, but in a lecture of Ernst Käsemann, who was a pupil of Bultmann. This lecture, delivered in 1953, has become known to English readers as "The Problem of the Historical Jesus."[1] We shall treat this lecture in more detail later in this chapter.

It should not be supposed that the representatives of the "new quest" school are a uniform group of critics. They differ widely with respect to particulars. As Perrin has put it, "They all began by accepting Bultmann's general position and . . . they all nonetheless agreed that he had not settled the question of the historical Jesus."[2]

This school is in reality fighting a battle on two fronts. It stands with Kähler and Bultmann in resisting most intensely the approach of the liberal lives and what it regards as their modern successors. On the other hand, it finds certain inadequacies in the treatment

---

[1] Ernst Käsemann, *Essays on New Testament Themes,* trans. W. J. Montague (Naperville, Ill.: Allenson, 1964), pp. 15-47.

[2] Perrin, "The Challenge of New Testament Theology Today," *Criterion,* IV (Spring 1965), 29.

of Bultmann. The movement is not nearly as critical of Bultmann, however, as it is of the liberal life-of-Jesus movement. In fact, the most notable representatives of the school have come from the circle of Bultmann's own students. Consequently, they have great respect for his work, and most of them would feel that "critics of Bultmann" is too strong a phrase to designate them. They would likely prefer to be characterized as Fuller describes them. "Käsemann and his colleagues have been able to seize upon certain features of Bultmann's scholarship which had often been overlooked."[3]

Bultmann as he wrote was most keenly aware of what the creators of the liberal lives of Jesus were trying to do. Along with his predecessor Kähler, he sought to demolish the arguments of this school. For this reason Bultmann is often pictured as a complete skeptic with regard to our recovery of the Jesus of history. He did not have to demonstrate in his argument that we could have some knowledge of the historical Jesus. Men had been attempting to do that for centuries. He wanted to demonstrate that from his point of view the procedure of these liberal lives was improper, and that our knowledge was much more modest than it was formerly thought to have been. Therefore, while he allows the inclusion of some historical material with respect to Jesus, he does not develop it.

Let us look briefly at these intimations of a more positive note in Bultmann. "Side by side with an apparently almost total scepticism about the historical Jesus there are other statements which would seem more hopeful. He does insist, as we have seen, that the kerygma is the interpretation of a real historical person."[4] The statements of a more positive nature come out in his *Jesus and the Word.* The kind of historical treatment that he was seeking to avoid was that founded upon a desire to construct a continuous chronological biography of the modern sort. The kind of psychological development of Jesus' life that the liberal theologians tried to trace was to him objectionable, for it merely avoided the question of what faith ought to be.[5] But while he rejected every attempt to reconstruct the personality of Jesus, he did not therefore discard the question of history altogether. "Little as we know of his life and personality, we know enough of his *message* to make for ourselves a consistent picture."[6]

The critics of the new quest have seized upon this historical

---

[3] Reginald H. Fuller, *The New Testament in Current Study*, p. 38.
[4] *Ibid.*, pp. 38-39.
[5] *Ibid.*, pp. 39-40.
[6] Bultmann, *Jesus and the Word*, p. 12.

element in Bultmann's treatment of Jesus and have sought to develop it. They do not do it, however, as the liberal life-of-Jesus movement sought to do, but they develop their thought in full recognition of the work of form criticism and Bultmann. Thus, the amount of historical material that they find in the Gospels is much less than that found by the liberal movement, but the writers in this group feel the necessity of forming a synthesis between the kerygma and the historical Jesus.[7]

APOLOGY FOR THE NEW QUEST: JAMES M. ROBINSON

We will discuss Robinson first, not because he comes first in time, but because he has given a systematic defense of the methodology employed by the critics in this school. He begins by noting that the word "historical" in the phrase "historical Jesus" has attained a technical meaning in New Testament scholarship. It is precisely the meaning given to the term by Kähler and agreed to by Bultmann, i.e., "What can be known of Jesus of Nazareth by means of the scientific methods of the historian."[8] He goes on to describe the source of the original quest of the historical Jesus. It was, at least in part, a protest movement. It was an attempt to set Jesus of Nazareth over against the presentation of him made in the Bible, the creed, and the church.[9]

There was, however, an additional methodological conception behind the original quest. This is to be seen in its idea of history. "The nineteenth century saw the reality of the 'historical facts' as consisting largely in names, places, dates, occurrences, sequences, causes, effects."[10] Such additional important factors as "the distinctively human, creative, unique, purposeful, which distinguishes man from nature," received slight attention.[11] In addition to this basic difference in the two conceptions of history, it is to be observed that when we are dealing with the subject of God, our task is even further complicated. It became obvious that when one talked about "Jesus of Nazareth as he actually was," he was talking about something far different from "the historical Jesus," or as Robinson puts it, "the historian's Jesus."[12]

This all leads Robinson to make two statements about the historical Jesus. (1) "We can know very little about the histori-

---

[7] James M. Robinson, "The Historical Question," *The Christian Century*, LXXVI (October 21, 1959), 1210.
[8] Robinson, *A New Quest of the Historical Jesus*, p. 26.
[9] *Ibid.*, pp. 27-28.
[10] *Ibid.*, p. 28.
[11] *Ibid.*
[12] *Ibid.*, p. 31.

cal Jesus."[13] By this he means that the scientific methods of historians will hardly be able to present us with a biography of Jesus.
This, according to Robinson, should not disturb the believer, because the knowledge of Jesus that is based on the historians'
inquiries is little more significant than the knowledge of God
gained by that avenue. He further notes that Christian faith for
the greater part of its existence has not been dependent upon
this kind of research. (2) "Christian faith is not interested in the
historical Jesus."[14] By this he means that throughout its history,
Christianity has been both ignorant of and uninterested in the
kind of knowledge of Jesus that can be gained by methods of
historical, scientific investigation.

Robinson mentions in passing those men who were primarily
instrumental in bringing to an end the original quest, including
in particular Wellhausen, Wrede, and Schmidt. He notes that
form criticism is often given the credit for the end of the original
quest, but he feels that form criticism is more of a result of what
had happened in the preceding generation of German scholarship, which really caused the demise of the original quest.[15]

He proceeds to demonstrate this by a series of contrasts between the nineteenth and twentieth centuries. The source of these
contrasts between the two centuries is to be seen in the discovery
of the kerygma. When history survived at all, it survived only as
kerygma. Accordingly, nineteenth-century historians assumed the
general historical reliability of the Gospels and eliminated only
such elements as they felt were blatant cases of doctrinal embellishments. Here the miraculous elements and so-called "Paul-
inisms" were particularly suspect. The situation is completely the
reverse in the twentieth century. Now the kerygmatic nature of
the Gospels is assumed, and historical credibility is assured only
when the details "cannot be explained in terms of the life of
the Church."[16] As a consequence, with respect to historical trustworthiness the situation today is the converse of that in the nineteenth century. Today, the demonstration of objective, factual
source material in the New Testament, the church's kerygmatic
book, is the more difficult to demonstrate. In the nineteenth century, the demonstration of theological tampering was the more
difficult to demonstrate.[17]

While the liberal lives of Jesus found their point of departure

13 *Ibid.*
14 *Ibid.*, p. 32.
15 *Ibid.*, pp. 35-36.
16 *Ibid.*, pp. 37-38.
17 *Ibid.*, p. 38.

in "the historical Jesus," the twentieth century has found its point of departure in the kerygma. The kerygma has been a unifying element on the contemporary theological scene in the critical school, for it has satisfied both the demand for a concept of history different from that of the nineteenth century and the demand for a theological system based on that concept. "Thus both as witness to past event and as experience of present event, the kerygma is central in primitive Christianity and contemporary theology."[18]

This leads Robinson to another contrast of the endeavors of the two schools. The nineteenth-century quest, in his opinion, attempted "to avoid the risk of faith by supplying objectively verified proof for its 'faith.' " This Robinson regards as theologically illegitimate. He sees in this an attempt to ground faith in works, which results in righteousness not by faith, but by works. The twentieth-century quest, on the other hand, with its point of departure in the kerygma, "calls for existential commitment to the meaning of Jesus."[19]

It is at this point that we can see perhaps more clearly than anywhere else both the difference between the two quests and the source of the difference. The new quest is very deeply rooted in existentialism. "Authentic existence is selfhood constituted by commitment, and consists in constant *engagement*."[20] This is precisely what we see in the new quest, both in respect to its concept of history and in respect to its interest in the kerygma. On the other hand, the devotees of the new quest see in the original quest two primary defects: (1) An attempt to prove Jesus as an objective phenomenon "out there" but not involving oneself personally is regarded as illegitimate. (2) The subsequent attempt to deal with Jesus apart from using him as a means of understanding one's own existence is likewise rejected.[21]

Robinson next discusses some other attempts to get at the Jesus of history apart from those of the new quest. Here he has in mind primarily the work of two scholars and a new school of Gospel study. The first scholar he mentions is C. H. Dodd. He notes that Dodd professes to be able to trace the life of Jesus in the kerygma,[22] but that there are two very serious limitations to this kind of thought. He says that such an attempt to find history in the Gospels is based on a positivistic conception of his-

18 *Ibid.*, p. 43.
19 *Ibid.*, p. 44.
20 *Ibid.*, p. 46.
21 *Ibid.*, p. 47.
22 *Ibid.*, p. 48.

tory, which was at the roots of the original quest. The Gospels, on the other hand, are kerygmatic documents, and it is not legitimate to use either the kerygma or the kerygmatic Gospels to develop such a history.

In the second place, Robinson notes that inasmuch as the kerygma shows a complete lack of interest in the public ministry of Jesus, Dodd should not have tried to construct the kind of historical picture he does on the basis of the kerygma.[23]

Robinson is even more critical of Ethelbert Stauffer than he is of Dodd. He particularly takes him to task concerning the three new sources Stauffer claims he has found to aid him in writing a life of Jesus. With respect to the increased knowledge of Palestine, Robinson denies that Stauffer has anything new. He says Stauffer is working with the same material Renan wrote of a century ago. Furthermore, he feels that this knowledge has been well known ever since Gustav Dalman and Joachim Jeremias collected the bulk of it early in our century. He goes on to criticize the way Stauffer uses this information. His claim to synchronize this material with the Gospels is doubly wrong. In the first place, this presupposes that the Gospels are in chronological order, an idea Robinson will not allow. Furthermore, the indirect sources, apart from an attempted synchronization, have no chronology. The result of his efforts, according to Robinson, is merely a synchronization of the Synoptics with John, or to put it in other terms, the use of the Gospels in a pre-form-critical way.[24]

Robinson also criticizes the second new source claimed by Stauffer. He considers invalid Stauffer's assumption that where Jewish polemics and Christian sources agree we have historical fact. It must be recognized that these Jewish sources often depend on the Christian witnesses. Therefore, when the Christian sources were damaging to the Jewish position they would suppress them, but certain elements in the Christian sources that could be given anti-Christian meaning (Robinson mentions the example of the virgin birth) the Jews left standing. Therefore, historicity was not a primary factor in the inclusion or exclusion of Christian viewpoints in the rabbinic tradition.[25]

The third new source of Stauffer, the literature of Jewish apocalypticism, is not really new either. This kind of source played a major role in the work of Albert Schweitzer, and even the recent Qumran discoveries have failed to add anything to it.

[23] *Ibid.*, p. 56.
[24] *Ibid.*, pp. 60-61.
[25] *Ibid.*, p. 61.

Robinson concludes his treatment of Stauffer's work with the charge that in effect he has gone back to the quest of the nineteenth century and ignored the work of the past fifty years.[26]

Robinson finally denies that there has been any shift in scholarly attitude toward the Gospels that would make a return to the old quest possible. He notes, for example, that the current trend has been to devaluate the work of Luke as an historian. He further comments that the increased estimate on the historical value of John has not placed it in a new historical category, but has merely raised it to the same general category as the Synoptics. Furthermore, the recognized increase in the historical value of John has been attended by a decrease in some cases of the historical estimate of the Synoptics. As a consequence, the origin of the new quest is to be found neither in the theories developed by Dodd or Stauffer nor in any revolutionary conception with respect to the view of the sources.[27]

Next Robinson deals more particularly with the new quest itself as it relates to various factors. He first discusses the possibility of the new quest. "Such a possibility *has* been latent in the radically different understanding of history and of human existence which distinguishes the present from the quest which ended in failure."[28]

In delineating the different understanding of history, he notes that "historicism" has ceased to be regarded as the primary element in historiography. Also "psychologism" has ceased to be regarded as the primary element in biography. These were the two primary elements in the old quest, and for that reason it has ceased to be tenable. Today it is realized that history must be thought of in terms of encounter. "History is the act of intention, the commitment, the meaning of the participants, behind the external occurrence."[29]

The new concept of selfhood is equally important. Selfhood is not to be thought of in terms of one's heritage and development. Rather selfhood, considered from the modern point of view, is to be thought of in terms of commitment to a context. "Selfhood results from implicit or explicit commitment to a kind of existence, and is to be understood only in terms of that commitment, i.e., by laying hold of the understanding of existence in terms of which the self is constituted."[30]

---

26 *Ibid.*, pp. 62-63.
27 *Ibid.*, pp. 64-66.
28 *Ibid.*, p. 66.
29 *Ibid.*, p. 67.
30 *Ibid.*, p. 68.

What effect has all of this had on New Testament study? Robinson answers that it has resulted in a study of the New Testament kerygma as a source for Jesus' history and his selfhood. To be sure, the church altered the sayings and scenes; but precisely at the point where we are most interested, that of the kerygma, the church would have been careful to preserve Jesus' intention and his understanding of existence. We cannot be certain, of course, of any particular saying that is handed down to us, but the quality of the material the church has passed on to us makes it particularly suitable to our encountering the meaning of history and the understanding of existential selfhood.[31]

> We have, for example, in the parables, in the beatitudes and woes, and in the sayings on the kingdom, exorcism, John the Baptist and the law, sufficient insight into Jesus' intention to encounter his historical action, and enough insight into the understanding of existence presupposed in his intention to encounter his selfhood.[32]

The above data bring Robinson to two conclusions. The new quest must be regarded as completely different from the original quest. It must not be based on an effort to resurrect old theories inherent in that quest. The second conclusion he reaches is that the Gospels, and the kerygma contained in them, do make possible a new kind of quest based on modern views of history and the self. Therefore, "Jesus' understanding of his existence, his selfhood, and thus in the higher sense his life, is a possible subject of historical research."[33]

What is the motivation for a new quest? "Man's quest for meaningful existence is his highest stimulus to scholarly enquiry; consequently, a serious quest of the historical Jesus must have meaning in terms of man's quest for meaningful existence."[34] Robinson is particularly eager to press this point, for he feels that unless there is a complete realization of this fact, the new quest will not enlist the best minds in current theological circles. But still more is involved in the background to this question than a quest for meaningful existence. It is the old problem of the relation of the historical Jesus to the Christ of faith. The original quest made the mistake of attempting to separate the historical Jesus from the Christ of faith. There is also a danger involved for those who have placed an emphasis on the kerygma. It is the danger of attempting to separate the Christ of faith

---

[31] *Ibid.*, p. 69.
[32] *Ibid.*, pp. 69-70.
[33] *Ibid.*, p. 72.
[34] *Ibid.*, p. 75.

from the historical Jesus. This could result in the replacing of history with a myth and the substitution of a heavenly being for Jesus of Nazareth.[35]

Since the work of Bultmann in 1941 on mythology, it has become apparent to all who follow him that the kerygma must be encountered existentially if its true meaning is to be grasped. But this has raised a further question. "Does one encounter in the kerygma a symbolized principle, or interpreted history?"[36] The first of the alternatives was seized upon by the History of Religions school. Bultmann, it will be recalled, came out of that school and thus had this idea in his theological background. But he came to realize that the symbol of the History of Religions school could only demonstrate what ought to be, not what was possible. Robinson notes what therefore caused Bultmann to shift away from his History of Religions position.

> Only as witness to God's intervention in history could the myth or symbol be the good news that eschatological existence is possible within history. In this way Bultmann's study of the New Testament *kerygma* compelled him to move beyond the view of it as the objectification of a religious idea, and come to recognize in its "happenedness" its essence.[37]

Conceived of in this way, "The *kerygma* is not the objectification of a new 'Christian' religious principle, but rather the objectification of a historical encounter with God."[38]

All this leads the advocates of the new quest to go one step further. What went on in the early church was a " 'historicizing' process taking place within the *kerygma* . . . leading to the writing of Gospels." This has led these critics to seek in the kerygma not a principle, but "Jesus as the event in which transcendence becomes possible."[39]

Next, Robinson contends that in addition to the possibility of the new quest and its legitimacy, it is also necessary. He states his case very precisely, both in relation to the liberal theologians and the Bultmannian school.

> The formal error of the nineteenth-century quest was to assume that in the Jesus "according to the flesh" one could see undialectically, unparadoxically, unoffensively Jesus as Lord, whereas one can only see Jesus "born of a woman, born under the law." But the formal error of the last generation in eliminating

[35] *Ibid.*, p. 78.
[36] *Ibid.*, p. 81.
[37] *Ibid.*, p. 82.
[38] *Ibid.*, p. 84.
[39] *Ibid.*, pp. 84-85.

the quest has been to ignore the relevance for the Christian dialectic, paradox, and offence, of seeing Jesus causally bound within the historical reconstruction of first-century Judaism, and yet encountering in him transcendence: "born of a woman, born under the law, to redeem those who were under the law."[40]

At this point Robinson confronts the mythologizing of Bultmann most directly. He admits that mythological concepts are used to get the message of the kerygma across, but he denies that the primary intention of the writers is to get across ideas; it is rather to communicate "the existential meaningfulness of a historical person."[41]

The important point is not that the kerygma preserves for us the precise details of Jesus' life. The important point is that the kerygma is based on an evaluation of Jesus, an historical person. Here the difference in the historiography of the nineteenth and twentieth centuries comes to the fore. The new quest is not interested in the kind of historiography lying behind the original quest, which was concerned primarily with the discovery of objective, verifiable facts. It is interested in existentialist historiography, which is concerned primarily with the meaning of historical events.[42]

With this background, Robinson comes finally to a discussion of the procedure of a new quest. He notes first of all that many of the key factors that motivated the original quest have disappeared. For example, the new quest cannot be based in anticlericalism as was the original quest. The secularization of society has been so thorough that anticlericalism has ceased to be an important issue; furthermore, the advance in biblical scholarship has been so great that criticism by someone outside of the field is almost impossible. Also, various theological trends that motivated the original quest have disappeared. In this connection he notes that orthodoxy has lost its hold on Western civilization; that historical skepticism about the existence of Jesus has been driven from the field; that the rationalistic attempt to eliminate the miraculous element from the miracle stories is no longer popular; and that the interest in Jesus as a "charming personality" who taught an ethical system has become meaningless to modern man, who is aware of the depth of his own problems.[43]

The purpose of the new quest is to be found in an attempt to compare the kerygma with Jesus' existential selfhood. It asks the

---

40 *Ibid.*, pp. 86-87.
41 *Ibid.*, p. 87.
42 *Ibid.*, p. 90.
43 *Ibid.*, p. 93.

question: Is the kerygma's understanding of existence the same thing as we find in the historical action of Jesus as seen in his existential selfhood?[44]

We cannot obtain the needed information via the old quest, which is interested primarily in the chronological and developmental in Jesus' life. "Rather the whole person is reached through encounter with individual sayings and actions in which Jesus' intention and selfhood are latent."[45]

The new quest does not attempt to break with the past completely. It is, for example, very much dependent upon the historical-critical method. It is very receptive to what this methodology has to say about philology, comparative religions, and the social-historical. But while it makes good use of these methods, it looks upon the results of these efforts not as being ends, but rather as means. "Contemporary methodology consists precisely in the combination and interaction of objective analysis and existential openness, i.e., it seeks historical understanding precisely in the simultaneous interaction of phenomenological objectivity and existential 'objectivity.' "[46]

What then in the mass of material that we have about Jesus in the Gospels can be accepted as authentic? Robinson has a twofold negative criterion. That material can be accepted as authentic which can be accounted for neither on the basis of primitive Christian preaching, nor on the basis of Judaism.[47] This gives rise to another question. Is the material thus arrived at either of sufficient quality or quantity to make it of any significance? Robinson's answer is Yes. The material thus arrived at is of sufficient quality and quanitity "to make an historical encounter with Jesus possible. His action, the intention latent in it, and the understanding of existence it implies, and thus his selfhood, can be encountered historically."[48]

This brings up a further problem for the new quest. When one encounters Jesus via the historical methodology of the new quest and via the kerygma does he find the same result? Some have felt that these two approaches are incompatible, but Robinson thinks otherwise. The compatibility of these two approaches for him is the working hypothesis of the new quest, i.e., "If an encounter with the kerygma is an encounter with the meaning

---

44 *Ibid.*, p. 94.
45 *Ibid.*, p. 95.
46 *Ibid.*, p. 96.
47 *Ibid.*, p. 99.
48 *Ibid.*, p. 105.

of Jesus, then an encounter with Jesus should be an encounter
with the kerygma."[49]

In the concluding portion of his book, Robinson deals with a
few of the problems, particularly as they relate to the antithesis
between Jesus and Paul seen by critics at the beginning of the
twentieth century. He proceeds to show how the new quest is
able to solve these problems, and concludes, "Paul's description
of his Christian existence is rooted in the kerygma, in which
Jesus' transcendent selfhood is proclaimed."[50]

The concluding sentence of Robinson's book is instructive
as a summary of the methodology and goal of the new quest.
"The selfhood of Jesus is equally available to us — apparently
both via historical research and via the kerygma — as a possible
understanding of our existence."[51]

With this summary of the methodology and procedure of the
new quest behind us, let us proceed to an analysis of the works
of four other leading figures in the school. Since we have treated
Robinson's summary of the methodology to considerable extent,
we shall summarize the work of these men only in terms of the
six questions at the end of Chapter One.

ERNST KÄSEMANN

The lecture of Käsemann, it will be recalled, was the event that
marked the beginning of the "new quest" investigation. In this
lecture Käsemann dealt with most of the issues confronting us,
but most particularly with the first question, on the possibility of
knowing the historical Jesus. He notes at the beginning the direct continuation of the thought of Kähler in the work of Bultmann. "In essence, Bultmann has merely, in his own way, under-
pinned and rendered more precise the thesis of this book [Käh-
ler's]."[52] So it is at the point of the relationship of the kerygma
to history that Käsemann takes up his discussion exactly as
Kähler and Bultmann before him had done.

He notes that the significance of Jesus for faith was the great
overriding factor in the life of the early church. He feels that
this was so much the case that it almost completely replaced his
earthly history. "The living experience of him which later generations enjoyed made the facts of his earthly life simply irrelevant,
except in so far as they might serve to reflect the permanent ex-

---

[49] *Ibid.*, p. 111.
[50] *Ibid.*, p. 125.
[51] *Ibid.*
[52] Käsemann, p. 16.

perience."[53] In this connection, Käsemann questions whether it is legitimate at all to use the formula "the historical Jesus," for he is afraid that it may awaken the hope that we will be able to write a life story of Jesus.[54] The central and supreme desire of the early church was to get across its message. This is obvious to Käsemann from the way in which the Gospels are written. They are not written merely as a report of historical events, but at their heart lies the kerygma. "It interprets out of its own experience what for it has already become mere history and employs for this purpose the medium of its preaching."[55] The importance of the contemporary significance of history is already to be seen at work in the Gospels. "To state the paradox as sharply as possible: the community takes so much trouble to maintain historical continuity with him who once trod this earth that it allows the historical events of this earthly life to pass for the most part into oblivion and replaces them with its own message."[56] Käsemann is consequently convinced that any attempt to construct a neat chronological picture of the life of Jesus in which we see his development by cause and effect is doomed to failure.[57]

But he is not content to rest his case here. He does not feel we are justified in adopting attitudes of defeatism and skepticism concerning the life of Jesus. If this should happen, we could lose interest in the earthly Jesus, which would be unfortunate from three standpoints. In the first place, we would lose sight of the primitive Christian concern that there be an identity between the exalted Lord and the earthly Jesus. Second, there is a chance that we would arrive at a docetic position in which we would be unconcerned with the earthly Jesus. Third, Käsemann maintains that in the Synoptic tradition itself there are fragments that simply must be recognized as being historical.[58]

It is against this background that Käsemann gives us three axioms.

> (1) It is not . . . historical interest but concern with the task of proclamation which has been responsible for passing on the relatively few genuine words of Jesus and combining them with the kerygmatic resources of the community — that is, for bringing our Gospels into existence. (2) The very reason why the historical facts of the life of Jesus as good as perished from the primi-

---

[53] *Ibid.*, p. 23.
[54] *Ibid.*
[55] *Ibid.*, p. 20.
[56] *Ibid.*
[57] *Ibid.*, p. 45.
[58] *Ibid.*, p. 46.

tive Christian message was the community's awareness that its mission was one of proclamation. (3) Apart from a few fragments of the preaching and activity of Jesus which are only accessible to us through the proclamation of the community, and even then have to be separated out under very great difficulties, the Gospels are, both in form and content, documents of primitive Christian preaching; documents, therefore, of faith in the Risen Lord and consequently also of church dogma. Here and there some material may in practice go back to an earlier stage, but in principle our Christian history begins with the Easter faith of the disciples. What lies behind that is only accessible now by theoretical reconstruction — and this applies above all to the Jesus of history himself.[59]

Before giving Käsemann's more positive analysis of the way we may arrive at what is historical, let us look at his evaluation of two current positions. That of Bultmann is of course most immediately available to him. He notes that "Bultmann's radicalism is provoking a reaction."[60] He goes on to list three particular points on which current criticism turns. (1) Efforts are being made to show that there is much more authentic tradition in the Synoptics than the position of the Bultmannians would allow. (2) Some are attempting to show that at least the most primitive elements in the passion and Easter tradition are reliable. The primary concern is to prevent a complete disjunction between the kerygma and the tradition. (3) Such critics of Bultmann "arrive ... at the systematic conception of a 'salvation history' running parallel to universal history, embedded in it but yet separable from it, having its own laws and continuity and finding its vehicle in the history of faith and of the Church as the new divine creation."[61]

On the other hand, Käsemann is very critical of any attempt to create a life story of Jesus as the liberal theologians had attempted to do. He feels that anyone who attempts to do this has ignored the fruits of the historical criticism of the past two centuries. This could only result in the rise of a more drastic form of criticism.[62] Käsemann is, however, aware of the dangers in abandoning the liberal position.

> The very people who have hitherto been the opponents of the liberal quest of the historical Jesus are obviously going in fear and trembling lest the doors should for the first time be really

---

[59] *Ibid.*, pp. 60-61.
[60] *Ibid.*, p. 16.
[61] *Ibid.*, pp. 16-17.
[62] *Ibid.*, p. 23.

opened to radical scepticism and lest, with the abandoning of any direct attack on the historical question, the historical reality of revelation itself should be endangered.[63]

What then should be our procedure for determining what is historical? First of all we must arrive at an adequate conception of history. History must not be thought of only in terms of what happened in the first century of our era. Interpretation of those facts is of supreme importance. He notes that both rationalism and supernaturalism have made efforts to establish the facts, but have arrived at diametrically opposite presentations of Jesus.[64] Interpretation, consequently, becomes the key. History is significant only when it can address us in our contemporary situation. "Mere history only takes on genuine historical significance in so far as it can address both a question and an answer to our contemporary situation."[65]

Furthermore, it must be asserted once again that the Gospels do contain historical elements. Käsemann points out that in spite of their different conception of history, and in spite of their desire for proclamation, it is to their interest in the history of Jesus that we are indebted for both the origin and the form of the Gospel narratives. It is similarly this interest in history that differentiates them from the rest of the New Testament and from other contemporary literature.[66] His personal view he states as follows. "My own concern is to show that, out of the obscurity of the life story of Jesus, certain characteristic traits in his preaching stand out in relatively sharp relief, and that primitive Christianity united its own message with these."[67]

We come then to the actual work of determining what parts of the tradition are historical. One must at first discard the notion that the Synoptic tradition is generally reliable. The question is not whether we should employ criticism, but rather how far we should carry it.[68] But even criticism has problems, for apart from the parables there is no formal criterion by which we may identify the material that comes authentically from Jesus. He sees the values of form criticism, but its concern is primarily with the *Sitz im Leben* of the narratives and not with their historical individuality. Its chief value is therefore negative in that it can rule out anything as authentic that can be accounted for on the

---

[63] *Ibid.*, p. 17.
[64] *Ibid.*, pp. 18-19.
[65] *Ibid.*, p. 21.
[66] *Ibid.*, p. 25.
[67] *Ibid.*, p. 46.
[68] *Ibid.*, p. 34.

basis of the *Sitz im Leben*.[69] The discovery of positive criteria is much more difficult. Ultimately Käsemann comes down to the position that Robinson later appropriated in his apology. "In only one case do we have more or less safe ground under our feet; when there are no grounds either for deriving a tradition from Judaism or for ascribing it to primitive Christianity."[70]

The attitude of Käsemann toward the miraculous in the life of Jesus is well summarized in the following statement. "No one has ever been compelled (in the true sense) to make his decision between faith and unbelief, simply because someone else has succeeded in representing Jesus convincingly as a worker of miracles."[71] He subsequently proceeds to a more careful analysis of the miraculous, which results for him in a complete rejection of miracles in the life of Jesus. He notes that there has been a two-fold attack on miracle in the modern era. In the first place, the world view of modern man finds the idea of miracle offensive. In the second place, historical research coupled with the study of comparative religion has revealed some significant things about the miracle stories of the Gospels, of which three are particularly significant. (1) There is indication of development in the stories within the context of the Gospels themselves. (2) There are many analogies to the miracle stories in the literature of classical antiquity. (3) They show a fixed form of presentation so that they represent a technique rather than a report.[72]

On the basis of this evidence, he concludes that most of the miracle stories of the Gospels are legends. Their origin may be accounted for on rationalistic bases, and their presence in the Gospels need not disturb our world view. "We can no longer employ them as objective proofs for the intervention of God in history."[73]

Käsemann's analysis of the significance of miracle in the ancient world is instructive, and for that reason we quote him at length.

> The concept of miracle current in the ancient world was not primarily, as ours is, towards the suspension of causality but towards the occurrence of an epiphany. In a miracle there is an encounter with the divinity and its power, which in its self-manifestation is reaching out to take hold of me. It is not merely that *something* extraordinary is happening but that I encounter

[69] *Ibid.*, p. 35.
[70] *Ibid.*, p. 37.
[71] *Ibid.*, p. 19.
[72] *Ibid.*, pp. 48-49.
[73] *Ibid.*, p. 51.

someone, be it deity or demon. . . . In such a situation, we are not merely receiving instruction about something which might be considered in an objective and detached way; but, because a power is reaching out for us, we are being summoned to make a decision which may express itself either as faith or as unfaith (hardness of heart).[74]

Käsemann goes on to note some shifts that occur in the New Testament itself from this conception in the ancient world. When miracles are used as objective evidence to convince, this basic conception of miracles was already being abandoned.[75] Furthermore, Paul and John make less of miracle than do the Synoptics. In Paul the proof of the Spirit lies not in miracle but in ministering obedience; and in John, faith which has its base in miracle is deprecated, as may be seen in 2:23ff.; 6:14f., 26f.[76]

He claims that miracles as they occur in the New Testament are intelligible only to believers and are not convincing to the unbeliever. That they are so closely linked to those who have faith has caused historical criticism to give up the majority of the miracle stories and question the status of the rest. "It forces us to acknowledge that in turn we are faced primarily with the preaching of primitive Christianity — the message of which is that in Jesus the divine love has taken the field and showed itself to be a life-giving power."[77]

Käsemann does not deal as extensively with the resurrection as he does with miracle, but this is no doubt because from his point of view it partakes of the same general character. "Nothing is settled about the significance of the resurrection tidings for me personally, simply because the evidence for the empty tomb has been shown to be reliable."[78] He evidently prefers to think of the resurrection appearances as visions, because he says in another context that the record of I Cor. 15 was not able to satisfy the next Christian generation probably because the appearances were too much like "visions." As a result, subsequent New Testament writers took steps to correct this inadequacy.[79]

Mythology plays a much less significant place in the writings of the new quest than it did in Bultmann. These writers have come to realize that Bultmann's demythologizing has in some places produced the same results as those of the History of Re-

---

[74] *Ibid.,* p. 52.
[75] *Ibid.,* p. 53.
[76] *Ibid.,* p. 51.
[77] *Ibid.,* pp. 53-54.
[78] *Ibid.,* p. 19.
[79] *Ibid.,* p. 51.

ligions school. Robinson in particular has pointed this out. "When
the kerygma was demythologized, it tended to reduce itself to an
objectification of the religiosity of the apostles. Thus one was
returned to the position of Wilhelm Bousset, who held that the
Lord of primitive Christianity was the symbolic objectification of
the cult deity of a mystery religion."[80]

We could perhaps most accurately describe the position of
Käsemann in terms of the quantity of material he finds in the
Gospels that partakes of the character of kerygma, history, and
myth. By far the largest quantity is kerygma. There is a smaller
quantity of history and myth. In spite of its kerygmatic emphasis,
primitive Christianity "is also making it clear that it is not minded
to allow myth to take the place of history nor a heavenly being
to take the place of the Man of Nazareth."[81] What we do find in
places is an "historification of mythical material."[82] A particular
example of this process is seen in the way Matthew sets about
making his infancy narrative correspond to that of Moses.[83]

What is the position of Käsemann with respect to the comparative historical value of John and the Synoptics? He begins by
calling our attention to the considerable variation among all four
accounts. Kerygma is primary, history is secondary. "Above all,
we cannot help being struck by the fact that the Gospels alone
present the tidings of the Christ within the framework of the
story of the earthly life of Jesus."[84] This then puts the historical
element in all of the Gospels under suspicion.

There is, however, a difference between the Synoptics and
John. He believes the Synoptics had every intention of giving
to their readers reliable tradition about Jesus, but he denies that
the author of John had the same intention. He notices the great
differences in this Gospel from the others. (1) John does great
violence to the narrative material. (2) He ignores the Synoptic
tradition. (3) He gives the material an entirely different arrangement. (4) He gives the discourses a completely different construction. Käsemann goes on to state that such gross differences
in the presentation of the material could not result from self-
deception, but that they must be accounted for on the basis of
a deliberate resolve of the author.[85]

Käsemann proceeds to characterize each of the Gospels with

---

[80] Robinson, "The Historical Question," p. 1209.
[81] Käsemann, p. 25.
[82] *Ibid.,* p. 26.
[83] *Ibid.*
[84] *Ibid.,* p. 21.
[85] *Ibid.,* p. 22.

respect to its historical reliability. In John, "The merely historical only has interest and value to the extent to which it mirrors symbolically the recurring experiences of Christian faith."[86] In other words, the historical Jesus is not of primary importance. His significance at the time of the author's writing is.

Käsemann discounts the comparative historical element in Mark to a greater degree than has anyone we have encountered since the beginning of the twentieth century. Mark writes his story of Jesus as a series of secret epiphanies in which the Son of God comes down to earth. It is the depiction of a series of battles between the God-man and his enemies. Thus, "The history of Jesus has become mythicized."[87]

Matthew, on the other hand, is dominated by a desire to make the life of Jesus conform to the mold of primitive Christian eschatology.

> The whole life history of Jesus as Matthew presents it is not only seen from the standpoint of eschatology, but basically shaped by it. It is precisely here that the story of Jesus has been interwoven with traditional material which can only be described as being in itself unhistorical, legendary and mythical.[88]

Käsemann regards Luke's Gospel as the first "life of Jesus." For this reason he gives particular place to such things as causality, teleology, and psychological insight. We thus have in Luke a depiction of salvation history in which "Jesus is the founder of the Christian religion."[89] Luke makes the history of Jesus conform to the eschatology of Luke's own time. "If, in the other Gospels, the problem of history is a special form of the problem of eschatology, in Luke eschatology has become a special form of the problem of history."[90]

With regard to the central significance of Jesus, Käsemann is convinced that the distinctive element to be found in Jesus must be found in his preaching.

> Jesus did not come to proclaim general religious or moral truths, but to tell of the *basileia* that had dawned and how God was come near to man in grace and demand. He brought, and lived out, the liberty of the children of God, who only remain the Father's children and only remain free so long as they find in this Father their Lord.[91]

---

[86] *Ibid.*
[87] *Ibid.*
[88] *Ibid.*, p. 27.
[89] *Ibid.*, p. 29.
[90] *Ibid.*
[91] *Ibid.*, p. 45.

It is thus that Jesus has become Lord for Christians. For both before and after his resurrection he revealed himself to them, "By setting them before the God who is near to them and thus translating them into the freedom and responsibility of faith."[92]

GÜNTHER BORNKAMM

Perhaps the most influential book from the point of view of the new quest is one written by Günther Bornkamm.[93] This is true not only because the author treats the subject more comprehensively, but also because his was one of the earliest treatments of the subject (the German edition of this book was published in 1956). Bornkamm begins his analysis of the possibility of writing a biography of Jesus where most members of the postliberal critical school do — with a reference to Schweitzer's book. He notes that Schweitzer's book is at the same time a memorial and a funeral oration to the liberal quest. He finds the reason for this as have others in the nature of the Gospels, which "unite to a remarkable degree both record of Jesus Christ and witness to him, testimony of the church's faith in him and narration of his history."[94]

It is in keeping with this that he denies the possibility of constructing a life of Jesus along biographical and psychological lines. He feels that any attempt to do this resorts to the acceptance of the records in an uncritical way, or in the use of an imagination that is just as uncritical.[95] Bornkamm shows his acceptance of the results of form criticism when he says that the events of Jesus' life as portrayed in the Gospels are told in pericopes, or brief, disconnected anecdotes. Thus it is completely wrong to attempt to put these stories together in a sequential fashion. Each one must stand by itself as an attempt to tell the entire history of Jesus. One must not depend on the context of a given passage to shed light on its meaning, because the anecdotes lack historical connection. One must not seek commentary on a given incident from some other passage, but he must treat it as an independent unit.[96]

Bornkamm arrives at this position largely on the basis of an analysis of the Gospels. He says it would be a mistake to regard the Gospels as having been written primarily to fulfil an historical interest. Whatever historical interest is found in them is an interest

---

[92] *Ibid.*, p. 46.

[93] Günther Bornkamm, *Jesus of Nazareth*, trans. Irene and Fraser Mc-Luskey and James M. Robinson (New York: Harper, 1960).

[94] *Ibid.*, p. 14.

[95] *Ibid.*, p. 24.

[96] *Ibid.*, p. 25.

that must be thought of in terms of faith.[97] The dominance of faith over the tradition is very marked from the viewpoint of Bornkamm. This is so much the case that we are not in possession of a single story in the Gospels that is not in some degree a confession of the early Christian community. This points out for Bornkamm the great difficulty of any attempt to get at the "bare facts of history."[98]

This situation illustrates for him not only the difficulty of the task before us, but the results of the two extreme positions in the history of criticism. The conservative camp has accepted everything in the Gospels as historical. In so doing, it has not given recognition to the nature of the Gospels. It has not paid attention to the fact that they are primarily confessions. On the other hand, critical scholarship, in accepting as authentic only that part of the tradition whose historicity cannot be doubted, has made of the Gospels something completely different from what they are.[99]

The church's faith must then be recognized as the primary — but not the only — factor in the writing of the Gospels. This is apparent to Bornkamm from an analysis both of the Gospels and of Paul and other New Testament writers. One need not deny that the Gospels contain historical recollections from the past, but it cannot be maintained that a chronological interest is at their heart. With regard to Paul and other New Testament writers, Bornkamm asserts that they knew very little of the material that we have in our Gospels.[100]

Bornkamm finds the evidence of the church's faith most clearly in what he calls "legends" and "legendary embellishments" as they increase from one Evangelist to the next. Narratives that are particularly subjects of this kind of development are the infancy narratives of Matthew and Luke and the Easter stories of all four Gospels. He sees these narratives as standing midway between the other sections of the Gospels and the phantasies of the apocryphal gospels.[101]

At this point, however, Bornkamm is conscious, as are all the other members of the new quest school, of the possibility that such a position may lead to a complete loss of interest in investigating the historical problem. He further criticizes two groups to whom this has in effect happened. The first group he identifies as members of "critical biblical scholarship," by which he means

---

[97] *Ibid.*, p. 23.
[98] *Ibid.*, p. 14.
[99] *Ibid.*, p. 15.
[100] *Ibid.*, p. 17.
[101] *Ibid.*, p. 19.

those who center their interest completely on the kerygma to the exclusion of history. Of them he says, "They consider the entanglement of confession and report, of history and faith in the Gospels so indissolubly close, that they consider every quest of the historical Jesus entirely vain."[102]

On the opposite side, he criticizes the "supporters of believing tradition," because they dismiss the use of critical scholarship from the first and insist that as a starting point one must accept the given tradition as completely reliable. His discussion of this second position is very brief, for he feels that critical research is here to stay and that any attempt to defeat it is meaningless.[103]

The possibility of skepticism, on the other hand, is a more menacing one — and, as a matter of fact, more threatening to Bornkamm. As a consequence, he directs himself to that question in more detail. He begins by assuring us that the Gospels do not justify our adopting a position of either skepticism or resignation. Historical criticism, he feels, has helped here by showing that our approach must not be along biographical or psychological lines. While the Gospels do not present history in the sense of a series of happenings in the chronological course of a life, as would a modern biography, this does not mean that we can completely throw out historical investigation. While we are not justified in attempting to construct on the basis of the Gospels a unified picture of Jesus' inner and outer development, our Gospels "do speak of history as occurrence and event."[104]

He is confident that a certain amount of the historical can be gleaned from the Gospels, "despite the fact that on historical grounds so many of the stories and sayings could be contested in detail, despite tendencies evidently active in the tradition, despite the impossibility of finally extracting from more or less authentic particulars a more or less assured whole which we could call a life of Jesus."[105]

What then is the conclusion at which Bornkamm arrives with regard to the writing of a biography or history of Jesus? He summarizes it for us very well.

> What then is shown us in this style of transmission? Surely these are all characteristics of a popular and unhistorical transmission, evidence that the Gospel tradition, in origin and purpose, is directed to the practical use of the believing Church, to whom mere history as such means very little. Surely the histo-

[102] *Ibid.*, p. 22.
[103] *Ibid.*
[104] *Ibid.*, pp. 24-25.
[105] *Ibid.*, p. 25.

rian is forced thereby to criticise this tradition, which often enough is silent where he seeks an answer, naïvely generalises where he enquires after the individual element in each case, and frequently blurs the distinction between history and interpretation. These are legitimate questions. And yet we must never lose sight of the fact that, precisely in this way of transmitting and recounting, the person and work of Jesus, in their unmistakable uniqueness and distinctiveness, are shown forth with an originality which again and again far exceeds and disarms even all believing understandings and interpretations. Understood in this way, the primitive tradition of Jesus is brim full of history.[106]

On the question of miracle, Bornkamm has a great deal to say. The purpose of the miracles is to show that Jesus does not fail those who come to him in the expectation of help.[107] But before we can study the miracles as such, we must understand two preliminary facts. In the first place, there is strong evidence in the Gospels themselves that Jesus did not wish to be known as a miracle-worker. There are instances, for example, when he withdraws from the people, and others in which he asks those who have been healed to be silent (Mk. 1:35ff.; 1:44, etc.).[108]

In the second place, Bornkamm denies that belief in miracles is important for faith. This he maintains was true in the life of Jesus, and it remains true today. In the Gospels themselves there are strong indications that miracles are not to be looked upon as essential to faith. John in particular points this out. Jesus leaves the crowds who are coming to him only because of the signs he works (Jn. 2:3ff.). His reply to the nobleman who wishes his son healed accuses him of wanting a miracle for faith (4:48); and he commends those who, unlike Thomas, believe in the absence of miracle (20:29). In addition, he refused to give the "sign" the Pharisees demanded (Mk. 8:11f., etc.). These instances are enough to demonstrate to Bornkamm that Jesus did not ask for faith that was based on his ability to work miracles. This would eliminate the need for trust and obedience as is indicated, for example, in the story of the temptation.[109]

Furthermore, Bornkamm insists that belief in Gospel miracles is not important to us today. "It is altogether absurd to consider recognition of their historicity as a proof of faith, and denial of

---

106 *Ibid.*, pp. 25-26.
107 *Ibid.*, p. 130.
108 *Ibid.*, p. 132.
109 *Ibid.*, pp. 132-33.

their historicity as disbelief, although such an assumption is widespread among many 'Christian' circles to this day."[110]

With respect to the analysis of the miracles themselves, Bornkamm feels that "It would be difficult to doubt the physical healing powers which emanated from Jesus, just as he himself interpreted his casting out demons as a sign of the dawning of the kingdom of God (Lk. 11:20; Mt. 12:28)."[111] On the other hand, it cannot be denied that in many instances legendary traits have been added to these stories.[112]

The "nature miracles" are the group in particular that give evidence of these legendary accretions. Three factors especially should be noted. (1) There is an indication of growth in the passing on of these stories in the Gospels themselves. (2) The stories are paralleled in ancient non-Christian literature.[113] (3) Many of these appear to have been made after analogies to and upon themes of the Old Testament.[114]

The resurrection of Jesus, Bornkamm says, should not be treated as an historical fact as are other events of the past. The last historical fact that is available to the historian is the Easter faith of the disciples.[115] This is underlined for him in an analysis of the Easter narratives in the Gospels. As against the singleness of the Easter *message,* he sets the plurality of the Easter *narratives.*[116] He notes that these narratives differ considerably in detail. Not only is this the case, but he sees within the Gospels a development from a tradition that originally made the resurrection and ascension one event, to a later tradition that separated the two by a period of time that Jesus spent on earth, after which he ascended to heaven.[117]

As against this multiple and differing sequence of narratives in connection with resurrection, he points out the relatively uniform presentation of the passion narrative.[118]

All this leads Bornkamm to believe that the primary factor in the Easter narratives is not the physical nature of the body of the risen Christ, but rather is to be found in the *message* of Easter. He is very cautious at this point lest he be interpreted to mean that

[110] *Ibid.,* p. 131.
[111] *Ibid.,* pp. 130-31.
[112] *Ibid.,* p. 131.
[113] *Ibid.*
[114] *Ibid.,* p. 208.
[115] *Ibid.,* p. 180.
[116] *Ibid.,* p. 181.
[117] *Ibid.,* p. 183.
[118] *Ibid.,* p. 182.

Easter is *only* a product of the faith of the community. "Certainly the form in which it comes down to us is stamped with this faith. But it is just as certain that the appearances of the risen Christ and the word of his witness have in the first place given rise to this faith."[119] Bornkamm apparently does not believe in a physical resurrection, but neither does he wish to speculate on what kind of resurrection gave rise to the Easter faith.

Regarding the question of mythology in the New Testament, Bornkamm is in complete agreement with Bultmann. He even goes to considerable lengths to defend him against his critics.[120] The differences that arise between them are more on the basis of theological variation. But here again, while he agrees with Bultmann in theory, it appears that the importance of myth to his interpretation as compared with that of Bultmann has lost much of its force. Thus, for example, he maintains that the birth stories of Matthew and Luke are so different from one another and so affected by Jewish and Christian messianic conceptions that they are useless as historical resources.[121] On the other hand, one will find statements like this: "The Gospels are the rejection of myth. To whatever extent mythological conceptions from time to time find access to the thought and faith of the early Church, they are given once and for all the function of interpreting the history of Jesus as the history of God with the world."[122] This, we see, is very similar to the idea of Käsemann.[123]

In Bornkamm's view, the problem of history in all the Gospels is a complicated one. Nevertheless, for Bornkamm the Synoptics stand on a much higher level historically than does John.[124] The Gospel writers were the first to formulate the tradition about Jesus into a continuous narrative. Of these, as far as we know, Mark was the first. With him as well as with his successors, the determinative interest was theological, not historical. Faith dominated the tradition rather than the converse.[125] But while the Synoptics pose problems, the Gospel of John must be placed in an entirely different class. "The Gospel according to John has so different a character in comparison with the other three, and is

---

[119] *Ibid.*, p. 183.
[120] Günther Bornkamm, "Myth and Gospel: A Discussion of the Problem of Demythologizing the New Testament Message," *Kerygma and History*, ed. and trans. Braaten and Harrisville, pp. 172ff.
[121] Bornkamm, *Jesus of Nazareth*, p. 53.
[122] *Ibid.*, p. 23.
[123] Käsemann, p. 26.
[124] Bornkamm, *Jesus of Nazareth*, p. 14.
[125] *Ibid.*, pp. 218-19.

to such a degree the product of a developed theological reflection, that we can only treat it as a secondary source."[126] Bornkamm is not willing to push this to the extreme of abandoning John as an historical source. He admits that historical reports are contained within the Gospel, but says that each of them must be examined by itself to determine its worth. Furthermore, Jesus' words and history are so intermixed with the Easter faith that to an even greater extent than is the case with the Synoptics, it would be unwise for us to place any great confidence in the history presented there.[127]

The question of date clinches the argument for Bornkamm. Because John was written about A.D. 100, Mark was written about A.D. 70, and the other two Synoptics in the years immediately after Mark, i.e., from about A.D. 75-95, the story that the Synoptics tell is to be preferred to that of John on the basis of date alone.[128]

With regard to the significance of Jesus, Bornkamm directly challenges the contention of Bultmann. It is not adequate from Bornkamm's point of view to regard Christ as one who merely gives to us self-understanding. The proper question is not as Bultmann puts it, "How do I understand myself?" but rather as Paul puts it, "Where am I?" In response to this question it may be asserted that the believer's existence is taken into Christ (Gal. 2:20). By this Bornkamm does not mean to imply a transport, but refers rather to "God's having surrendered his Son up to the real curse and death of my life. Thus, God is for us. . . . Hence he makes us righteous before him (Rom. 8:31ff.)."[129]

It is therefore inadequate from Bornkamm's point of view to regard redemption as "a new qualification of my own history." It is rather "a new history which is no longer mine."[130] It thus surpasses in meaning one's own history and understanding of existence. Bornkamm interprets it in light of Rom. 8:31ff.

> It has its past, its present, and its future. Its past, the "whence" from which as a believer I come, means now: God sent his only Son; God has given him up for us all. Its present, its "wherein," means: Christ dwells within you, God is for us . . . , Christ is with us. . . . Its future, its "whither," means: How will he not give us all things with him, who will separate us from the love of God?[131]

---

[126] *Ibid.*, p. 14.
[127] *Ibid.*, p. 215.
[128] *Ibid.*
[129] "Myth and Gospel," p. 192.
[130] *Ibid.*
[131] *Ibid.*, p. 193.

He comments also on Bultmann's interpretation of resurrection from the dead. Again Bultmann interprets this to mean a new understanding of one's self, a new qualification of one's history. Bornkamm is aware of what he regards as the danger of thinking of the future in objective terms. However, he concludes, "The interpretation may never surrender what the message of the resurrection from the dead intends to express — namely, that the destiny and realization of my existence lies beyond the possibilities of my self. They signify the description and end of my history and thus the disclosure of a new history in Christ."[132]

On the basis of these comments, it can be seen that while Bornkamm and Bultmann disagree on matters of interpretation, they both derive the significance of Jesus via existentialist analysis.

ERNST FUCHS

Some would consider it inappropriate to include Fuchs and Ebeling in a chapter on the new quest, since they go beyond the position of the other scholars to deal with an existentialist interpretation of the New Testament rather than an existentialist interpretation of the kerygma. The theological position at which they arrive has been called by some the "New Hermeneutic."[133] We shall nevertheless include them in this chapter, because they do come from the circle of Bultmann's pupils and they share many concerns with the others included here.

Fuchs and Ebeling do not deal at any great length with either miracles or mythology. The reason for the slight attention given to miracle is doubtless that they share Bultmann's completely negative opinion on this subject and therefore consider lengthy further treatment unnecessary. Their reason for neglecting comparatively the question of mythology is that they are more particularly involved with the concern of faith with the historical Jesus and not as completely involved in the kerygma as was Bultmann.[134] Accordingly we shall not discuss these questions in connection with these two authors.

In his treatment of the possibility of writing a biography or history of Jesus, Fuchs gives recognition to what everyone in the critical school has accepted since Kähler — the kerygmatic character of the Gospel accounts. He points out that this early Christian kerygma says something that Jesus himself did not say, and furthermore, that it says something Jesus could not have said. He bases this conclusion on a comparison of Jesus' words with the

132 *Ibid.*, p. 195.
133 Perrin, pp. 30, 33.
134 *Ibid.*, p. 33.

early Christian theology, at three levels. There is first of all a difference between the theology of the early church in general and Jesus' proclamation. Second, the theology of Paul carries this a step further. And finally, in the Fourth Gospel we have an absolute shift from a proclamation of Jesus in the Synoptic Gospels, to Jesus' proclamation of himself in John.[135] Fuchs, who agrees completely with the methods of form criticism as exhibited in Bultmann's *History of the Synoptic Tradition,* concludes that the oldest documentary layer in the tradition outside of the passion narrative itself was a collection of individual sayings, parables, and miracle stories, identical with Q.[136]

Fuchs proceeds to analyze the three levels in the New Testament on which the historical Jesus can be seen. He develops his discussion of each of these levels on the basis of a question. At the first level the question is, "What does faith think in John's Gospel?"[137] To this Fuchs gives the following answer:

> Faith thinks what it confesses: that God was present in Jesus ([Jn.] 14:9), since Jesus was God's word which wishes to give us life (1:1-18). Faith thinks what it believes: that Jesus was the word of love, which makes every question superfluous because the Father fulfils the Son's request (16:23). Jesus' prayer in John 17 arises from the anguish of love. This hymn of the dying Jesus is the Song of Songs of God's faithfulness. God is faithful because, in the Son, he gives nothing less than himself (5:26f.). For the Father loves the Son. This most of all is what we are accustomed to forget.[138]

According to John, therefore, knowledge of faith and confession of faith must not be separated. God has given man knowledge of himself in Jesus and therefore man has something to confess, because when faith "really sees Jesus, then it sees the Father. . . . Because the Father is at work in Jesus, 14:10f."[139]

At the next level on the path to the historical Jesus, Fuchs asks the question, "How does faith think in Paul?"[140] He summarizes the concept as follows: "Whereas in John's Gospel thought was made dependent on faith, in Paul's case it almost appears as if he were making faith dependent on thought."[141] Paul takes his point of departure from the law. The law of Moses

---

[135] Ernst Fuchs, *Studies of the Historical Jesus,* trans. Andrew Scobie (Naperville, Ill.: Allenson, 1964), p. 49.

[136] *Ibid.,* p. 37.

[137] *Ibid.,* p. 169.

[138] *Ibid.,* pp. 171-72.

[139] *Ibid.,* p. 172.

[140] *Ibid.,* p. 169.

[141] *Ibid.,* p. 173.

held sway until the time for the revelation of faith in Christ. With the coming of Christ, however, all are free for faith. The law and faith, however, should not be regarded as contradictory concepts, for even now the evildoer is damned by the law, while he may be saved by faith. After the believer has made faith his own, he is constantly exhorted to self-examination. As a result, the ones who on this basis of self-examination conform to faith, receive in faith the strength they need.[142] Consequently, "According to Paul, faith is concerned with everything that we are able to answer for morally, when we lay claim to Christ's power."[143] This calls for constant self-examination "to see if I am concerned with the demonstration of the Spirit and of God's power in my active and passive conduct."[144] "*How* does faith think? Not scrupulously but conscientiously, by testifying to everyone through his own determination that God acts for him."[145]

Finally he asks, "Where does faith think in Jesus?"[146] Here we are most immediately concerned with the question of the historical Jesus and his proclamation. At this point Fuchs differentiates very carefully between sayings of Jesus and proclamations of Jesus. He states that we cannot have any certainty that any genuine saying of Jesus has been preserved for us. On the other hand, we can feel more confident in trying to determine what Jesus' proclamation may have been about. Consequently, while Fuchs thinks it is unlikely that Jesus ever preached of the rule of God or of repentance, it is just as likely that he thought on these subjects. What we have then in our Gospels on these subjects "are stylized formulations of the early community or of the evangelists."[147] From them, however, by careful analysis we may separate the christological additions and get back to Jesus' thought.

Furthermore, in the conduct of Jesus we have a good clue to what is historical. Over against Jesus' conduct Fuchs sets the miracle stories of the Gospels and the titles ascribed to Jesus, which may be attributed to dogmatic considerations of the early church. If, however, we find agreement between Jesus' conduct and his words, we may be more certain that we are in touch with the historical Jesus, since actions were more apt to move the early Christian community toward imitation than were words.[148]

---

142 *Ibid.*, pp. 174-77.
143 *Ibid.*, p. 178.
144 *Ibid.*
145 *Ibid.*, pp. 178-79.
146 *Ibid.*, p. 169.
147 *Ibid.*, p. 179.
148 *Ibid.*, pp. 21-22.

On the subject of the resurrection, Fuchs is quick to point out that our primary source cannot be the Gospels, but rather must be Paul. He notes, for example, that the Gospels are at least twenty years later than Paul and fifty years later than the life of Jesus. Furthermore, while the Gospels may contain authentic traditions, these traditions are anonymous, whereas with Paul we know that the assertions he is making are his own.[149] Fuchs is particularly interested in I Cor. 9:1 and its context, from which he believes certain important things may be established. (1) From the way Paul asks the question in I Cor. 9:1, and from the series of rhetorical questions in which it is set, it is apparent that "it was generally accepted at that time that Paul had . . . experienced a vision or appearance of Jesus."[150] (2) "That it was not absolutely necessary for an apostle to have previously known Jesus personally (cf. also II Cor. 5:16)."[151] (3) "That such experiences were probably the mark of each of the apostles, for the circle of those who had such experiences was considerably greater than the circle of those who were at that time included with the twelve (I Cor. 9:1, 5; cf. 15:5-8)."[152] (4) "We have in I Cor. 9:1 a confirmation of the statement in Rom. 10:9 that at that time *only* the resurrected Christ was regarded as Lord."[153] It was believed that after the resurrection God revealed Jesus as Lord and Christ.

What gave rise to the idea of the resurrection? Fuchs looks to the primitive Christian community, which lived in the near expectation of the coming of the rule of God, as is seen for example in the preaching of John the Baptist. It is in the primitive Christian community, frightened by the events of the passion, that we see the origin of the resurrection vision. As Fuchs puts it, "In my opinion the Easter visions are nothing other than the expression of such expectations."[154]

With regard to the historical value of John as compared with the Synoptics, Fuchs begins by emphasizing his belief that the Gospels originated primarily out of kerygmatic considerations. One therefore should not regard the Gospel writers as compilers of materials, but rather as men who used materials to contribute to a theological plan. He notes, for example, that the framework of Mark's Gospel carries a resemblance to Paul's theology. This also applies to a lesser degree to Matthew and Luke.

---

149 *Ibid.*, pp. 14-15.
150 *Ibid.*, p. 15.
151 *Ibid.*
152 *Ibid.*
153 *Ibid.*, p. 16.
154 *Ibid.*, p. 183.

John, on the other hand, except that it like the others includes a passion narrative, is completely independent in its composition. For this reason, although it contains some historically interesting details, it must be placed in a class by itself.[155]

Fuchs uses a comparison of the Synoptic Gospels and John to establish the kerygmatic content of both sets of writings. If one were tempted to say that the statements of the Synoptics are historical in the sense that Jesus spoke of what he would *become,* one would still be confronted with the undeniable difference of the Synoptics from John.[156] The Jesus of the Synoptics is concerned primarily with an expansion of the law. He is very critical of the Jewish religious teachers because they are involved in the minutiae of the law and do not pay adequate attention to the more weighty matters.[157] John, on the other hand, writes of the meaning of love for Jesus. "For faith Jesus' word has become . . . the new command of love."[158]

The significance of Jesus can be traced, says Fuchs, in four steps: (1) Jesus' own decision, (2) belief in Jesus, (3) bringing of the historical Jesus into language, (4) existential interpretation of that language. Let us review each of these briefly.

With respect to Jesus and his decision, Fuchs is emphatic in denying that Jesus claimed any unique or special position before God. His decision is to be found centrally in his recognition of the *time* of the rule of God. He made this rule of God his own. As a consequence, "He understood himself as the *witness of a new situation,* as the authentic witness for the exposition of the future of the rule of God; an exposition which is now valid in his own presence. . . . He therefore summoned men, his contemporaries, to the rule of God."[159]

The second step has to do with faith in Jesus. Jesus had not demanded faith in himself. He only demanded faith in what he proclaimed because he regarded it as God's sentence for the present.[160] But soon Jesus himself became the basis of faith. "Jesus would in the future speak to this community as its Lord. From the *witness* of faith in God there had arisen the *basis* of this faith."[161] Fuchs summarizes the matter well in the following.

Through his word Jesus conveyed to his hearers his own in-

---

155 *Ibid.,* p. 19.
156 *Ibid.,* p. 50.
157 *Ibid.,* p. 58.
158 *Ibid.,* p. 57.
159 *Ibid.,* pp. 23, 224.
160 *Ibid.,* p. 76.
161 *Ibid.,* p. 226.

dividual certainty of God. He therefore portrayed to them in
his word the faith that remains faith until he himself became
in his person the lasting portrayal of the faith which God had
intended for them.

We asked *where* faith thinks. Now we have to say: Faith thinks
in the place where Jesus' word and person become the portrayal
of faith. *How* does faith think? Faith thinks as Paul thought, in
conscientious self-examination. *What* does faith think? Faith
thinks of God, by holding fast to the word of love, which
corresponds to Jesus' certainty of God.[162]

This, however, is not the end of the story, for the historical
Jesus comes into language once again in the writing of the
Gospels.[163] Thus we have the sequence: the *witness* of faith, the
basis of faith, the bringing of the historical Jesus into language.[164]

The fourth step is the interpretation of this language of the
New Testament. Fuchs believes the task of the expositor is "to
work out an existential interpretation of the documents."[165]
Fuchs' own existential interpretation he summarizes in the following way.

The message of the New Testament says to the individual that
the responsibility for the present sets him free for a future in
which man is relieved of the burdens of the past. . . . The end
of history occurs in my own present. . . . This is what it would
mean to have faith in God. . . . If the believer lives out the
present as the gift and work of God, then he also gives up the
past of his own works in favor of the future, without allowing
himself to be led astray by death.[166]

Norman Perrin has pointed out the significant shift here from
an emphasis on the kerygma in Bultmann and other of his students
in the new quest school to an emphasis on hermeneutic. "A concern for an existentialist interpretation of the kerygma has been
modified by a concern for the historical Jesus until it has become
a concern for an existentialist interpretation of the New Testament."[167]

GERHARD EBELING

Ebeling deals at considerable length with the possibility of
knowing the historical Jesus. He organizes his discussion around
three questions. "(1) What is the meaning of the phrase 'his-

---

162 *Ibid.,* p. 184.
163 *Ibid.,* p. 76.
164 *Ibid.,* p. 190.
165 *Ibid.,* p. 217.
166 *Ibid.,* p. 218.
167 Perrin, p. 33.

torical Jesus"? (2) What came to expression in Jesus? (3) Has faith in Jesus Christ a basis in Jesus himself?"[168] With regard to the first of these questions, Ebeling says that the technical meaning of the words "historical Jesus" connotes Jesus as he may be known via historical investigation without any of the touches that have been added via church tradition. In other words, this means the true or the real Jesus.[169]

There is nothing exceptional about this kind of investigation, for it is what we mean when we talk about any figure of history. The difficulty does not lie in the result we seek, but rather in the peculiar character of the sources we employ. These sources show the particular interest that faith and preaching find in Jesus. Thus the "historical Jesus" stands in contrast to the "dogmatic Christ," the "biblical Christ," the "Christ of faith."[170]

Pushing the investigation a step further, he finds primarily three elements in the dogmatic or kerygmatic tradition that do not belong to the historical Jesus. (1) We must exclude from our consideration of the historical Jesus all elements of interpretation added as a result of the postresurrection faith. (2) Elements that are given in the form of historical reports, "yet cannot by any means be considered as historical statements about Jesus," must be eliminated. He has particularly in mind here such things as the resurrection, the appearances of Jesus thereafter, and the ascension. (3) Finally, we must eliminate anything that has the character of confessional statements about Jesus' person and work.[171]

All this serves to point out a major problem for Ebeling. Our fundamental task must be to attempt to bridge the gap between the historical Jesus and the dogmatic Christ. Ebeling starts on a path to the solution of this problem by means of the second question, "What came to expression in Jesus?"[172] This he regards as the proper question concerning the past. The facts, the explanation of the facts, and so forth, are not of primary importance. What came to expression is of primary importance.[173] His answer here is very simple. "Faith came to expression in Jesus."[174] The primary significance of Jesus in this regard is that he is a witness or a

---

168 Gerhard Ebeling, *Word and Faith,* trans. James W. Leitch (Philadelphia: Fortress, 1963), p. 288.
169 *Ibid.,* p. 290.
170 *Ibid.*
171 *Ibid.,* pp. 290-92.
172 *Ibid.,* p. 296.
173 *Ibid.,* p. 295.
174 *Ibid.,* p. 296.

communicator of faith to us. But Ebeling is very much concerned that we do not separate the historical Jesus from what came to expression in Jesus. "Indeed, it must be laid down as fundamental that . . . where Christology is concerned nothing may be said of Jesus which does not have its ground in the historical Jesus himself and does not confine itself to saying who the historical Jesus is."[175]

Ebeling then takes up the third question, "Has faith in Jesus Christ a basis in Jesus himself?"[176] He says that the fundamental problem of the old quest was that while it was interested in demolishing the traditional church picture of Jesus, it ended with the realization that it had nothing to put in its place. This in turn gave rise to another problem. How was one to understand the transition that took place from the historical Jesus to the Christ of faith? Therefore, when historical criticism reached a point where it felt it must assert a complete discontinuity between the two, in its attempt to understand that discontinuity it found itself forced once again to search for the continuity. "For it is undeniable that a connection exists between Jesus and the primitive Church."[177] To put it in Ebeling's terminology, "The witness of faith became the ground of faith."[178] But the ground of faith is not to be found only in the witness of faith. "The ground of faith is certainly to be brought to expression also by historical study, because it came to expression in history."[179] Ebeling therefore concludes that faith in Jesus Christ has a basis in Jesus, and that as a result historical study is necessary.

What then can we say about the historical Jesus? Ebeling points out two extremes that are for him unwarranted. The first is the idea that we can construct a biography of Jesus the way the liberal theologians had attempted to do. However, he does not feel we are justified in forsaking the historical question as if Jesus were completely hidden from us behind the New Testament witness.[180] What would be the result if research should demonstrate that there is no continuity between the Jesus of history and the Christ of faith? "If the quest of the historical Jesus were in fact to prove that faith in Jesus has no basis in Jesus himself, then that would be the end of Christology."[181] On the other hand,

---

175 *Ibid.,* p. 298.
176 *Ibid.*
177 *Ibid.,* p. 301.
178 *Ibid.*
179 *Ibid.,* p. 304.
180 *Ibid.,* p. 205.
181 *Ibid.*

Ebeling demonstrates the importance of the attempt to hold these two elements together by asking the question, "Would it not be significant if it could be historically shown that Jesus and faith are inseparably joined together, so that whoever has to do with the historical Jesus has to do with him from whom and in view of whom faith comes?"[182]

Ebeling agrees with the contentions of form criticism. That is, he feels that the biographical framework of the Gospels is a product of the Evangelists' own composition. It is only in the passion narrative that we find a relatively reliable sequence of events. On the other hand, the narratives of Jesus' childhood, for example, cannot be regarded as other than late and legendary. For the first time in the Gospel of Luke we see a semihistorical interest, but even here the interest in history is secondary.[183]

Going beyond the Gospels as a whole to their parts, Ebeling feels we are closer to the historical in the sayings and conversations of Jesus than in the stories about him. Here once again we find what we have seen repeatedly in this chapter. Where the particular sayings by Jesus cannot be accounted for on the basis of the Jewish thought world or as a result of the faith of the early church, we are more certainly in touch with an historically reliable tradition about Jesus.[184] But Ebeling again shows the restlessness of the members of this school when he reiterates the impossibility of constructing "a biography of Jesus which is chronologically coherent and psychologically transparent."[185]

What then specifically in the sayings and conversations does he feel is historical? He lists three things. First of all there is an emphasis on the nearness of the rule of God. This nearness is not to be taken in the apocalyptic sense, but rather, "The essential thing in the nearness of the rule of God is the rule of the God who is near."[186] Furthermore, Jesus' call to repentance does not end with fear, but it "is wonderfully transformed into a call to Joy."[187] Second, Jesus' emphasis on the will of God must be taken as historical. This will is not to be found in casuistry, but rather in freedom. It is something that enables us to distinguish between what is trivial and what is important. "He taught the will of God in such a way that we are impelled to say, Yes, this is how it is. We

---

[182] *Ibid.*
[183] Gerhard Ebeling, *The Nature of Faith,* trans. Ronald Gregor Smith (Philadelphia: Fortress, 1961), pp. 51-52.
[184] *Ibid.,* p. 52.
[185] *Ibid.*
[186] *Ibid.,* p. 53.
[187] *Ibid.,* pp. 53-54.

are given courage to believe, and that means, courage to be free."[188] Finally, there is in the historical Jesus a call to disciple-ship. Once again, his emphasis was unique, in that it was not primarily a call for pupils or revolutionaries, but rather a call for men to faith, a call for men to share in his way.[189]

Ebeling writes on the subject of the resurrection of Jesus at considerable length. He notes three kinds of narratives that deal with this subject in the New Testament. There are first the miracle stories of the Gospels. These narratives contain a great deal of precise and particular detail; however, a harmonization of the accounts is not possible, even those in the Synoptic Gospels, to say nothing of John. While they contain very old traditional material, it is obvious to Ebeling that they have been elaborated by legend that is much later.[190]

A second kind of narrative is very brief. These are merely formulas of confession and are marked, in contrast to the first kind, by a lack of concrete details. Ebeling gives Acts 2:24 and 3:15 as typical examples of this type.[191]

The third type is by all odds the most important for Ebeling. It is the passage by Paul in I Cor. 15. He mentions first of all that this passage was written about twenty-five years after Jesus' death. Furthermore, Paul is quoting a tradition that he has received, which makes the source of his information even earlier than that. Ebeling contrasts the statements of Paul here with those of the Gospels by calling the former "sparse, sober and reliable state-ments."[192] On the basis of his comparison of these two sets of accounts, he concludes that pious imagination played a part in the writing of the Gospels. There is in fact a sense in which the Gospel accounts stand halfway between Paul and the apocryphal gospels. To be certain, the apocryphal gospels go much further, but even in the canonical Gospels there are theological tendencies at work, for example, the need to cope with the suspicion that Jesus' body had been stolen.[193]

It is likely that there were at first two types of tradition: stories of the appearances, and stories of the empty tomb. As time passed, these two traditions were combined and intermingled. To Ebeling the stories of the appearances were the earlier of the two and those of the empty tomb are to be regarded as later additions.

---

188 *Ibid.*, p. 55.
189 *Ibid.*, pp. 55-56.
190 *Ibid.*, pp. 63-64.
191 *Ibid.*, p. 64.
192 *Ibid.*, pp. 64-66.
193 *Ibid.*, p. 66.

He picks up a theme that we found very early in our study. He notices, as have others we have studied, that the appearances of Jesus were not to neutral witnesses, but always to believers. At any rate, all of those to whom he appeared became believers. Therefore, for Ebeling, "The point of the appearances is precisely the arising of faith in the Risen One."[194]

Finally, Ebeling compares the resurrection appearances in the Gospels and in Paul. While he admits that the Gospel appearances are sharply distinguished from visions, he concludes that if we are to accept the experience of Paul on the road to Damascus as a vision, there is no reason why we should differentiate the Pauline experience from those in the Gospels. As a matter of fact, he denies that Paul differentiated them.[195]

Ebeling does not deal at any great length with the comparison of the Synoptics and John, but he says enough to make his position clear. Typically, he emphasizes that the Gospels are not to be taken simply as historical documents, and that the Synoptics stand on a higher level than John with respect to historical accuracy. He notes the similarity of the Synoptic Gospels, and as a consequence the reason for their being grouped together and attaining the name "Synoptic." However, the meaning of this term must not be overemphasized. "This means that they confront the reader with all their differences and contradictions, which cannot decently be harmonised. When they are considered as witnesses to faith, this diversity need not be a disturbance."[196] We have already noted that of these Synoptic Gospels, the Gospel of Luke appears to be the best from an historical point of view, for it manifests a "quasi-historical interest."[197]

The Gospel of John, on the other hand, maintains even less interest in history than do the Synoptics. Its presentation of the events is so independent and so completely different from that of the Synoptics that one should not expect to find in it an historical account. Ebeling points out that the Synoptics, with the exception of one passage in Matthew (18:6) which he regards as secondary, never speak of Jesus as making himself the object of faith, whereas in John faith becomes linked to Jesus as its object.[198]

Jesus' significance according to Ebeling is that the witness of faith now becomes the basis of faith.[199] But this, in turn, needs

194 *Ibid.*, pp. 66-68.
195 *Ibid.*, p. 69.
196 *Ibid.*, p. 50.
197 *Ibid.*, p. 52.
198 *Word and Faith*, p. 234.
199 *The Nature of Faith*, p. 62.

further explanation. The question here is what faith in Jesus means. We are not to think of Jesus as the object of faith, but rather we must think of ourselves as entering upon his way. "To participate in him and his way, and thus to participate in that which is promised to faith, namely, the omnipotence of God."[200] Considered in this way, Jesus bore witness as to the meaning of being involved with God in death as well as life. It thus becomes our task in faith to follow Jesus, not in the sense of the old liberal theology, of mimicking his outward conduct, but rather in our innermost being we must be related to God, we must commit ourselves to him.[201]

The result of such experience can best be expressed as openness to the future. "Only that which has a future is real. That which has no future is nothing. Salvation in the strict, ultimate, that is, eschatological sense, comes to him to whom in his nothingness the future is opened."[202]

Ebeling goes on to a position very similar to that of Fuchs. Thus he too comes to a place where an existential interpretation of the New Testament replaces an interest in the existential interpretation of the kerygma. And like Fuchs, he is as a result very deeply involved in the area of hermeneutics. His position may be summarized in his own words. "The text by means of the sermon becomes a hermeneutic aid in the understanding of present experience."[203]

SUMMARY

We attempt a summary here with even greater hesitation than previously, for the diversity among these authors is more difficult to define than that which we have encountered in any other group that we have considered in a single chapter. There are, however, some very common elements which it would be profitable to note briefly.

1. IS IT POSSIBLE TO WRITE A BIOGRAPHY (HISTORY) OF JESUS?

These authors all approach this subject from the point of view of the character of the Gospels. The Gospels must not be regarded as historical documents. They are primarily documents of faith; documents of preaching; primarily kerygmatic in their purpose. It is therefore not legitimate to use them the way the liberal theologians did. In looking for the historical, one must rule out

---

[200] *Ibid.,* p. 71.
[201] *Ibid.,* pp. 73-74.
[202] *Ibid.,* p. 124.
[203] *Word and Faith,* p. 331.

accounts that give evidence of being tampered with for theological reasons; one must realize that the documents are in nature theological and then subsequently investigate the possibility of finding some history in them.

Certain modern concepts and techniques have contributed to this position. Form criticism is acknowledged by all these authors as having changed the current picture. Its value with respect to the construction of a life of Christ, however, from their point of view is mainly negative. It has shown that a biographical account of Jesus' life is impossible. It has furthermore shown that a psychological analysis of Jesus' development is equally impossible to demonstrate on the basis of the Gospels.

Furthermore, these authors have found the old quest objectionable from their own philosophical point of departure. These thinkers are all existentialists. Their philosophical starting point has had an effect on all of their thought, but in connection with this question it has most particularly caused them to attack the positivistic historicism of the old quest.

But more is involved here than dissatisfaction with the old quest. There is a certain uneasiness with the position of Bultmann, or more properly, with where the position developed by Bultmann may ultimately lead. There is a fear that contemporary theology may go to the point where it makes a complete break between the Jesus of history and the Christ of faith. This would be a modern return to the ancient heresy of docetism. These authors want no part of that. Furthermore, these authors feel that while our confidence in the historical reliability of the Gospels has been greatly shaken, there are elements in the Gospels that we must accept as being historical. They differ as to the content of this historical "core," but they all insist that it is there.

One other item here deserves our attention. They have a rather common basis for deciding what in the Gospels may be authentic. When a tradition cannot be accounted for (1) on the basis of early Christian preaching, or (2) on the basis of contemporary Judaism, its claim to authenticity must be taken with all seriousness. From this basic position each of the authors proceeds to develop his particular construction.

2. WHAT IS THE PLACE OF MIRACLE IN THE LIFE OF JESUS?

Miracle has ceased to be a problem for some of the members of this school. The last two authors we considered do not even deal with it at length. Fuchs and Ebeling are thus satisfied that miracle has no proper place in the Gospels. Even among the others there is not the thoroughgoing attempt to rationalize the miracles that we found in the liberal lives. There appear to be three reasons for this. (1) Miracles from their point of view cannot be regarded as important for faith. In some sense, they really destroy what faith demands. This was true in Jesus' day, and it remains true today. (2) They regard the attitude of Jesus as instructive here. There are repeated indications in the Gospels that Jesus did not wish to be known as a miracle-worker, and even when he performed healings he often instructed those healed to be silent about it. Furthermore, there are instances in which Jesus refuses to perform any miracles. (3) Miraculous happenings are always confined to the circle of believers. This indicates to these authors that faith may be more a cause for the rise of a miracle story than the occurrence of a miracle cause for the rise of faith.

Some of these authors do, however, make use of certain of the arguments used by the liberal scholars. For example, Old Testament parallels and the occurrence of similar accounts in other religious literature are noted. They advance a step beyond the liberals, however, in analyzing the miracle stories on the basis of a comparison of parallel Gospel accounts. This must be acknowledged as a contribution that form criticism has made to their position.

3. HOW SHOULD THE RESURRECTION OF JESUS BE INTERPRETED?

The advocates of the new quest are in agreement with the liberal writers that a physical resurrection of Jesus is out of the question. There is unanimity of opinion here that what is presented in the Gospels is not a physical resurrection, and that at the base of it are simply visions.

These authors develop their position on the basis of several observations. In the first place, they note that the appearances all involve believers or people who as a result became believers. Furthermore, they occurred to an early community that lived in expectation of the rule of God in light of the life of Jesus. As a consequence, it is the fact of the Easter faith with which we must primarily deal, not the fact of the resurrection.

In the second place, these authors note a basic difference between the passion narratives in the Gospels and the Easter narratives. While the passion narratives are more or less uniform, the Easter narratives are impossible to reconcile with one another. The accounts demonstrate to the satisfaction of these authors that while we are dealing with history in connection with Jesus' death, we are involved with something less objective when confronted with his resurrection.

Finally, they deal with a series of problems that we may call evidences of development in the concept of the resurrection in the New Testament itself. Thus, in I Cor. 15 we find the earliest account of the resurrection in the New Testament. This, as compared with what we find later in the Gospels, is marked by restraint. There is no express statement as to the nature of the resurrection; and even more significantly, the appearance to Paul is listed with the others with no indication that it was of a different nature. Since Paul's experience is elsewhere called a vision, these authors conclude that all other appearances must have been of the same character. Further, there is an indication in some of these authors that the stories of the appearances are older than those of the empty tomb, which leads them to assert that belief in the empty tomb was a subsequent development.

4. WHAT IS THE NATURE AND PLACE OF MYTHOLOGY IN THE NEW TESTAMENT?

It is obvious from the way they treat the subject of mythology that the exponents of the new quest stand after Bultmann, not before him. It will be recalled that in the liberal lives little place was found for mythology. The writers in this school are well aware of the work of Bultmann, and while they accept his work to varying degrees, their concern is to link myth more closely to history than to the kerygma. Myth is not to be thought of as an objectification of the piety of the apostles or as an attempt to get across religious ideas, but rather it is used to interpret the history of Jesus. In accordance with this, they reject any idea that the Gospels are mythical in total. Myth when it is used has the purpose of giving the meaning of an historical personage for present existence.

5. WHAT IS THE HISTORICAL VALUE OF JOHN AS COMPARED WITH THE SYNOPTICS?

The writers of the new quest have far less confidence in the historical value of the Synoptics than did the liberals. This is once again to be attributed to their emphasis on the kerygma as standing at the center of the Gospels. It would seem that the Synoptics for these writers stand about where the Gospel of John did for the liberal writers, though of course for a different reason. On the other hand, the greater part of the material we find that can be considered historical comes to us from the Synoptics, even though they must be subjected to a much harsher criticism than the liberals are willing to give them.

This lowering of the historical estimate of the Synoptics, however, has not been attended by a general rise in the historical estimate of John in this school. Among most of these writers, John continues to be of less value than the Synoptics. The only exception is Robinson. He notes that in some circles there has been a raised estimate of the historical value of John in the current century, but he too denies that this has resulted in the legitimate use of the Gospel of John as being a primary historical source better in quality than the Synoptics. It has merely lifted John to the level of the Synoptics. In this position, however, he is not supported by the other four writers.

6. WHAT IS THE CENTRAL SIGNIFICANCE OF JESUS?

There is perhaps a greater difference here among the writers of this chapter than anywhere else. Yet, basic to all their analysis there is a common element — existentialist interpretation. Robinson feels that more is available to us via the new quest than an understanding of human existence as Bultmann contended. He feels that we have available to us Jesus' existential selfhood. This is available to us through the kerygma. But it is equally available to us through critical analysis of the Gospels in the authentic sayings of Jesus.

Käsemann is most particularly concerned with the problem of history, but even he cannot completely avoid the question of Jesus' significance. Jesus proclaimed how the kingdom of God had come near. This placed its demand upon man, for now he was put into the "freedom and responsibility of faith."[204] This freedom could and can be maintained only as long as man finds in God his Lord, as Jesus proclaimed during his life.

Of all the writers in this chapter, Bornkamm confronts Bultmann most openly. He does not feel that a conception of Jesus that views him merely as one who enables man to understand himself is adequate. Christ is not one who gives "a new qualification of my own history." Rather he gives "a new history which is no longer mine."[205] Therefore, the believer is brought to the point of recognizing that the realization of his existence lies beyond his own possibilities. Instead there is revealed to him a new history in Christ.

The views of Fuchs and Ebeling are certainly the closest among these writers. For them Jesus' significance is that the *witness* of faith has become the *basis* of faith. Here one must be quick to point out what is meant by the basis of faith. Jesus is not to be thought of as an object of faith. Rather, we are to enter

[204] Käsemann, p. 46.
[205] Bornkamm, "Myth and Gospel," p. 192.

upon his way and thus to participate in the omnipotence of God. But they do not stop here and suggest that we have an existential encounter with Jesus. The historical Jesus came into language in the New Testament; thus, what we must seek is an existential interpretation of the New Testament. This idea has led some observers to designate the New Hermeneutic of Fuchs and Ebeling as "Neo-liberalism."[206]

AN EVALUATION

Because we have chosen to develop our study in the chronological sequence that we have, we have left no opportunity for rebuttal of the new quest by subsequent writers in the critical school. For this reason, we shall here note some thoughts of those critical scholars who find themselves in basic disagreement with the approach of the new quest. The most severe criticism of the new quest has come from those in the Bultmannian tradition, and those to the left of it who continue to orient faith toward the kerygma rather than toward the historical Jesus.

One of the most precise criticisms of the new quest is found in a recent article by Harvey and Ogden.[207] These authors challenge the claim of the new quest to its novelty both in respect to the theology of Bultmann and in respect to the nineteenth-century quest. Their attack is directed particularly against James Robinson, but much of what they say would apply to others in the school. Let us note first, briefly, the denial that the new quest is new in relation to the theology of Bultmann.

According to these authors, Robinson says two basic things about the quest of the historical Jesus as developed from Bultmann's perspective. It is in the first place impossible, for the sources do not make available to us such information. But such a quest is also illegitimate, according to Robinson's analysis of Bultmann, because we cannot find any identifiable continuity between the proclamation of Jesus and the kerygma of the early church.[208] Robinson realizes, however, that while the above analysis is true to a degree, it cannot stand without qualification; and as a consequence he proceeds to identify two Bultmannian positions. Bultmann's earlier position is indicated by the summary just given, i.e., nothing can be known of the historical Jesus and

---

[206] Perrin, p. 33.

[207] Van A. Harvey and Schubert M. Ogden, "How New Is the 'New Quest of the Historical Jesus'?" *The Historical Jesus and the Kerygmatic Christ,* ed. and trans. Braaten and Harrisville, pp. 197-242.

[208] *Ibid.,* p. 202.

there is no continuity between the Jesus of history and the Christ of the early church. The second Bultmannian position is to be seen as an "undercurrent" in Bultmann's earlier works, but more fully developed more recently. This position is the converse of the first and it says that something *can* be known of the historical Jesus and that there *is* a kind of continuity between the Jesus of history and the Christ of the early church.[209]

Harvey and Ogden proceed to criticize this analysis. They first of all deny both that there has been a shift in Bultmann's position and that there has been an undercurrent running against the mainstream. Bultmann himself has noted several things that the sources reveal concerning Jesus' person and work, even if they hide from us his "personality."[210] Therefore, Bultmann has never regarded the quest of the historical Jesus as impossible.

Furthermore, these authors deny that Bultmann ever regarded such a quest as illegitimate. He regards a quest as illegitimate only if the one who undertakes it seeks to establish faith via historical investigation. In this connection, these authors also criticize the attribution to Bultmann of the new historical method that lies behind the new quest. What Bultmann professes to find via his encounter with Jesus is an understanding of human existence. What the new quest, and particularly Robinson, professes to find is Jesus' existential selfhood.[211]

Harvey and Ogden also deny that the new quest is new in relation to the old quest of liberalism. They challenge the assertion that the old quest sought to prove faith on the basis of historical facts. They quote a passage from Harnack to support their position. Even the Ritschlians made a distinction between fact and value. While it may be admitted that some of the members of the original quest put too much reliance on an historical picture of Jesus, these authors ask if the new quest is any less prone to seek security by this improper means.[212]

These authors push further an analysis of the new historiography that is claimed to be at the basis of the new quest and to make a second avenue of approach to Jesus' selfhood possible. They see a choice between two possibilities. If the new quest seeks to establish that which faith knows already, the results of such a quest are a foregone conclusion. If, on the other hand, what the new quest seeks has not been found, what assurance have we

---

209 *Ibid.*, p. 203.
210 *Ibid.*, pp. 204-05.
211 *Ibid.*, pp. 207, 209, 221.
212 *Ibid.*, pp. 226-28.

that the result of such a quest might not disconfirm the kerygma and thus make faith impossible?[213]

This brings up a further point with respect to the new quest. It is subject to criticism not only on the basis of its motivation, but also with respect to its object. "Is the new quest for the *existentiell* selfhood of Jesus different from the old quest for the 'inner life' of Jesus, his 'personality?' And if it is impossible to recover Jesus' 'inner life' — as Robinson claims — is it any easier to recover Jesus' *existentiell* selfhood?"[214]

These writers agree that the new quest may be based on a more profound anthropology, as Robinson claims, but they insist that the difference is not as great as the new questers claim. The difference of the new from the original quest in this respect appears to be largely linguistic. The critics of the new quest proceed to demonstrate their contention by comparing a quotation from Harnack with one from Robinson.[215]

It is next questioned whether it is possible to get at the selfhood of a man, as Robinson claims to do, apart from the positivistic matters that involved the original quest. It seems to these writers that such matters as chronology, names, dates, and actions are essential to such a quest. If this be the case, the new quest lands in precisely the place of the original quest.[216]

Finally, these authors challenge the validity of the new quest from the point of view of psychology. Back of the quest lies the assumption that one can demonstrate a man's faith by an analysis of his speech and actions. "Unless we assume a priori that Jesus' selfhood was more consistent with his life and thought than that of other human beings — and as an a priori assumption it can hardly serve the purposes of historiography — surely we must remain silent concerning his own 'openness to transcendence.' "[217]

Harvey and Ogden apply this principle specifically to Robinson's assertion that the cross was "the ultimate realization" of Jesus' "eschatological selfhood." This they feel can be stated only on the basis of the chronological assertion that Jesus never during his life "faltered or changed his mind."[218]

There are others, however, even among those who orient faith to the kerygma, who see some basic positive contributions of the critics in the new quest school, even while they remain very critical

---

213 *Ibid.*, pp. 229, 230, 234.
214 *Ibid.*, p. 234.
215 *Ibid.*, pp. 234-35.
216 *Ibid.*, pp. 236-37.
217 *Ibid.*, pp. 240-41.
218 *Ibid.*, p. 241.

of the school. (1) Its renewed interest in the historical Jesus has checked a tendency in Bultmann's thought which if followed out might lead to a docetic Christology. (2) The new quest has demonstrated that a return to pre-form-critical days is impossible. (3) The movement has given renewed emphasis toward the development of criteria for determining what is authentic in the sayings and deeds of Jesus. (4) The movement has demonstrated that the debate concerning faith or kerygma and history has not come to an end.[219]

---

[219] Hugh Anderson, *Jesus and Christian Origins*, p. 183.

BIBLIOGRAPHY

Anderson, Hugh. *Jesus and Christian Origins.* New York: Oxford University Press, 1964.

Barth, Karl, "Rudolf Bultmann — An Attempt to Understand Him." *Kerygma and Myth.* Vol. II. Ed. Hans Werner Bartsch. Trans. Reginald H. Fuller. London: S. P. C. K., 1962. Pp. 83-132.

Beck, Dwight Marion. *Through the Gospels to Jesus.* New York: Harper, 1954.

Bornkamm, Günther. *Jesus of Nazareth.* Trans. Irene and Fraser McLuskey and James M. Robinson. New York: Harper, 1960.

——, "Myth and Gospel: A Discussion of the Problem of Demythologizing the New Testament Message." *Kerygma and History.* Ed. and trans. Carl E. Braaten and Roy A. Harrisville. Nashville: Abingdon, 1962. Pp. 172-196.

Bousset, W. *Jesus.* Trans. Janet Penrose Trevelyan. New York: Putnam, 1906.

Braaten, Carl E. and Roy A. Harrisville, ed. and trans. *The Historical Jesus and the Kerygmatic Christ.* Nashville: Abingdon, 1964.

Bruce, F. F., "Form Criticism." *Baker's Dictionary of Theology.* Ed. Everett F. Harrison. Grand Rapids: Baker, 1960. Pp. 227-28.

Bultmann, Rudolf. *The History of the Synoptic Tradition.* Trans. John Marsh. New York: Harper, 1963.

——. *Jesus and the Word.* Trans. L. P. Smith and E. H. Lantero. New York: Scribner, 1958.

——. *Jesus Christ and Mythology.* New York: Scribner, 1958.

——, "New Testament and Mythology." *Kerygma and Myth.* Vol. I. Ed. Hans Werner Bartsch. Trans. Reginald H. Fuller. London: S. P. C. K., 1964. Pp. 1-44.

——, "The Study of the Synoptic Gospels." *Form Criticism.* Trans. Frederick C. Grant. New York: Harper, 1934. Pp. 11-76.

Case, Shirley Jackson. *The Historicity of Jesus.* Chicago: University of Chicago Press, 1912.

——. *Jesus: A New Biography.* Chicago: University of Chicago Press, 1927.

Dibelius, Martin. *From Tradition to Gospel.* Trans. Bertram Lee Woolf. New York: Scribner, 1935.

Ebeling, Gerhard. *The Nature of Faith.* Trans. Ronald Gregor Smith. Philadelphia: Fortress, 1961.

——. *Word and Faith.* Trans. James W. Leitch. Philadelphia: Fortress, 1963.

Fuchs, Ernst. *Studies of the Historical Jesus.* Trans. Andrew Scobie. Naperville, Ill.: Allenson, 1964.

Fuller, Reginald H. *The New Testament in Current Study.* London: S.C.M., 1963.

Goguel, Maurice. *The Birth of Christianity.* Trans. H. C. Snape. New York: Macmillan, 1953.

——. *The Life of Jesus.* Trans. Olive Wyon. New York: Macmillan, 1933.

Harnack, Adolf. *What Is Christianity?* Trans. Thomas Bailey Saunders. New York: Putnam, 1901.

Harrison, Everett F. *Introduction to the New Testament.* Grand Rapids: Eerdmans, 1964.

Harvey, Van A. and Schubert M. Ogden, "How New Is the 'New Quest of the Historical Jesus'?" *The Historical Jesus and the Kerygmatic Christ.* Ed. and trans. Carl E. Braaten and Roy A. Harrisville. Nashville: Abingdon, 1964. Pp. 197-242.

Jaspers, Karl and Rudolf Bultmann. *Myth and Christianity.* New York: Noonday, 1958.

Jeremias, Joachim. *The Problem of the Historical Jesus.* Trans. Norman Perrin. Philadelphia: Fortress, 1964.

Kähler, Martin. *The So-Called Historical Jesus and the Historic Biblical Christ.* Trans. Carl E. Braaten. Philadelphia: Fortress, 1964.

Käsemann, Ernst. *Essays on New Testament Themes.* Trans. W. J. Montague. Naperville, Ill.: Allenson, 1964.

Kinder, Ernst, "Historical Criticism and Demythologizing." *Kerygma and History.* Ed. and trans. Carl E. Braaten and Roy A. Harrisville. Nashville: Abingdon, 1962. Pp. 55-85.

Klausner, Joseph. *Jesus of Nazareth.* Trans. Herbert Danby. New York: Macmillan, 1925.

Künneth, Walter, "Bultmann's Philosophy and the Reality of Salvation." *Kerygma and History.* Ed. and trans. Carl E. Braaten and Roy A. Harrisville. Nashville: Abingdon, 1962. Pp. 86-119.

Mackinnon, James. *The Historic Jesus.* New York: Longmans, Green, 1931.

Mackintosh, Hugh Ross. *Types of Modern Theology.* New York: Scribner, 1964.

Ogden, Schubert M. *Christ Without Myth.* New York: Harper, 1961.

Perrin, Norman, "The Challenge of New Testament Theology Today," *Criterion,* IV (Spring 1965), 25-34.

Redlich, E. Basil. *Form Criticism.* London: Duckworth, 1939.

Richardson, Alan. *The Miracle-Stories of the Gospels.* London: S.C.M., 1941.

Robinson, James M., "The Historical Question," *The Christian Century,* LXXVI (October 21, 1959), 1207-10.

———. *A New Quest of the Historical Jesus.* London: S.C.M., 1959.

Schweitzer, Albert. *The Quest of the Historical Jesus.* Trans. W. Montgomery. New York: Macmillan, 1910.

Scott, Ernest Findlay. *The Validity of the Gospel Record.* New York: Scribner, 1938.

Stauffer, Ethelbert. *Jesus and His Story.* Trans. Richard and Clara Winston. New York: Knopf, 1960.

———, "The Relevance of the Historical Jesus." *The Historical Jesus and the Kerygmatic Christ.* Ed. and trans. Carl E. Braaten and Roy A. Harrisville. Nashville: Abingdon, 1964. Pp. 43-53.

Taylor, Vincent. *The Formation of the Gospel Tradition.* New York: Macmillan, 1933.

Troeltsch, Ernst. *The Social Teaching of the Christian Churches.* Trans. Olive Wyon. New York: Macmillan, 1931.

Vos, Geerhardus. *The Self-Disclosure of Jesus.* Grand Rapids: Eerdmans, 1953.

Zahrnt, Heinz. *The Historical Jesus.* Trans. J. S. Bowden. New York: Harper, 1963.

INDEX OF SUBJECTS

203

INDEX OF AUTHORS